The Complete Idiot's Guide® to The Great Recession

The Complete Idiot's Guide® to The Great Recession

by Tom Gorman

ALPHA

A member of Penguin Group (USA) Inc.

ALPHA BOOKS

Published by the Penguin Group

Penguin Group (USA) Inc., 375 Hudson Street, New York, New York 10014, USA

Penguin Group (Canada), 90 Eglinton Avenue East, Suite 700, Toronto, Ontario M4P 2Y3, Canada (a division of Pearson Penguin Canada Inc.)

Penguin Books Ltd., 80 Strand, London WC2R 0RL, England

Penguin Ireland, 25 St. Stephen's Green, Dublin 2, Ireland (a division of Penguin Books Ltd.)

Penguin Group (Australia), 250 Camberwell Road, Camberwell, Victoria 3124, Australia (a division of Pearson Australia Group Pty. Ltd.)

Penguin Books India Pvt. Ltd., 11 Community Centre, Panchsheel Park, New Delhi—110 017, India

Penguin Group (NZ), 67 Apollo Drive, Rosedale, North Shore, Auckland 1311, New Zealand (a division of Pearson New Zealand Ltd.)

Penguin Books (South Africa) (Pty.) Ltd., 24 Sturdee Avenue, Rosebank, Johannesburg 2196, South Africa

Penguin Books Ltd., Registered Offices: 80 Strand, London WC2R 0RL, England

Copyright © 2010 by Tom Gorman

International Standard Book Number: 978-1-59257-959-4
Library of Congress Catalog Card Number: 2010905601

12   11   10   8   7   6   5   4   3   2   1

Interpretation of the printing code: The rightmost number of the first series of numbers is the year of the book's printing; the rightmost number of the second series of numbers is the number of the book's printing. For example, a printing code of 10-1 shows that the first printing occurred in 2010.

Printed in the United States of America

Most Alpha books are available at special quantity discounts for bulk purchases for sales promotions, premiums, fund-raising, or educational use. Special books, or book excerpts, can also be created to fit specific needs.

For details, write: Special Markets, Alpha Books, 375 Hudson Street, New York, NY 10014.

Publisher: *Marie Butler-Knight*
Associate Publisher: *Mike Sanders*
Senior Managing Editor: *Billy Fields*
Senior Development Editor: *Phil Kitchel*
Production Editor: *Kayla Dugger*

Cover Designer: *William Thomas*
Book Designers: *William Thomas, Rebecca Batchelor*
Layout: *Brian Massey*
Proofreader: *Laura Caddell*

Contents

Introduction

In 2008 and 2009, the United States experienced its worst financial crisis and economic recession since the Great Depression of the 1930s. Across the board, residential and commercial real estate values, and the value of stocks, bonds, and other securities, plunged from their highs of the preceding years. Americans and investors around the world collectively lost trillions of dollars in wealth, and the crisis touched off what has become known as the Great Recession, which affected tens of millions of households in the United States alone.

While the crisis originated in troubled mortgages and the securities based on them, those financial instruments are far from the whole story. Nor is the story limited to the financial markets. The "real economy," which produces products and services and provides employment and income, entered a contraction that began in December 2007 and ended with positive economic growth in the third quarter of 2009. At more than 18 months, the Great Recession was well over the post–World War II average of 10 months. Even as I write this and the economy appears to be on the mend, few are forecasting a speedy return to the old status quo, let alone robust growth.

The financial crisis and Great Recession amounted to a worldwide story (sort of an international financial thriller), because nations are far more economically interdependent than ever before. The story of this financial and economic crisis is thus complex in its characters, settings, events, plotlines, and potential endings—and it is not over. None of us—no economist, financial advisor, or business or political leader—knows how the future of the U.S. and world economy is going to play out. However, with the right information in hand, we can make an educated forecast and plan our financial and professional lives accordingly.

This book explains the crisis and the recession in plain English. This book also explains the many terms that most other sources leave unexplained, leaving many of us wondering what Alt-A mortgages, mortgage-backed securities, and credit default swaps are—and why we should care! I'll also occasionally explain more familiar terms, such as inflation, unemployment, and housing starts, when the need arises—for example, when government agencies change the way they calculate them.

Speaking of government agencies, they can cause confusion. There's the Treasury, Federal Reserve, Federal Deposit Insurance Corporation (FDIC), Fannie Mae, Freddie Mac, and many others. What do these agencies and the people who run them do? What part, if any, did these agencies play in creating, ignoring, or worsening the crisis and recession? What did they do and what can they do to address these matters? How might their actions affect our financial futures? This book will answer these questions.

This guide will help you understand the Great Recession of 2008–2009, what happened, who caused what, and what may happen in the years ahead. Most economists agree that the United States and quite possibly the world economy may face a few years of slow economic growth. A return to recession is even possible. Much of the prosperity the United States enjoyed from 2002 to 2007 was financed with consumer credit in all its forms, and the availability of credit will not return to precrisis levels for some time. Income—and the employment that provides it—will take even longer to recover. Also, many consumers will probably shift away from debt-financed consumption in order to pay down their debts and increase their savings. While this shift will benefit the U.S. economy in the longer term, it will dampen growth for at least several quarters.

U.S. citizens may also face a lower standard of living for years to come, as global competition for markets and resources intensifies and we pay for past errors such as piling up unprecedented amounts of debt to finance government and household expenditures, and misallocating capital to speculation rather than investment. A lower U.S. standard of living would take getting used to, but it will remain high relative to those of most economies, and extremely high by world standards. Meanwhile, the government will likely try to boost demand, household income, and business investment and to support the stability of financial institutions. These can be politically charged decisions, and I will explain why people support or oppose them.

Speaking of politics, as readers of *The Complete Idiot's Guide to Economics* know, I recognize the political dimension of economics in both theory and policy. Stated simplistically (which is how economic arguments are often stated), at one extreme are conservatives, who believe the government should avoid taxation and regulation, let markets alone determine the winners and losers in an economy, and keep social programs for the economically unfortunate to a minimum. At the other extreme are liberals, who believe government should do all it can to ensure an even (or "fair") distribution of income, goods, and services, and should even own businesses or industries if that's what it takes. Of course, conservatives support regulation when it benefits business, and liberals enjoy the range of products, services, and material comforts that only a market economy can provide.

Most of us stand somewhere between those two extremes. We believe in maintaining an economy in which markets are free of heavy government control but are regulated to temper the excesses or damage that completely free markets can create. Whether we like it or not, the United States and most industrialized nations actually maintain mixed economies, which are characterized by substantial government expenditures on goods and services. So to the extent possible, I will leave politics at the door of our briefing room. When the political dimension is unavoidable and omitting it would not serve you as a reader or me as an author, I will point out the various political viewpoints regarding a policy, development, or forecast as well as my own view. That way, you can consider the various viewpoints and form your own opinion.

Finally, I want to point out that we have plenty of reasons to be optimistic. The business cycle—the alternating pattern of expansion and contraction in economic activity—is here to stay. It is caused mainly by the recurring mismatch between supply and demand, which no market economy (or state-controlled economy) has been able to eliminate. Attempts by governments in market economies to soften the effects of the business cycle have met with some success in the past, but our policy options are now somewhat limited. Yet strong demand and vigorous growth will return, even if no one knows precisely when. In the meantime, it helps to understand where we are, how we got here, and where we might be headed.

How to Use This Book

This book is divided into seven parts:

Part 1, The Causes of the Crisis, explains the origins of the financial crisis and how it touched off the Great Recession. It shows the connections between the housing bubble, the financial markets, the banking systems, and the economy.

Part 2, Government Responds to the Crisis, details the steps the U.S. government—both the Federal Reserve and the U.S. Treasury and Congress—took under Presidents Bush and Obama to contain the financial crisis and to keep the economy from sliding into another Great Depression. This part also discusses economic events and responses in other nations at the time.

Part 3, Lessons from Past Recessions and Expansions, examines the major economic cycles of the 1970s, 1980s, and 1990s, as well as the savings and loan crisis of the late 1980s. It also examines the Great Depression of the 1930s, the response of the government under President Franklin D. Roosevelt, and the long-lasting legacy of that response.

Part 4, The Impact on Consumers and Households, shows how the Great Recession affected ordinary people, particularly in terms of unemployment, and how the economic trends of the past three decades left them ill-equipped to deal with the recession.

Part 5, The Impact on Industries and States, shows how the Great Recession affected certain industries and states, particularly the auto industry and a few key states. This part also examines the loss of manufacturing jobs in the United States over the past 40 years and why that has been such a serious development.

Part 6, Structural Problems in the U.S. Economy, looks at some of the most pressing issues facing Americans, including federal taxes and deficits, the Social Security and Medicare "time bombs," and the health-insurance system. Ways to establish sustainable economic growth are also examined in this part.

Part 7, The Economy Going Forward, looks at the emergence of the U.S. and other economies from the Great Recession, and provides a "report card" on the U.S. government's handling of the financial crisis and recession.

Even if we are a good many years away from the next financial crisis and major recession, the events of the late 2000s represent the culmination of a number of things that have not been right in the U.S. economy for some time. Those things transformed what could have been a fairly "normal" cyclical recession into the worst economic downturn since the Great Depression, and those things have not been fixed.

So to survive and prosper, we'll have to be lucky as well as smart. Americans have been lucky. Here's hoping that we can also learn from the events of the past, and develop better policies and a stronger economy for the future.

Extra Bits

Throughout the book, you'll see nuggets of extra information, neatly packaged in sidebar boxes. Here's what to look for:

WHAT'S THAT?

These boxes explain economic and financial terms in plain English.

WHAT TO DO?

These boxes provide bits of advice, warn of potential misunderstandings, and point to further sources of information.

Acknowledgments

Thank you to everyone who helped make this book possible: Marie Butler-Knight, publisher at Alpha Books, and the entire editorial team (Mike Sanders, associate publisher; Phil Kitchel, senior development editor; Kayla Dugger, production editor); Mike Snell, my agent; my wife, Phyllis, and my sons, Daniel and Matthew; my professors and instructors at New York University's Stern School of Business; and my past employers, colleagues, and clients.

Trademarks

All terms mentioned in this book that are known to be or are suspected of being trademarks or service marks have been appropriately capitalized. Alpha Books and Penguin Group (USA) Inc. cannot attest to the accuracy of this information. Use of a term in this book should not be regarded as affecting the validity of any trademark or service mark.

The Causes of the Crisis

The financial crisis of the late 2000s seemed to come out of nowhere to most people, which, I suppose, is why it was called a crisis. But that market meltdown was several years in the making, and driven by forces that were long apparent to many observers as they were building to a head. In hindsight, it appears that the crisis shouldn't have come as a surprise to anyone. There were just too many things going in the wrong direction for an economy as large, productive, and wealthy as that of the United States.

This first part examines those things and the forces that led to the financial crisis and the recession. These three chapters trace the key drivers of the crisis and describe the major events of the crisis and why they occurred. One of the major reasons to examine these events, particularly now that we have had time to gain some perspective on them, is to prevent them, or at least recognize them the next time they appear. Because they almost certainly will, if not in exactly the same form.

How Did We Get into This Mess?

In This Chapter

- The four fatal factors that created the crisis
- Financial incentives for people's behavior
- How easy money fed the housing bubble
- The effects of subprime loans on the mortgage market

As with most events, there's a short version and a long version of the financial crisis. Here's the shortest version I know: Many lenders lent money to many borrowers who couldn't pay it back, and when they couldn't pay it back, those lenders couldn't pay *their* bills—and then people who didn't get paid by those lenders couldn't pay *their* bills, and so on. When enough people can't pay the people they owe, then people who do have money won't lend it to anyone. When that happens, credit markets freeze, financial markets panic, and economic growth stops.

But that short version doesn't say why *so many* people and businesses beyond the actual lenders and borrowers were hurt by the financial crisis. Why did so many people lose their money and jobs because of events in the housing and mortgage markets? Why did such a long and severe recession follow the financial crisis?

The answer is threefold. First, a huge amount of money—about $1.3 trillion—was loaned to noncreditworthy borrowers. Second, mortgages, including those of noncreditworthy borrowers, were bundled into securities and sold to thousands of institutions and investors around the world, which spread the risks of default on those mortgages throughout the financial system. Third, certain public policies allowed or even encouraged some of these activities, and steps taken by the government could not stop all of the economic fallout. The next two chapters and Part 2 cover these three issues. In this chapter, we look broadly at the key drivers of the financial crisis.

Four Fatal Factors and the Key Players

Essentially, four fatal factors brought about the *financial crisis* of 2008:

1. Low interest rates and easy money

2. The housing bubble

3. New types of mortgages, subprime borrowers, and bad credit policies

4. Widespread distribution of mortgage-backed securities and derivatives

Before we examine these factors, let's meet the key players in the crisis and consider the incentives that drove them (and drive most of us):

- *Families and individuals* know that a house is usually a good investment and that mortgage interest is tax-deductible, which encourages them to buy their homes rather than rent.

- *Real estate agents*, who represent the seller, are paid a percentage of a home's selling price, which motivates them to negotiate the highest prices possible without scuttling the sale.

- *Real estate developers* are also motivated by high home prices, which gives them an incentive to build as many homes as possible during a boom, as well as larger homes (the much-maligned "McMansions") and luxury condominiums.

- *Mortgage lenders* want to do as much business as possible, so they lend as much money as they can, assuming (usually) that it will be repaid.

- *Investment bankers* can make more money by developing new financial instruments and by using high levels of debt to leverage their earnings. (I'll explain how leverage works in Chapter 3.)

- *Investors* want high returns, so if home prices are rising faster than stock prices, they will invest in homes even if they don't intend to live in them. Rising home prices can also lead them to believe that mortgage-backed securities carry very little risk.

- *The federal government* wants a growing economy with strong demand, but not strong enough to fuel inflation. So the government encourages easy credit to help drive demand for goods and services, as long as it believes inflation is under control.

WHAT'S THAT?

The term *credit crisis* refers to a lack of funds to lend, or to an unwillingness of banks and other parties to lend funds. A **financial crisis** is a more widespread event characterized by lack of confidence in the financial markets, widespread selling of securities, and an unwillingness or inability to invest.

Now these players and incentives had been in place for decades. What changed were the four fatal factors that brought about the crisis.

Fatal Factor #1: Low Interest Rates and Easy Money

In the 1990s and the 2000s, there was too much money available for speculation on, respectively, technology stocks and housing. As a result, we experienced a tech-stock bubble in the 1990s and a housing bubble in the 2000s.

There was "too much money" because in each of those decades the Federal Reserve (the Fed) departed to a degree from its former monetary policy. The Fed—the U.S. *central bank*—regulates the banking system in the United States. Monetary policy influences the supply of money in the economy, which affects economic growth. In general, low interest rates increase the money supply and encourage growth, and high interest rates decrease the money supply and temper growth.

WHAT'S THAT?

A **central bank** is usually a government owned and operated "bank for banks," which regulates the banking system, makes loans to banks, sets interest rates, and implements economic policies. The Bank of England and the Bank of Japan are, like the U.S. Federal Reserve, also central banks.

Under its former monetary policy, the Fed would raise interest rates relatively early in an economic expansion to keep the economy from "overheating." Higher rates make loans costlier, which makes it harder for consumers and businesses to obtain loans to buy goods and services, which *decreases* demand and hampers or halts economic growth. This is often referred to as the Fed "taking away the punch bowl as the party gets going."

Why would the government do that? To control inflation. When the economy overheats, businesses and consumers bid up the price of goods and services, and as unemployment decreases workers can push for higher wages. Both of these forces can generate inflation—a decrease in the purchasing power of a currency.

Traditionally the Fed *lowers* interest rates when the economy slows down, making it easier for consumers and businesses to obtain loans to purchase goods and services. That boosts demand, which creates jobs and heads off a recession or fuels an expansion.

The Fed didn't completely abandon this monetary policy, but it departed from it under Fed Chairman Alan Greenspan and kept interest rates relatively low during the expansions of the 1990s and 2000s, even as the economy heated up. From January 2001 to June 2003, the Fed cut the *Federal Funds rate* from 6.5 percent (its May 2000 peak) to a low of 1 percent in June 2003—where it remained until June 2004. Indeed, at its next peak, the Fed Funds rate reached 5.25 percent in June 2006 (well below the previous 6.5 percent peak in 2000). Inflation during the six-year expansion from 2002 through 2007 averaged 2.7 percent, which the Fed viewed as comfortably low or at least tolerable.

WHAT'S THAT?

The **Federal Funds rate** (or Fed Funds rate) is the interest rate that the Federal Reserve charges on overnight loans to member banks. This rate is actually "targeted" and set through market forces rather than actually being "set" by the Fed.

The low interest rates of those years made large sums available to the mortgage market, which helped to fuel the housing bubble. The Fed's hesitancy to raise rates also fostered expectations that low interest rates would continue in the future and keep the mortgage and housing markets bubbling along. Those rates and expectations also fueled record levels of consumer debt, particularly credit card debt.

Many observers, myself included, expected the bursting of the tech-stock bubble back in 2000 to usher in a severe recession. (I'll discuss the tech-stock bubble in Chapter 4.) Instead, the United States entered a mild eight-month recession in March 2001. After that recession came the six-year Bush expansion, which lasted from November 2001 through November 2007. During this expansion, easy money helped fuel the housing bubble, which replaced the tech-stock bubble and kept the U.S. economic carousel spinning.

Fatal Factor #2: The Housing Bubble

The second fatal factor was the housing bubble, which occurred from 2002 until April 2007, when average nationwide housing prices peaked. Generally, bubbles follow an eightfold path (but they don't lead to Nirvana):

1. People start setting a value on an item—stocks, houses, whatever—that's historically well beyond the item's intrinsic worth. *Initially* this occurs for seemingly rational reasons, usually because the price has been bid up by high demand and limited supply.

2. People come to expect the price of the item to rise rapidly and indefinitely, and it does grow rapidly for a time.

3. As the bubble expands, people formerly not in the market enter it (think cabbies day trading stocks in the 1990s); they have little expertise in the market and simply want easy, outsized profits.

4. People speculate on the prospect that prices will rise fast enough for them to realize strong appreciation so they can sell before the bubble bursts.

5. Earlier (and savvier) market participants take their profits and exit the market.

6. People in the market run out of new buyers at the overvalued prices and try to sell quickly before the bubble bursts, often at lower prices than they expected.

7. A situation of many sellers and few buyers drives down prices and causes the market to collapse, at which point the bubble bursts.

8. Prices return to levels more in line with the true value of the item, and the market remains sluggish until demand recovers. In this stage, the early participants may re-enter the market and buy at bargain prices.

WHAT TO DO?

The next time a bubble in stocks, housing, precious metals, or any other asset comes along, either sit on the sidelines or be very aware of the "bubblelike" conditions. In order to make money from a bubble, you must enter fairly early and leave when you have hit your target for appreciation. Entering or leaving too late can be financially ruinous.

In the early stages of a bubble, the skyrocketing prices can seem justified. The U.S. housing markets that experienced the fastest appreciation were places many people saw as desirable, with good climates and growing economies, such as California, Florida, and Las Vegas. So there can be a thin line between "high prices driven by strong demand" and "irrational exuberance." That's why bubbles are far easier to see in hindsight than while they are still expanding.

Yet there were clear indicators of a bubble in the U.S. housing market in the 2000s, if you examined some fundamental data. For instance, the ratio of home prices to rental costs reached a 36-year high in 2006. That's an indicator of how far prices had risen beyond the intrinsic value of a house as shelter. The ratio of average home prices to average incomes reached similar highs, meaning that homes were not affordable without incurring large amounts of debt—beyond the mortgage debt. In other words, mortgage payments rose so high relative to incomes that many homebuyers didn't have enough money for food, fuel, and other necessities, unless they borrowed against their equity or used their credit cards. One of the best indicators of the bubble was that many people with no real estate experience entered the market with hopes of making a quick buck *and* borrowed money to purchase houses and condos they never intended to live in.

In addition to those indicators, there was the mortgage mania that accompanied the housing bubble. Since almost all U.S. housing purchases are financed with mortgages, the bubble could not have happened without madcap mortgage-industry practices.

Fatal Factor #3: New Mortgages and Bad Credit Policy

Mortgage and finance companies developed newfangled mortgages for homebuyers who would not qualify for standard mortgages. Dating from the late 1930s, standard mortgages have featured a 20 percent down payment and a 30-year term, and mortgage lending was a conservative business, with the loan secured by a valuable asset (the home being financed). Then legislation enacted by Congress in 1982 to deregulate the savings and loan industry permitted the adjustable rate mortgage (ARM).

ARMs became popular because they typically give borrowers a lower initial interest rate than a fixed-rate mortgage. There was (and is) nothing necessarily wrong with ARMs, but if they're not handled carefully, they can be dangerous to both borrowers and lenders. If interest rates rise substantially, ARMs can expose borrowers to sharp increases in their payments and increase the risk of default. If rates fall to low levels, the lender can lose money because his funding costs were higher than the current rate on the mortgage. Thus, an ARM should have a reasonable "collar"—a maximum-rate ceiling (or "cap") and a minimum-rate floor, which is often the initial rate at which the loan was made.

However, during the bubble, rates were low and many ARMs were written without reasonable caps. Note that ARM rates are tied to specific interest rates set in the credit markets, such as the London Interbank Offered Rate (LIBOR), which the borrower may not be familiar with, and usually feature a margin added to the rate, such as LIBOR plus 2 or even 3 percent. In such negotiations, lenders typically have more knowledge of rates and rate movements than do borrowers, who are therefore at a disadvantage in negotiations. Thus, when rates reset at higher levels at the times specified in the mortgage agreements, payments often became too costly for the borrowers. This situation, known as "payment shock," affected many borrowers in the 2000s, who then became unable to make their payments.

While prime and subprime mainly describe the borrowers, the terms are also used to describe these borrowers' mortgages. Mortgage loan classifications, which are essentially defined by Fannie Mae and Freddie Mac, can become somewhat technical. In general, a prime mortgage is one in which borrowers' monthly payments are one fourth to one third or so of their monthly incomes; these borrowers have good credit histories and detailed income, employment, and credit documentation. Subprime borrowers are those who fail to meet those guidelines, who have low credit scores, or who seek high loan-to-value mortgages.

Mortgage loans are generally described as conforming or nonconforming. Conforming loans are those that meet Fannie Mae's and Freddie Mac's underwriting guidelines, loan limits, and regulatory parameters. Nonconforming loans do not meet these conditions; for instance, mortgages that go beyond the loan limits ("jumbo mortgages") are nonconforming.

Alt-A mortgages are those with features like zero down payment and no income verification. They often offer borrowers "teaser" rates that typically have little relation to the rate they will pay after the term of the teaser rate runs out, usually a period ranging from a few months to a year or two. Alt-A mortgages are *technically* not subprime loans, but are, according to Freddie Mac's Glossary, "inferior to prime pools, often as a result of lack of documentation and perhaps a small credit-related blemish." However, in practice, these mortgages were directed toward noncreditworthy borrowers, partly because the bubble required new market participants in order to keep expanding. The borrowers and lenders who signed these Alt-A mortgages and subprime mortgages created unprecedented numbers of defaults and foreclosures.

Not requiring a down payment radically departs from sound mortgage-lending policy. A down payment gives the owner equity in the house from the start *and* something to lose if financial trouble arises and he thinks about walking away. It also demonstrates the ability to save (or acquire) a substantial sum, and thus represents a level of financial responsibility (or at least access to someone with that responsibility).

An institution's *credit policy* defines who it will lend to and under what terms, and stipulates the information and standards required for proof of creditworthiness. As credit policy, requiring no down payment is bad enough, but not requiring proof of income borders on insanity—unless, of course, you are lending someone else's money. As we'll see in Chapter 3, that's exactly what happened, and unethical mortgage professionals took advantage of that.

WHAT'S THAT?

A bank or company's **credit policy** is a set of rules and procedures that guide its employees and managers in making lending decisions.

Much has been written and said about the role of irresponsible or dishonest subprime borrowers in the mortgage crisis. People who borrow money that they can't pay back are clearly wrong; however, the lender is the professional who sets his own credit policy and determines who he lends to, and the fact is that lenders were as dishonest as borrowers, if not more so. After all, subprime borrowers could have somehow believed they would get better-paying jobs or hit it big in Vegas. Moreover, many borrowers couldn't understand the deals they agreed to and believed what they were told by those nice folks down at the mortgage origination office. The mortgage professionals who originated, approved, and resold their loans, however, knew exactly what they were doing.

Much has also been written and said about the efforts of politicians and Fannie Mae and Freddie Mac to expand homeownership to lower-income citizens. Those efforts clearly occurred and definitely contributed to the crisis, and we'll examine how in Chapter 3.

WHAT TO DO?

Be sure to understand whatever you sign, and ask for a plain-English explanation of every contract. Even though you may think that a lender would not do anything to harm his or your financial status, it's been proven that a good number of them will.

Fatal Factor #4: Mortgage-Backed Securities and Derivatives

Mortgage-backed securities (MBSs)—and, to an extent, the derivatives linked to them, called credit default swaps—transformed a bad financial situation into a full-blown crisis. Credit default swaps are so complex that even the people who bought and sold them didn't understand them, so I'll cover them in Chapter 4 and in chapters to follow. Also, with one exception that I will mention, they haven't done much actual damage (yet). However, it wasn't MBSs but MBSs based on subprime mortgages that caused the actual crisis. (I'll use the term subprime to include Alt-A mortgages, as most writers do, because, despite Freddie Mac's definition, not-prime means subprime.)

MBSs are a subset of a type of security known as a collateralized debt obligation (CDO). In general, a CDO is a security formed of a bundle or "package" of debt obligations. The obligations are most often consumer debt, such as home mortgages, car loans, or credit card balances. These obligations are genuine assets because they represent an income stream—the payments from the borrowers who must by contract pay the mortgages, car loans, or credit card balances.

There are economically sound motivations for developing, selling, and buying these securities:

- The banks or finance companies that extended the loans get paid less than the full amount owed, but they get paid faster and thus have more money to lend to more borrowers.

- The investment bank that bundles the loans into securities and sells them to investors earns a fee for doing so.

- The investor who purchases the CDO obtains a relatively low-risk investment secured by contractually agreed-upon income streams (hence the term *collateralized* to describe these securities, and *securitization* to describe the process by which they are created).

A CDO is also often referred to as an asset-backed security (ABS) because the securities are backed by the loans, which are financial assets to the creditors. Historically, CDOs were low-risk investments because the original lenders could ensure that a high percentage of the borrowers—say, 96 or 97 percent—would repay their loans. Banks, mortgage lenders, and auto-finance and credit card companies had developed highly accurate methods of evaluating borrowers and forecasting default rates.

However, that didn't apply to a lot of the MBSs being sold to investors as the subprime mortgage market expanded from 2001 to 2005. Those subprime mortgages—essentially riskier loans extended to noncreditworthy borrowers—were used to back thousands of MBSs in a process that I'll describe in Chapter 3.

For now, the key point here is threefold. First, the widespread packaging of subprime loans into MBSs represented a departure from earlier practice in which a lower volume of those loans were securitized—that is, bundled into securities. Second, subprime loans were combined in securities in ways that increased the risk of the securities while also disguising that risk, at times in unethical ways. Third, reputable bond rating agencies, such as Moody's and Standard & Poor's, led some investors to believe these securities were far less risky than they were, as we'll see in Chapter 4.

So risky subprime mortgages embedded in thousands of MBSs distributed by at times unethical financial professionals to ignorant investors formed a house of cards destined to collapse when subprime borrowers could no longer make their payments (when the "teaser" rates on their ARMs expired and their monthly payments ballooned). On top of all that, this occurred in an environment in which incomes remained flat even during an expansion, consumer debt financed a lot of consumer spending, and homeowners tapped "equity" resulting from paper gains created by the housing bubble.

The Rest of the Story

Of course, these four fatal factors don't tell the whole story. They are meant to sketch the outlines of the crisis and the key drivers of it. There are many other factors linked to these. Also, any one of these factors in and of itself would not jeopardize the broader economy. As noted, the basic motivations were often sensible. More than any one or even two factors, it was the combination of all four in an environment of high debt, flat incomes, and lax regulation that made them deadly. That environment made them not merely combustible but explosive.

Everyone should understand that this crisis didn't "just happen." The four factors and the environment in which they mixed came about due to specific government policies. In a developed *mixed economy*, policies determine the type and degree of regulation, the incentives for buying a home, the supply of money, the price of loans, the type and level of taxation, and the conditions for everything from starting a business to hiring employees to declaring bankruptcy. Policies are created by elected and appointed officials. Every policy aims to achieve certain goals by influencing certain parties in certain ways. Although unintended outcomes often occur and policies may fail to achieve their goals, it's essential to understand the effects of policies and how they might affect you and your future.

WHAT'S THAT?

In a **mixed economy,** the government and the private sector each play a significant role. Like most industrial economies, the U.S. economy is mixed. In contrast, a free-market economy has no government involvement in transactions, and a socialist economy is essentially government-controlled.

Finally, if you really want to understand the origins of the crisis, try to identify and examine the things that changed over the past 15 to 20 years. I mentioned that during those years monetary policy became looser during expansions, and mortgage-backed securities based on subprime loans became more common. Other changes include increased government encouragement of homeownership for lower-income families and Wall Street investment banks going public in the late 1980s and the 1990s, as well as unprecedented levels of household and government debt.

In the next chapter, we turn from the causes of what happened to exactly what happened in the housing market.

The Least You Need to Know

- Easy credit and relatively low interest rates allowed the housing and mortgage markets to grow rapidly from 2002 to 2006.

- Bubbles occur when people bid the price of an item beyond its actual value, believe that prices will continue to rise, and enter the market believing they can make a quick killing before prices collapse—which prices in a bubble always eventually do.

- Mortgage-backed securities provide funds to the housing market, fees for the packagers of the securities, and low-risk returns for investors; however, lenders abandoned sound credit policy, originators passed along bad loans, and packagers securitized and sold them and thus misused MBSs.

- No single policy, event, or group of people created the crisis. It was the result of various elements interacting in an environment that contained certain imbalances and posed certain risks, neither of which were addressed by either the public or the private sector. That environment, however, was created mainly by public policies.

The Housing Crisis— Markets Gone Wild

In This Chapter

- Policies that favor the housing market
- How the mortgage market changed
- How subprime mortgages morphed into risky securities
- The bubble bursts: effects and aftereffects

In this chapter, we dive more deeply into the housing and mortgage crises to examine how the interplay between rising housing prices and easy mortgage money led to the housing bubble. That bubble burst when interest rates rose, homeowners couldn't make their increased payments, speculators and homeowners rushed to sell, and home prices collapsed. The effects flowed into the financial markets through the medium of mortgage-backed securities. Credit markets seized up, easy money dried up, and confidence in markets plummeted as the solvency of many financial institutions was threatened.

This chapter also examines how mortgage originators and rating agencies fell down on the job, and the roles of Fannie Mae and Freddie Mac.

Encouraging Homeownership

The U.S. government encourages homeownership mainly through the tax deductibility of mortgage interest (up to a total of $1 million on first and second homes). This was not an original intent of the tax code, because *all* interest used to be tax deductible. Although many homeowners don't itemize deductions (which you must do in order to claim the deduction), the deductibility of interest means a lot to most homeowners—and to the real estate and homebuilding industries.

Other U.S. policies also favor homeownership. With the Tax Reform Act of 1986, Congress eliminated the tax deductibility of interest on *other* forms of consumer credit, such as auto loans, personal loans, and credit card balances. This boosted the popularity of the home-equity line, on which you can deduct up to $100,000 in interest from your income for tax purposes. Also, a capital-gains tax provision allows profits up to $250,000 ($500,000 for a married couple) on the sale of a home to be tax-free. In addition, property taxes are deductible, which shelters homeowners from that expense.

Most politicians view these policies favorably because homeownership generally benefits the U.S. economy (and, of course, voters). In any developed economy, population increases and household formation drive the baseline level of economic growth. When people buy their homes rather than rent, they need a lot of "stuff"—appliances, lawn mowers, tools, pools, and so on—that they don't need if they rent. It's a recipe for a true consumer society, and it's the result of policy decisions.

Of course, the real estate industry—developers, real estate agents, and the construction trades—support and benefit from those policies, too. So do banks, mortgage lenders, and property and casualty insurance companies, who in a sense have government-subsidized markets of borrowers and policyholders.

WHAT TO DO?

Understand both the positive and negative effects of government policies. Many people forget the positives (and not just subsidies for homeowners). They fail to see how much they benefit from policies that put in place roads and other infrastructure, national security, police protection, courts, and the entire system of laws and financial markets. Without those things, there can be no productive modern society.

Mortgage Market Changes

Like everything else, the mortgage business used to be simpler. From the 1940s into the 1970s, savings and loans and other relatively small banks took deposits and loaned much of the money to homebuyers. The local banker, personified by George Bailey in the classic Christmas film *It's a Wonderful Life*, supported strong communities and values such as family life, neighborliness, and plain old decency. To an extent, these values became linked in the public mind with homeownership, despite later portrayals of soulless suburbia. The psychology of the public aside, this much is certain: by the 1990s, the George Baileys of the world had left the field to the profit-hungry bankers personified by Bailey's nemesis, Mr. Potter.

After the U.S. savings and loan crisis of the late 1980s (a subject covered in Chapter 8), the mortgage market changed dramatically, if gradually. The S&L crisis resulted in the closure or failure of over 1,500 thrift institutions from 1986 through 1995. This left more of the home-financing market to mortgage finance companies, mortgage originators and brokers, large commercial banks, and others who often had less stake in the communities.

Meanwhile, the market for securitized mortgage loans was poised for rapid growth. (Securitization is the process of bundling numerous small loans—such as mortgages, auto loans, or credit card balances—into securities that are then sold to investors.) From 1995 to 2003, the portion of conventional loans being securitized grew from 46 percent to 76 percent, while that of subprime loans grew from 28 percent to 59 percent.

Securitization facilitates resale of the loan, gets it off the lender's *balance sheet*, and ends the direct relationship between borrower and lender. When that relationship is severed, lenders and borrowers have less stake in one another's situation, which can tempt some lenders to take advantage of borrowers and some borrowers to take advantage of lenders. In business, it's much easier to leave someone you don't know holding the bag, as opposed to someone you do know.

WHAT'S THAT?

A bank or company's **balance sheet** shows its financial position at a given point in time, such as the last day of the calendar year. It shows assets, liabilities, and owners' equity, which is assets minus liabilities. In contrast, an income statement shows revenues, costs, and earnings—or financial performance—during a given period, such as a year.

Origination Sins

When the housing market heated up in the early 2000s, the number of mortgage originators and brokers exploded. These outfits had existed before and served as useful middlemen, bringing together borrowers and lenders. At least initially in the housing bubble, much origination occurred in home-equity loans. These deals are easier to do than mortgages because the owner already occupies the home and just wants to borrow against his equity. But these loans were made not only against the homeowner's equity from the down payment and mortgage payments, but also against "equity" generated by the rapidly rising prices.

For example, if you buy a house for $250,000 and put 20 percent down, you'll have a $200,000 mortgage and $50,000 in equity. If in three years the price rises to $350,000, then (the logic went) you have $150,000 of equity. But two thirds of that is a paper gain that you'd realize only if you actually sold the house for $350,000. Yet lenders cheerfully loaned and borrowers cheerfully borrowed real money against such paper gains.

Also, an article in the Jan./Feb. 2006 *Federal Reserve Bank of St. Louis Review* pointed out that slightly over one half of subprime loans nationwide had been for cash-out refinancing at that point. (Cash-out refinancing enables borrowers to borrow against the equity in their home with a new mortgage for a higher amount than they owe on their existing mortgage. The borrower then pays off the existing mortgage and pockets the difference between the amount of that mortgage and the amount he borrowed.)

Mortgage originators marketed these loans aggressively, and many people used their homes as ATM machines in this way. These loans helped fuel the housing bubble by reinforcing the expectation of rising home prices. Worse, they gave people money to buy yet another house or condo. Think about it: rising home prices provided paper gains against which people borrowed to further bid up home prices. Of course, more people borrowed against their home equity for home renovations, college tuition, and cars and other major purchases. Yet the overall effect was huge amounts of debt taken on in expectation of eternally rising home prices.

Many mortgage loan originators and brokers were honest and useful. They served as new sales channels for financial institutions and enabled borrowers to shop among lenders. But they and the lenders started doing deals with no money down, no income verification, and unrealistic teaser rates, and those mortgages were included in securities that were sold to investors who were not aware of the risks involved. When bad mortgages could be passed on to unsuspecting investors, then the originators and lenders did not have to originate good mortgages—only mortgages they could pass on.

Bad mortgages passed on to others who developed risky securities from them were the time bombs in this scenario. And as the largest packagers of securities, Fannie Mae and Freddie Mac played a major role in this.

Meet Fannie and Freddie

Fannie Mae, the Federal National Mortgage Association (FNMA), was established by Congress in 1938 to provide local banks with federal money to make mortgage loans. The government aimed to shore up a U.S. housing market devastated by foreclosures in the Great Depression. Fannie Mae and Freddie Mac buy primary mortgage loans (meaning no equity lines of credit or second mortgages) to hold in their portfolios *or* to securitize and resell as mortgage-backed securities. In the latter process, they guarantee the mortgage loans and collect fees for securitizing and selling the bundled mortgages. The purpose of this is to expand the pool of funds in the mortgage market, which Fannie and Freddie did.

Freddie Mac, the Federal Home Loan Mortgage Corporation (FHLMC), was chartered by Congress in 1970 to provide competition for Fannie Mae—an odd way to do so, considering both were created by the government with the same purpose and advantages. Freddie Mac was "chartered by Congress as a *private company* serving a public purpose" originally, and has been listed as a publicly held company since 1984. Back in 1968, President Lyndon Johnson had Fannie Mae converted to a government-sponsored enterprise (GSE) and a public company to get it out of the federal budget, which was stressed by the funding demands of the Vietnam War. Both Fannie and Freddie are GSEs, as explained later in this chapter.

 WHAT'S THAT?

The term **private company** distinguishes an organization from a public agency or government organization. Private companies are "publicly held" when their stock is owned and traded by the general public. Private companies are "privately held" when they are owned by an individual or partnership and do not sell stock to the public.

Now let's clear up three points that many people find confusing:

Fannie Mae and Freddie Mac *do not make loans to homeowners.* Instead, they buy mortgages from lenders and either hold those mortgages in their portfolios or "package" them into mortgage-backed securities (MBSs) and sell them to investors. They do this to increase the cash available for mortgage loans and thus expand U.S. homeownership.

Fannie and Freddie *are not government agencies.* Instead, they are GSEs, an ambiguous status. They are publicly held companies, which ranked 53 and 54 among the Fortune 500, based on their 2007 financial results, but they have unique advantages over purely private-sector competitors. Key among these are access to U.S. Treasury funds, exemption from state and local taxes, lower funding costs, and huge market share based on their history and "special status." Through political contributions and lobbying, they also maintained close ties with elected officials (as do purely private-sector financial institutions).

Fannie and Freddie *did not cause the subprime mortgage crisis, but they did contribute to it.* The vast majority of mortgage loans—the actual loans, including subprime loans—were made by private lending institutions. (State, city, veterans', and other public housing agencies also make mortgage loans to or otherwise assist unqualified borrowers.) In 2006, 84 percent of subprime loans were made by private institutions. Until 1992, the GSEs almost exclusively purchased standard loans. Then in 1992, the Department of Housing and Urban Development set low-income loan targets for the GSEs. Thus, the GSEs contributed to the crisis by *purchasing* subprime loans, but it was the private sector that extended the loans. So in that sense, the GSEs were "enablers" of the subprime lenders and borrowers. The GSEs increase in subprime lending sprang from their ambitious—or, perhaps, overreaching—goals as well as from political pressures.

Subprime Strategies and Political Pressures

As GSEs, Fannie and Freddie were responsible both for maximizing shareholders' returns (as are all public companies) and for promoting U.S. homeownership. This whipsawed them between shareholder demands for high returns, and pressures from politicians to expand housing to lower-income families.

Here's what happened: In 2000, Fannie Mae announced vast expansion plans, focused on purchasing mortgages made to riskier, low-income borrowers over the coming decade. These were in addition to the earlier, periodically increasing subprime purchase targets issued by the Department of Housing and Urban Development going back to 1992. Under both the Clinton and George W. Bush administrations, Fannie and Freddie were pressured to expand homeownership to lower-income segments of the population. Democrats were motivated by their impulse to assist lower-income segments of society, while some Republicans wanted to pitch a "big tent" to attract traditionally Democratic voters and, in the 2000s, to act upon George W. Bush's call for "an ownership society." Also, as noted earlier, homeownership is generally good for the economy and is supported by most politicians, as are the housing and home finance industries.

As the major players in mortgage securitization, the GSEs strongly influenced the mortgage industry—but only up to a point. Against the backdrop of rising prices and easy credit, from 2001 to 2004 the overall subprime market—not the GSEs' share—grew from $160 billion to $540 billion (a *235 percent* increase) according to *Inside Mortgage Finance*, a trade publication quoted in *The New York Times* of October 5, 2008. However, in the last three years of the housing bubble, 2004 through 2006, "the private sector securitized almost two thirds of all U.S. mortgages, supplanting Fannie and Freddie."

Did Fannie and Freddie *cause* the subprime crisis? Despite the certainty of commentators answering "yes" or "no," and their ability to quote seemingly convincing anecdotes and statistics, the "enabler" role appears to be supported by the facts and figures. To say the GSEs bear no responsibility would be naïve, given their expertise, market share, subprime volume, goals, and responsiveness to political pressure. Yet it's also naïve to blame them wholly for the crisis—or even the MBS aspects of it—given the large role of purely private-sector mortgage originators and lenders in the subprime market and of investment bankers in the MBS market.

The GSEs acted as enablers by increasing their subprime securitization activity in the late 1990s and early 2000s, which sent the housing and mortgage markets clear signals that there was plenty of money available for subprime lending. This in turn created moral hazard exploited by private-sector parties. Moral hazard refers to the tendency of some people to exploit a shield, or to exercise less care in situations in which they are shielded from negative consequences. For instance, if you have auto theft insurance, you may be less careful about where you park your car. You may even prefer that the car be stolen, if its value has fallen below the insured book value. The GSEs may well have created moral hazard to the extent that lenders and investors in MBSs believed that they would be bailed out or insured for losses. They would clearly have reason to believe that regarding MBSs securitized by the GSEs, but more broadly, the notion that major banks had become *too big to fail* may also have created moral hazard even among private-sector lenders and investors.

 WHAT'S THAT?

A bank or other financial institution (or even a major company, such as an auto manufacturer) may be considered **too big to fail** if its going out of business would greatly disrupt the economy. The disruption could result from tens of thousands of people becoming unemployed, huge financial losses to depositors or investors, or follow-on effects on other companies that could go out of business. If a bank or company is considered too big to fail, the government will usually step up, for instance with financial assistance, to ensure that the business continues in some form.

Fannie Mae and Freddie Mac were charged with mismanagement and undercapitalization and taken over by a conservator on September 7, 2008. (A financial institution is undercapitalized when it does not have enough capital—in relation to its level of assets or debt—to meet levels set by regulators.) Some controversy surrounds this move by the Treasury, which Chapter 5 will examine. (To focus on the bigger picture, I am also leaving aside the early 2000s accounting scandal at Freddie Mac.)

Whatever the roles of the GSEs, the parties who contributed to the crisis also included the companies that gave high ratings to MBSs that did not deserve them.

MBSs Explained

As noted in Chapter 1, mortgage-backed securities (MBSs) are part of the broader type of securities known as collateralized debt obligations (CDOs) and asset-backed securities (ABSs). All of these securities are created in basically the same way: a financial institution purchases a large number of mortgages, auto loans, personal loans, or credit card balances and bundles or "packages" them into securities. The securities are relatively low risk because the borrowers are contractually obligated to pay the loans and lenders have accurate methods of assessing creditworthiness and default rates on consumer loans.

MBSs, however, became complicated because of the way they were structured. Rather than simply bundling whole mortgages, the investment banks broke down the mortgage payment streams into various categories and packaged them into separate securities. For instance, payments of interest were separated (or "stripped out" in financial parlance) and packaged into some securities, while payments of principal were stripped out and packaged into others. In addition, payments of interest or principal for various terms of the mortgages—for instance, interest payments for the first five years—were packaged into some securities and interest payments for the second five years were packaged into others. The same was done with principal payments.

Why do this? Because the investment bank can "design" securities to meet the financial needs of various investors. An investor with a five year horizon could buy an MBS with a five year term. One who thought that interest rates would rise could buy an MBS based on ARMs. And so on.

So how did subprime mortgages cause so much trouble? Picture a meat packing plant that packages bacon. Let's say pork bellies are delivered to the bacon plant every day, and some of them are "prime" and some are "subprime" and they're labeled that way.

The prime pork bellies get cut up into strips and packaged as bacon. Some of these strips are really lean and go into the best brands of bacon, and some are less lean and go into the next best brands, but they're all still prime.

But then we have those subprime pork bellies. Let's say there are three grades of subprime bellies: Subprime 1, Subprime 2, and Subprime 3. They're all fit for human consumption, but some more so than others (and some have a funky taste that *some* bacon-lovers love). Strips from these bellies are graded Subprime 1, 2, or 3 on the packages, so people know what they're buying, and they are priced accordingly, with Subprime 1 priced higher than 2, which is higher than 3. (If you're considering becoming a vegetarian at this point, it's okay!)

Now one day some bacon maven gets a bright idea. He says they can put strips from Subprime 1, 2, and 3 into one package—and charge the Subprime 1 price for that package. A co-worker points out that customers might smell that funky bacon, or even cook it and eat it and be grossed-out by the taste. But the bacon maven says most customers won't notice the Subprime 2 strips, and those that do will just ignore them and even ignore Subprime 3 strips, because no one will be getting sick and the price was right.

This is more or less what happened. Strips—of interest and principal payments, not bacon—were created from subprime loans, and strips from riskier subprime loans were packaged into securities with those of less risky subprime loans. (These strips were organized by their levels of risk into groups called *tranches*. That's a word from the French *trancher*, which means to cut and is also the root of "trench.")

The strategy for structuring the securities in this way was twofold. On the positive side, the idea was to arrange the strips so that if delinquencies started to occur in the subprime market, then the riskier tranches would default but the less risky ones would not. Thus, that MBS would not go into total default. (The lower-rated tranches would act as protective "trenches" and absorb the defaults and leave the higher-quality tranches unscathed.) As a relatively risky security, these MBSs would carry higher interest, so the investor would be compensated for that risk with higher interest rates.

But on the negative side, this became a method by which the investment banks obtained higher ratings for the entire security. In other words, in our bacon metaphor, the whole package of bacon was often labeled Subprime 1, even though it included strips of bacon rated Subprime 1, 2, and 3.

This is the way it worked because the rating agencies did not do their jobs thoroughly.

Rating Agencies: Asleep at the Switch

In the United States, a few companies rate almost all bonds and other debt securities issued by public companies. The two largest rating agencies are Moody's and Standard & Poor's (S&P). These are not government agencies, nor are they "agencies" in any true sense, although that's what they're called. (A true agency, such as a talent or insurance agency, is legally empowered to make certain decisions and take certain actions on behalf of the party it represents.) These companies rate debt securities for creditworthiness and risk, which helps the market price those securities. (Disclosure: In the 1980s, I worked for six months at Moody's, then a business unit of Dun & Bradstreet, in its information business—not the debt-rating business.)

Moody's and S&P's fees are paid by the companies whose securities they are rating, and this creates a clear conflict of interest. (One could claim the same of public accounting firms being paid by the companies they audit; however, accounting is a profession, like medicine and law, with strict educational and professional standards and governing bodies. This hardly makes them perfect, but the debt-rating industry lacks even those safeguards.) If a rating agency delivers a lower-than-expected rating, a client company may go elsewhere next time. That provides an incentive for the agency to "rate easy" in some situations.

In general, debt-rating agencies set their ratings based on information about the issuer's financial performance and strength, the nature of the security, and the purpose for which the money is being raised. Given that the MBSs in question were created from "strips" of various mortgages, often on the basis of complex, computerized risk-analysis programs, they could be difficult to rate. There is no income statement and balance sheet as there are for corporate entities issuing bonds, and no taxing or toll-collecting authorities as there are for state and municipal bonds. There is also no practical way to analyze the creditworthiness of all of the borrowers behind the MBS once their payments are stripped out and packaged in complex ways.

In other words, because of the way strips were combined, the actual risk of an MBS became obscured. This meant that for some investment banks and funds, securitization basically became a means of converting risky mortgages into artificially high-rated securities. By structuring the security with tranches of varying degrees of risk, the actual risks of the security became obscured. Then the bond rating agencies rated the entire MBS artificially high, by either assigning it the risk associated with the best strips within the security (as in our Subprime 1 bacon example), by conducting poor analysis, or by relying on the reputation of the investment bank that had structured the MBS.

So given high-risk and low-risk tranches in single securities, the inaccuracy and unreliability of the ratings, and the lack of *transparency*—that is, lack of the ability to see and understand the actual risk of the securities—the subprime defaults that began in 2006 created widespread loss of confidence in *all* MBSs, which by then had been purchased by thousands of banks, funds, and investors worldwide. If the subprime loans and strips from them had been sequestered only in lower-rated MBSs, then the higher-rated securities would have remained safe. Securitization practices created complexity that left few purchasers (or sellers) of MBSs understanding their value after the bubble burst. This problem persists in the form of "toxic assets" that banks cannot value or sell.

One "reason" given to date for the securities' complexity and unmeasured risk is that the algorithms used in constructing them could not accommodate the possibility of falling home prices. On the face of it, that's absurd. Virtually any properly constructed risk-management system accounts for possible downside developments. *That's the point of risk analysis!* We will delve more deeply into the reasons for the meltdown in the MBS market in Chapter 3.

 WHAT'S THAT?

Transparency indicates the degree to which a management team shows investors, employees, and other stakeholders what is really going on in the organization. Accounting rules and financial market regulations generally aim to promote transparency.

The Bubble Bursts

Five key events caused the housing bubble to burst in 2007. As noted in Chapter 1, interest rates rose steadily, with the Fed Funds rate (belatedly and too gradually) quintupling from 1 percent in mid-2003 to 5.25 percent in mid-2006, where it remained until September 2007. While not rapid and high enough to stop the bubble sooner, the increases ultimately took effect. In July 2007, mortgage rates finally peaked with the 30-year fixed rate at 6.75 and the 5-year ARM at 6.25. Those increases triggered subprime defaults when adjustable rates reset and borrowers' monthly payments skyrocketed.

Average nationwide housing prices peaked in April 2007, according to the Office of Federal Housing Enterprise Oversight (OFHEO). Shortly thereafter, subprime defaults increased. Over the next 12 months, average home prices fell 4.6 percent. Although that might seem like a small drop given the size of the crisis, in some regions homeowners had grown used to—and in some ways reliant upon—double-digit annual appreciation.

In 2005, nearly 28 percent of homes were purchased as investments rather than as residences; in 2006, that figure dropped to 22 percent (from 1.6 million to 1.1 million homes), a clear indication of a deflating bubble. Much of the record homebuying for investment represented pure speculation on the expectation of rapidly rising prices.

Defaults and foreclosures started hitting financial institutions in 2006 and 2007, with foreclosures increasing to more than 1.2 million homes in 2007, almost *80 percent* more than the 2006 level. In February 2007, HSBC, one of the world's largest banks, announced write-downs of $10.5 billion in MBSs related to subprime loans. In April 2007, large subprime lender New Century Financial Corp. filed for bankruptcy, as did American Home Mortgage Investment Company in August 2007. The fate of these institutions spooked investors as well as the mortgage market.

By mid-2008 the rating agencies had downgraded some $1.9 *trillion* worth of MBSs. However, the entire market of U.S. subprime mortgages totaled $1.3 trillion, well below that downgraded figure. This indicated that the contagion of subprime mortgages had spread throughout the MBS market and would take a toll on the financial markets, financial institutions, and the broader economy.

Financial stress—inability to pay financial obligations as they become due—brought down investment bank Bear Stearns in March 2008. In July 2008, the credit markets froze and financial markets saw heavy selling when Indy Mac, a major California mortgage lender, collapsed and was taken over by the federal government. That same month, Congress passed the Housing and Economic Recovery Act of 2008. (Part 2 describes the major steps the government took to address the crisis.) Investors had no way of knowing how broad and how deep the risk of widespread, massive defaults on mortgage-related obligations had become or how far it would spread. In September 2009, Lehman Brothers failed, Fannie and Freddie were taken over by regulators, and Congress began seriously debating the Emergency Economic Stabilization Act.

Mortgage Meltdown in the Rearview Mirror

Theoretically, the risk of default was supposed to be concentrated in the higher-risk tranches of the subprime MBSs, but widespread defaults placed all MBSs under suspicion. This occurred partly because so many MBSs had been sold to so many institutions and investors, and it became unclear just where the risks were and how extensive they were. So in reality, the subprime risks were not "sequestered" in their tranches, but instead caused contagion and fear of contagion to spread throughout the financial markets.

Consider this: the entire subprime mortgage market totaled $1.3 trillion, and yet after hundreds of billions in write-offs by financial institutions and hundreds more in government assistance, the end of the "toxic assets" and of the related write-offs was not in sight, even in mid-2009. Far from representing a sound risk-management and securitization strategy, these MBSs spread unknown levels of financial risk far and wide, with virtually nobody positioned to understand the full extent of the potential damage.

The Least You Need to Know

- Certain policies, such as the tax deductibility of mortgage interest and the creation of government agencies to purchase and guarantee mortgages, "subsidize" and encourage homeownership.
- Fannie Mae and Freddie Mac enabled, but did not actually cause, the credit and financial crisis.
- Bond rating agencies face an inherent conflict of interest because they are paid by the companies whose securities they are rating for sale in the public securities markets.
- Subprime MBSs composed of strips organized into tranches of varying degrees of risk were supposed to protect the entire security. However, the strategy was undermined by the lack of disclosure over their true risks, inaccurate ratings, and unanticipated numbers of subprime borrowers defaulting on their loans.

Debt Debacles and Financial Follies

In This Chapter

* How consumer and government debt contributed to the crisis
* Leverage on Wall Street and the impact on Main Street
* How investment banking as we knew it came to an end
* Credit default swaps explained

In this chapter, we turn to a more detailed look at the role of debt in the financial crisis of 2008. From 2000 to 2007, consumers and the federal government took on debt at unprecedented rates. For consumers, that included debt in addition to mortgages and home-equity lines. For the federal government, that meant new levels of deficit spending. This chapter explains why this run-up in debt occurred and with what effects.

We also look at the ways in which financial institutions used debt to leverage their earnings but left themselves vulnerable to losses. This chapter examines the role of Wall Street in the crisis and its impact on Main Street, and how investment banking as we knew it came to an end.

How Debt Became the American Way of Life

As I've mentioned, one good way to understand the origins of the crisis is to identify things that changed over the past 15 or 20 years. Among the most significant of these changes was the way households, the government, and financial institutions used debt—and the vast amounts they used.

Credit has many good uses. Businesses want to grow, and most businesses need credit to finance growth. Of course, growth is also financed out of profits, but what if the company wants to grow faster than its profits permit? That often occurs in a startup company, an established company facing a major opportunity, or any company in an expanding market. (To focus on debt, I'm leaving aside selling stock to raise money.) So a business will borrow to build an office or factory, buy computers, and hire workers to produce a product or service. The company intends to earn enough to pay its expenses, pay back the debt and the interest on it, *and* make a profit.

There are, of course, good uses of debt for households and governments. But the problem in the crisis was not use of debt by commercial and industrial companies or sensible use of debt by others. The problem was overuse of debt by consumers and use of debt by financial institutions to achieve what is known as *leverage*. I'll explain how leverage works in this chapter, but basically it means borrowing money to invest, and it was a major cause of the crisis. But first let's look at government debt, which also played a role in the crisis and has hampered the speed and strength of the recovery.

WHAT'S THAT?

Leverage occurs when an investor or business person borrows money and then invests it at a higher rate than the interest rate he or she must pay on the debt. This increases the rate of return on the investment—as long as nothing goes wrong.

I.O.U. (Signed) Uncle Sam

A government uses debt to finance budget shortfalls—called deficits—which occur when the government spends more than it collects in tax revenues. The U.S. government does not have to balance its budget, but by law, states must balance theirs. (After all, they cannot print money; the federal government can.) A deficit is the shortfall between revenues and expenditures in a period of time, usually a year. The national debt—roughly the cumulative total of past deficits—results from deficit spending by the federal government. Every year that the government runs a budget deficit, it adds to the national debt, which is the total amount of Treasury bills, notes, and bonds issued but not paid off by the U.S. government.

The U.S. national debt increased in every decade since 1900 except one (the 1920s). But before the crisis of 2008–2009, the most dramatic run-up occurred from 1984 through 2007—during a long economic expansion with only two recessions, one of them (in 2001) quite mild. That's significant because heavy deficit spending shouldn't be necessary in expansions, when tax revenues rise and economic stimulus is not needed. The following table shows the total national debt at the 10-year marks for the decades from 1950 to 2000 and at the end of 2008.

U.S. National Debt and Percent Increases 1950–2008

Year	National Debt	Percent Increase
1950	$257 billion	
1960	$286 billion	11.3
1970	$371 billion	30.8
1980	$908 billion	144.7
1990	$3.2 trillion	252.4
2000	$5.7 trillion	78.1
2008	$10 trillion	172.7

Source: U.S. Treasury

This analysis doesn't relate the debt to the size of the economy, and it leaves inflation aside. Instead, these figures portray the size of the deficit while side-stepping the difficulties of evaluating the deficits of specific presidents. Politicians often game their budget and deficit numbers by "borrowing" from Social Security, classifying certain costs (such as the war in Iraq under George W. Bush) as "off-budget," and other tactics.

WHAT TO DO?

Listen carefully. Some of the politicians who protest loudest about deficits when the opposition party is in office promote deficit spending when their own party is in. Ross Perot was the last politician who tried to explain the effects of deficits to voters—and he ran for president in 1992 and 1996.

Meanwhile, quite a few Republicans who want a government that's capable of providing only minimal services supported high deficit spending with the goal of "starving the beast"—that is, breaking the federal government. This strategy worked, in a sense, in that the high deficits limited U.S. policy options, such as stimulus spending and publicly financed health care during the 2008–2009 recession. High deficits still limit our options.

The trend is clear. Federal spending rapidly outpaced revenue in the 1970s, a time of sluggish growth and (until 1975) the Vietnam War. By 1980, the national debt was approaching $1 trillion. By 1990, it hit $3.2 trillion, with most of the increase on President Reagan's watch. Even with George H. W. Bush's tax increase and the Clinton expansion, the national debt increased almost 80 percent in the 1990s. Yet, as the table shows, the run-up in the 1990s was moderate compared with the increase during George W. Bush's two terms in office.

Three major controversies repeatedly arise regarding the national debt and deficit spending:

Deficits don't matter. It does matter when an entity always borrows heavily to fund its expenses. It may not kill a country, but government deficits and the interest paid on the debt they create suck up capital that could have gone to private investment. Also, unbridled spending sets a bad example for the populace and leads people to believe they can get something (specifically government services) for nothing. Deficit spending is best used to stimulate growth or to invest in infrastructure, but the United States has done it during most expansionary years and to finance current expenses, including wars, rather than long-term infrastructure investments.

We don't have to repay the national debt because we owe it to ourselves. We don't "owe it to ourselves" if we'll be dead before it's repaid. We're just shifting our expenses to future generations. Also, we now owe trillions to foreign nations and investors. In 2009, U.S. Treasury figures stated that $3 trillion is held by foreign entities, with $2 trillion held by the top five holders (China, Japan, the United Kingdom, Caribbean banking centers, and oil-exporting nations). Many citizens doubt our ability to conduct foreign policy without considering certain foreign creditors' potential responses.

No problem! U.S. securities are the world's safest. This has been true and, at the moment, remains so, but U.S. paper is backed only by the taxing power of the government. So foreign investors essentially hold pieces of paper with "I.O.U.—Uncle Sam" written on them. If the United States lacks the productivity and fiscal responsibility to back that up, investors may put their money elsewhere. And perhaps soon. The January 7, 2009, *New York Times* cited "the declining Chinese appetite for United States debt, apparent in a series of hints from Chinese policy makers over the last two weeks." China isn't saying U.S. debt is poor quality, but that they had other things to do with their money that year, such as funding their own $600 billion stimulus package.

The crisis showed that if something seems illogical, unsustainable, or mathematically unsound, seemingly sophisticated arguments don't make it otherwise. Unbridled deficit spending is all of those things. Yet consumers have also incurred unprecedented levels of debt.

Household Finance

Please bear three things in mind as we examine consumer borrowing before the crisis.

Consumer spending accounts for almost 70 percent of GDP. When economists say "consumers have run out of steam," they're saying they can't spend enough to keep the economy growing.

From 1970 to 2000 (the most recent census), a portion of total U.S. income was redistributed (or re-redistributed, if you prefer) from the bottom 80 percent to the top 20 percent of the population, and even more so to the top 5 percent, as shown in the following table. (Each quintile is 20 percent of the U.S. population.) Each of the bottom four quintiles lost share of income from 1970 to 2000, while the top quintile's share rose from 43.3 percent to 49.9 percent. Thus the top 20 percent of households made 50 percent of the nation's income. (The top 5 percent's share rose from 16.6 percent to 21.9 percent.)

These figures are from 2000, and the trend intensified under George W. Bush. According to the October 12, 2007, *Wall Street Journal*, the top *1 percent* of the population received 21.7 percent of all income in 2005 (up from 19 percent in 2004), while the bottom *50 percent* received 12.8 percent (down from 13 percent in 2004). People argue over whether this is "fair"; my point is simply that it occurred, and that it occurred as a result of policies.

Share of Income Received by Each Quintile and the Top Five Percent

Year	Lowest	Second	Third	Fourth	Fifth	Top 5%
2000	3.6	8.9	14.9	23.0	49.6	21.9
1990	3.9	9.6	15.9	24.0	46.6	18.6
1980	4.3	10.3	16.9	24.9	43.7	15.8
1970	4.1	10.8	17.4	24.5	43.3	16.6

Source: U.S. Census Bureau

Real income for the majority of the population remained virtually flat during the 2001–2007 expansion, and—this was the first expansion in which this ever occurred—never returned to or exceeded their prerecession peak.

> **WHAT'S THAT?**
>
> In economic terms, **real** means adjusted for the effects of inflation. So real household income and real GDP growth are the figures for income and GDP corrected for the effects of inflation. The unadjusted figures are called nominal income or nominal GDP growth.

Together, these facts about income explain a lot about households' borrowing during the run-up to the crisis. Some consumers borrowed for speculative reasons such as condo-flipping, and some to purchase luxury goods they couldn't afford. But most borrowed to maintain the middle-class lifestyles they had grown used to when incomes were growing for most households.

How do we know? Because broad consumer spending grew despite stagnant incomes during the Bush expansion. The only way that *could* happen was with borrowing. Speculation doesn't count as spending, and spending on luxury goods is dwarfed by spending on fuel, food, clothing, medical bills, and other necessities.

Should people have refused to borrow? Sure. That may have burst the housing bubble sooner, hastened the onset of a milder recession, and positioned us for a more robust recovery. But they did borrow. Credit was unlimited, housing was booming, and unemployment and inflation were low. Times were great, or at least they appeared to be.

From 2003 to the end of 2007, outstanding personal loans, auto loans, and credit card balances increased almost 25 percent, from $2.1 trillion to $2.6 trillion. Again, that's not counting mortgage and home-equity lines, and it's a record high. This is why offering consumers credit wouldn't get the economy moving in the recession of 2008–2009, and why banks were reluctant to lend. Consumers were loaned up, and very concerned about their prospects for continued employment.

Lead Balloon: A Whole Lotta Leverage

While the government and consumers lived beyond their means, financial institutions relied on leverage. Leverage is an investing strategy. It doesn't mean every kind of borrowing, nor does it just mean being in debt. Leverage means using debt to increase the rate of return you can earn on a given investment.

Here's a simple example: Let's say you buy shares of stock for $100,000 using your own money, and you sell them one year later for $120,000. You have made a return of 20 percent on your investment (20,000/100,000) in one year. Congratulations!

Now let's bring Mr. Leverage into the deal. Let's say you do the exact same deal, only you *borrow* half of the money you invested, or $50,000. You still earn $20,000, but your return on investment (ROI) increases to 40 percent (20,000/50,000). Double congratulations!

But wait: I left out the interest you had to pay on the borrowed money. So let's say that over that year you paid 10 percent interest, or $5,000, on that borrowed $50,000. That reduces your $20,000 return to $15,000 (20,000 – 5,000), *but* your ROI still increases from the original 20 percent to 30 percent (15,000/50,000).

A lever enables you to lift something higher than you could with your own strength. Similarly, financial leverage—or OPM, for Other People's Money—lifts your rate of return. For this to work, all you need is the ability to borrow money and an investment opportunity with a rate of return higher than the interest you must pay on that money.

Let's apply this to real estate. Suppose you have $100,000 and you want to buy a condo in Miami for $500,000. Let's say condos are appreciating at 20 percent a year. (Those were the days!) That means you can buy one condo with 20 percent down *or* two with 10 percent down ($50,000 on each). If you buy two, you can live in one and rent the second one to someone who'll pay your carrying costs (mortgage, taxes, and fees), then you can sell it in a year at a handsome profit.

If this works, you sell that second condo in a year and make $100,000, because its value rose by 20 percent from $500,000 to $600,000. And you invested only $50,000, for a whopping ROI of 200 percent (100,000/50,000). What can go wrong?

Well, housing prices could fall. If the condo's price *falls* by that same 20 percent and you must sell it, you lose money. You sell it for $400,000 (20 percent less than you paid) and you owe the mortgage lender $450,000 ($50,000 more than the price you received). The ROI has turned negative. Many people found themselves in this "negative equity" or "underwater" situation after the housing bubble burst.

Such sad situations become global disasters when major financial institutions leverage themselves to dangerous degrees—and they did.

WHAT TO DO?

Use leverage—and any borrowed money—wisely. The fact that you can borrow money to invest can seem like an easy route to riches, and it has been for some people. However, many people, including many supposedly expert investors and even major institutions, have gone broke when interest rates moved against them or their "sure-thing" investments soured.

Wall Street Lived Large with Leverage

What does housing have to do with Wall Street? Traditionally, not much. For decades, regulations separated commercial banking from investment banking, and the investment banks weren't in the mortgage business. It was MBSs that brought Wall Street to Main Street.

Commercial Banks, Investment Banks—What's the Difference?

In 1933, the Glass-Steagall Act separated commercial banking and investment banking. (That law was reversed in 1999 with the passage of the Gramm-Leach-Bliley Act.) The two types of banking businesses had been separated due to stock-market abuses in the 1920s and the effects they had on commercial banking.

A commercial bank takes deposits and makes loans (it also "buys" money to lend, but that's beside this point). Commercial banks traditionally do not put depositors' money at risk in the securities markets, but rather in loans extended to businesses and consumers. They are regulated by the Federal Deposit Insurance Corporation, also created by the Glass-Steagall Act, and by the Federal Reserve, while investment banks are not.

An investment bank places partners', investors', or shareholders' money at risk in the securities markets. It also does so in bond, stock, options, and foreign exchange trading, and in underwriting securities that companies use to raise money in the public financial markets. Also, since the 1980s, investment banks created many new risk-management products, including credit default swaps (discussed shortly).

The End of the Street

The investment banking business has come to an end, at least as we knew it and at least for now. This occurred with four major events:

- In March 2008, investment bank Bear Stearns was bought at a distressed price by commercial bank JP Morgan in a sale assisted by the Fed, which bought $29 billion of Bear Stearns's mortgage assets to facilitate the transaction.

- On September 15, 2008, Lehman Brothers went bankrupt after Fed Chairman Ben Bernanke and Treasury Secretary Henry Paulson tried to arrange a buyout by other banks without taxpayer funds; they wanted to signal that institutions were not "too big to fail" and could not count on bailouts. (But then they bailed out insurer American International Group the next day, as described later in this chapter.)

- Also, on September 15, 2008, Bank of America (BofA) announced it was purchasing Merrill Lynch, the world's largest retail broker, in a $50 billion transaction (unassisted by the government, at least at the time; after that, BofA received added assistance, as discussed in Part 2). Merrill sold itself to BofA—with strong "encouragement" from the government for the deal—to avoid deeper financial stress due to the MBS crisis.

- In September 2008, Goldman Sachs and Morgan Stanley—by then the only remaining independent major U.S. investment banks—applied for commercial banking charters. This brought them under Fed regulation but also made them eligible for bailout funds under the Troubled Asset Relief Program (discussed in Chapter 4).

High leverage stressed the investment banks. Banks of every kind must hold or have access to enough *capital* to meet their obligations to creditors and investors. They must pay their liabilities as they come due, which is called being *solvent*. Leverage ratios measure the relationship between a bank's liabilities and its capital. Leverage ratios skyrocketed from the 1980s to the 2000s, with Bear Stearns and Lehman Brothers running ratios over 30 to 1 and Goldman Sachs and Merrill Lynch in the 25 to 1 range. These ratios used to register in the 10 or 12 to 1 range or lower. Stated simply, the higher the ratio, the higher the level of debt relative to capital, and the higher the bank's exposure to risk.

 WHAT'S THAT?

Capital is the amount of assets or funds that a bank or company has after subtracting the money that it owes and other liabilities from its assets. The term can also refer to the amount of money that's invested in a company.

Until the mid- to late-1980s, investment bankers managed their businesses more conservatively, mainly because the firms were partnerships, not public companies. Thus in those days, partners'—rather shareholders'—money was at risk. They did relatively low-risk deals and investments, and held enough capital to cushion the effects of any bad ones. (One exception was Drexel Burnham Lambert, which imploded due to overinvestment in junk bonds in the 1980s.) But then investment banks started going public, which gave them shareholders' funds and greater access to the public debt markets.

One might hope that management would exercise the same degree of care—or an even greater degree of care—in handling funds that were not theirs; alas, not so. In two decades, Wall Street transformed itself from a bastion of generally sensible financial behavior to something resembling a casino. Actually, a casino makes sure that the odds favor the house—which the investment banks also did, but only up to a point. High leverage left them vulnerable to creditors and investors withdrawing funds as the crisis spread, and, given the risks they took, leverage ultimately brought a number of them down.

Credit Default Swaps: Bad Boys or Good Guys?

In coverage of the crisis, *credit default swaps* (*CDSs*) have received much attention—and scorn. CDSs are fairly complex risk-management tools that insure parties against credit risk (that is, the risk of default, hence the name credit default swap). CDSs do this in the form of a contract between two parties—that's a key point, and it's why swaps are "tools" or "instruments," not securities.

 WHAT'S THAT?

A **credit default swap (CDS)** is a contract between two parties in which one party, the protection seller, agrees to pay all or part of the losses realized by the other party, the protection buyer, if the issuer of a bond defaults. The protection buyer does not have to hold the bond. Default is defined in the contract and can range from missed payments to total bankruptcy.

One party to the contract, the protection seller, agrees to pay all or part of the losses realized by the other party, the protection buyer, if the issuer of the bond defaults. (However, the protection buyer may or may not actually hold the bond.) Default is defined in the contract and can range from missed payments to total bankruptcy. It's called a swap because the risk of default is being swapped by the protection buyer in return for payments from the protection seller.

A CDS is derivative. The value of derivatives is *derived* from another, underlying financial asset. For example, a stock option—a put or a call—is a derivative. (A put is a contract that allows the holder to sell a certain stock at a specific price by a specific future date; a call is a contract that allows the holder to buy a certain stock at a specific price by a future date.) A CDS functions as a tool for hedging risk and as an insurance policy, although neither party has to hold the bond being insured. If neither party holds the bond, it's like buying a life insurance policy on someone you (the protection buyer) barely know, with the party doing the insuring (the protection seller) not *necessarily* having the money to settle the claim if the third party dies. In the financial crisis, many protection sellers didn't have the money to pay up if default occurred.

At least that is how the CDS market developed over time. Indeed, the market morphed from a fairly sensible method of hedging credit risk, first developed in 1995 by JP Morgan, into something of a global financial casino. Banks and speculators were simply betting whether or not a default would occur on bonds that they were not holding.

Did CDSs Cause the Crisis?

In a word, no. As noted in Chapters 1 and 2, the crisis was rooted in subprime defaults and the loss of confidence in the MBS market. A good number of investors became concerned that financial institutions would have to pay billions on CDSs related to MBSs, but that did not occur. One major company that was stressed by its position in CDSs was American International Group (AIG), which the U.S. government bailed out for $85 million in September 2008 in exchange for almost 80 percent ownership of the company. However, AIG is actually an insurer and did have a financial interest in whether the defaults occurred.

CDSs did contribute to the overall atmosphere of fear, eroding confidence, and potential insolvency that plagued the markets for the first three quarters of 2008. People remain concerned about them, and with reason. One issue is the huge dollar amount of "notional outstandings" that can arise around CDSs (as high as $55 to $62 trillion in 2009 by some estimates). But these are not necessarily obligations that become due. Instead, the positions have been hedged—in effect, insured—in so many different ways that the true potential liability amounts to a fraction of that. But it's still a towering, potentially multitrillion-dollar sum. Therefore, regulators and financial institutions are working to stabilize and add transparency to this market, which may or may not actually occur.

Overall, debt and plain old financial mismanagement (along with—no surprise—greed) were main drivers of the financial crisis. It's sad that certain risk-management tools with actual usefulness were misused. Of course, it's even sadder that tens of millions of households, and quite possibly the federal government, incurred far more debt than they could reasonably handle. At the household, institutional, or government level, high debt really limits your options when economic difficulties arise.

The Least You Need to Know

- A decreasing share of income for the lower 80 percent of the population from 1970 to 2008 helped fuel consumer borrowing, particularly in the run-up to the 2008 financial crisis.

- The level of government borrowing over the past several decades has left the nation with a towering $10 trillion debt, 30 percent of which is owed to foreign governments and investors.

- Investment banking as we knew it came to an end due to large bets placed on MBSs and massive leverage, which weakened the institutions as well as creditors' and investors' confidence in them.

- Credit default swaps (CDSs) began in 1995 as a hedging strategy for investors in bonds, but over time changed from "insurance policies" to simple "bets" on whether or not a bond issuer would default. CDSs did not cause the crisis but did contribute to market uncertainty and exacerbated the crisis.

Government Responds to the Crisis

Part

2

Given the severity and suddenness of the financial crisis and the recession, the U.S. government had to take action. Only the president, Congress, the U.S. Treasury, and the Federal Reserve can create and implement national economic policies. Only Washington could mount a response that would calm the markets, restore faith in the banking system, and extend assistance to people undergoing layoffs and financial distress.

Ironically, given that so much of the criticism has come from the right, most of the policy responses were initiated before Barack Obama took office by President George W. Bush; Congress; Bush's Treasury secretary, Henry Paulson; and the Fed Chairman appointed by Bush (and reappointed by Obama), Ben Bernanke. The Obama administration continued virtually all of those policies and added an economic stimulus package to address the effects of the recession itself.

The first two chapters of this part examine the U.S. government's response to the financial crisis and the Great Recession and the broad effects and outcomes of those policies. The last chapter examines the effects of the crisis in Canada, Europe, and Asia, and their governments' responses.

Steps Taken by Bush and Obama

In This Chapter

- Government inaction, reaction, and action
- The saga of Fannie Mae and Freddie Mac
- The Economic Stabilization Act and TARP
- President Obama's stimulus package

Despite a string of government-assisted takeovers and bailouts, during the 2008–2009 recession credit remained scarce, markets moribund, and consumer and business confidence low. Persistent economic problems included increasing unemployment, slack demand, and cratering home prices. Both the Bush and Obama administrations faced the challenge of developing and implementing policies that would get the economy moving and help consumers and businesses survive until recovery kicked in.

This chapter and the next one review U.S. government actions in response to the crisis. This chapter covers actions taken mainly by the president and Congress, and the next chapter covers actions taken mainly by the Federal Reserve System, the U.S. central bank. Although the actions taken by the administration and Congress—that is, elected officials—overlap with those taken by the central bank, these are separate bodies that can and typically do act independently of one another. Broadly, the president and Congress enact and implement *fiscal policy* and the Federal Reserve enacts *monetary policy*.

This chapter also explains some of the limitations of policy, and looks at the bind that those limitations have created for economic policymakers.

Housing and Economic Recovery Act of 2008

As the real estate market continued to slide and job losses mounted, the Bush administration and Congress realized that they had to act. As a result, the Housing and Economic Recovery Act of 2008 was passed at the end of July to address the subprime crisis. The act included two main legislative initiatives.

WHAT'S THAT?

Fiscal policy affects the economy mainly through taxes, government spending, and budget allocations and is overseen and directed by Congress and the president. **Monetary policy** affects the economy mainly through changes to interest rates and the banking regulations (particularly those having to do with reserves banks must keep on deposit with the Fed).

First, the Federal Housing Finance Regulatory Reform Act established a new, independent regulator for the housing-related government-sponsored enterprises (GSEs): Fannie Mae, Freddie Mac, and the Federal Home Loan Banks. This regulator—the Federal Housing Finance Agency (FHFA)—was given increased powers to establish standards, restrict asset growth, increase enforcement, and put entities into receivership.

Second, the Hope for Homeowners Act created a new, temporary, voluntary Federal Housing Authority (FHA) program to back distressed homeowners' FHA-insured mortgages. The program required borrowers to share the equity created by the modified mortgage and any future appreciation. The program was authorized to insure up to $300 billion in mortgages and could serve as many as 400,000 homeowners. Hope for Homeowners (H4H) is set to run from October 1, 2008, to September 30, 2011, and the Congressional Budget Office estimates it will net nearly $250 million for taxpayers.

WHAT TO DO?

Visit www.hud.gov/hopeforhomeowners for more information on this mortgage assistance program.

Federal Takeover of Indy Mac Bank

In July 2008, the Office of Thrift Supervision, which regulates savings and loans, closed Indy Mac Bank of Pasadena, California, and placed it under FDIC conservatorship. With $32 billion in assets and 33 branches in southern California, Indy Mac (no relation to Fannie or Freddie) represented a significant bank failure. Depositors were insured by the FDIC.

The FDIC also launched a loan-modification effort for Indy Mac subprime borrowers facing financial distress. The program was viewed as only moderately successful because borrowers were hard to contact and resisted participation. But this early program did achieve a number of successes and provided lessons on how to conduct mortgage modification. The latter included developing the right mix of incentives for the lenders, borrowers, and other involved parties, and clearly communicating the program's benefits.

Government Takeover of Fannie Mae and Freddie Mac

On September 7, 2008, Fannie Mae and Freddie Mac were placed under conservatorship under the auspices of the FHFA. Given the GSEs' status, this is equivalent to bankruptcy protection. The step was taken given the GSEs' importance to the U.S. housing and mortgage markets, exposure to subprime and Alt-A mortgages, undercapitalization, and instances of past mismanagement. In various ways, the GSEs accounted for $5.2 trillion—or almost half—of the U.S. mortgage market at the time of the crisis. It is arguable that they did a decent job of managing their risks given the pressures they were under and developments in the housing market. Yet it's also arguable that with that kind of volume and market share, the GSEs are either just too large and powerful or should be managed in an unfailingly competent manner—probably both. In addition, Fannie and Freddie:

- Enjoyed market advantages over their non-GSE competitors, who lacked access to similar low-cost funds and to implied, if not actual, federal guarantees. This did distort the housing market to a degree, although the intent of having GSEs was to make homeownership more widely available than the unassisted market would make it.

- Spent huge sums lobbying politicians of both parties, expanded into the purchase of subprime loans, and grew to new proportions, thus crowding out some private financial institutions.

- Reportedly *decreased* their market share of subprime loans sold into the secondary market between 2004 and 2006, from 48 percent to 24 percent, according to *Inside Mortgage Finance* (as quoted in an October 18, 2008, McClatchy Newspapers article). Thus, the GSEs grew even while reducing their share of the subprime market from 2004 to 2006—that is, if their loans were properly classified.

- May well have held a large number of subprime and Alt-A loans in their sub-prime *and* prime databases. In testimony before the House of Representatives Oversight Committee on December 9, 2008, Edward Pinto, Fannie Mae's former chief credit officer, stated that 34 percent of both GSEs' loans should be classified as subprime, Alt-A, or other nonprime loans. While it came three months after conservatorship, his testimony—and the lack of lucid explanations in testimony from former senior executives of the GSEs—provided excellent justification for the federal takeover.

WHAT TO DO?

Be aware that much of the criticism of Fannie Mae and Freddie Mac can be classified as "political theater." Both of these organizations functioned well for years and fulfilled their mission of bringing more money into the mortgage market. Did they become more politicized and were they run badly in certain ways? Yes. Did they do as much as the purely private sector to create the housing crisis? No.

Pinto said that, "Fannie Mae and Freddie Mac went from being the watchdogs of credit standards and thoughtful innovators to the leaders in default-prone loans and poorly designed products." There had for several years been concerns about the health of the GSEs, but politicians of both parties sought to keep the housing market going. In his first term, George W. Bush and several members of Congress did seek to regulate the GSEs more tightly, which was reasonable given the GSEs' size and influence. This occasioned Democratic Congressman Barney Frank's oft-quoted 2003 remark that the GSEs were basically financially sound—which they may have been at the time, *if* one could rely on their financial statements.

GSE regulators leveled charges of accounting irregularities at Fannie and Freddie in the late 1990s and into the 2000s, stating that they had tweaked earnings statements to portray themselves as less risky; inappropriately deferred expenses into subsequent years; and hadn't properly accounted for derivatives. The latter resulted in a $125 million fine for Freddie Mac. Also, senior executives at the GSEs were lavishly compensated, given that they headed an essentially government-sponsored duopoly. For instance, in 2003, Fannie Mae CEO Franklin D. Raines received more than $20 million in total compensation.

Yet overall, the most compelling reasons to place the GSEs in conservatorship were their hundreds of billions of dollars in exposure to mortgage-related risks at a time of rising defaults and foreclosures; their combined $67 billion of losses dating from the bursting of the housing bubble; and their cratering stock prices in 2008—the latter providing an apolitical, market-driven verdict on their situation (although Fannie Mae did raise $7.4 billion in capital in Spring 2008 through sale of stock).

Fannie and Freddie's conservatorship was an open-ended proposition, in that it "will end when the FHFA finds that a safe and solvent condition has been restored," according to a Congressional Research Service report dated September 15, 2008. When that will be decided and by what criteria remain obscure, as does the longer-term future of Fannie and Freddie. However, residential mortgage GSEs have a well-established place in the U.S. home financing market. This is not to say that they should remain in place forever, but that any plans or attempts to change their basic mission, let alone to turn their responsibilities over to the purely private sector, should be made very carefully and with full disclosure regarding who would benefit.

Emergency Economic Stabilization Act of 2008

Congress hotly debated the Emergency Economic Stabilization Act (EESA) before passing it on October 3, 2008, as the last major legislation under George W. Bush. Supporters believed the government had to assist large, stressed financial institutions both to prevent failure and, equally important, to signal to international financial markets that the U.S. government *would* prevent failures. (After all, it was a U.S. subprime crisis.) Opponents objected to the amount of funds requested—$700 billion—with opposed legislators heeding the many voters who objected to bailing out the financiers who caused much of the crisis.

In the end, the legislators who opposed it "held their noses" and voted for passage of the EESA, which created the Troubled Asset Relief Program to administer the *bailout fund*.

> **WHAT'S THAT?**
>
> The **bailout fund** and the bailouts took the form of investments in stock, loans to banks, guarantees of loans, and purchases of distressed securities. A good portion of the funds were paid back, and the Treasury, which administered the program, made almost $13 billion in dividends, interest, and fees on the program as of December 2009.

Troubled Asset Relief Program

After the assist of Bear Stearns, the failure of Lehman Brothers, and the rescue of AIG, Treasury Secretary Henry Paulson and Fed Chairman Ben Bernanke asked Congress to finance a comprehensive approach to assisting financial institutions. They realized that the ad-hoc responses to stressed financial institutions could not continue.

This prompted the creation of the Troubled Asset Relief Program (TARP). All told, as of January 2010, some $375 billion in funds had been distributed to banks (and the auto industry) and $165 billion had been repaid. The creation of TARP generated a number of concerns—chiefly that the banks did not start making loans, did not rigorously account for their disposition of the funds, and paid out millions in bonuses after accepting these funds.

Those are legitimate concerns, but Congress's main purpose in enacting TARP was not for the funds to be loaned out, but for them to be used to remove "toxic waste"— mainly mortgages and MBSs—from banks' balance sheets. This meant either buying or guaranteeing the troubled assets, or modifying distressed homeowners' subprime mortgages, or both. As of President Obama's inauguration, neither had occurred.

The major impediment to the removal of "toxic waste" had been the apparent decision (or indecision) by the government and the banks *not* to take action to do so. One objection was that it was impossible or impractical to value the toxic assets on the balance sheets. No one really knew what they were actually worth, so the government couldn't purchase them—or so goes the logic. The issue of whether and how to value them was widely debated, but various ways of valuing them were suggested, as were various ways of protecting taxpayers' interest if the government were to take over those assets.

One popular and probably viable idea was the good-bank/bad-bank concept. This approach calls for the government to purchase or otherwise take possession of the distressed assets (again mainly mortgages and MBSs) and consolidate them into a "bad bank" that will hold the assets. This leaves the "good banks" with sound assets and the ability to do business. Meanwhile, the government "bad bank" waits for the economy and real estate market to improve and then sells the viable assets, recoups money for the taxpayers, and writes off the assets that cannot be sold. This approach was used (albeit on a far smaller, $160 billion problem) in the savings and loan crisis of the late 1980s with the creation of the Resolution Trust Corporation "bad bank" in 1989, which operated until 1995. (This is explained in detail in Chapter 7.)

Yet under TARP, very few of the toxic assets have been purchased by the government compared to the number estimated to be on the banks' books. Instead, the Treasury injected more than $200 billion into major banks in the Capital Purchase Program.

Capital Purchase Program

Under TARP, in October 2008 the Fed and Treasury started a Capital Purchase Program (CPP) to reinforce the solvency of major banks. In this program, the major vehicle for the "bailouts" of the banks, the Treasury purchased nonvoting preferred stock in a number of banks. This gave the government an ownership stake in the banks, but it did not mean that the government "controlled" them, since it's nonvoting stock.

Eight financial institutions decided to participate by the original November 14, 2008, deadline, and by then had requested a total of $125 billion in funds: Citigroup ($25 billion), JP Morgan ($25 billion), Bank of America ($20 billion), Merrill Lynch ($5 billion), Wells Fargo ($20 billion), Wachovia ($5 billion), Morgan Stanley ($10 billion), Goldman Sachs ($10 billion), the Bank of New York Mellon ($2.5 billion), and State Street ($2.5 billion).

By that November 14 deadline, about a dozen other, mostly smaller banks requested a total $125 billion in CPP funds, bringing the total TARP funds extended under the program to $250 billion. (By February 1, 2009, another $80 billion had gone to Citigroup and another $20 billion to Bank of America, along with another $100 billion to the latter in the form of guarantees for troubled assets.)

These injections of money into these banks ignited controversy on five counts:

- They made the government part owners of the banks, which amounts to partial nationalization. Although it is nonvoting stock, some observers believed that the banks would alter their policies to please the government and distort their market behavior. Considering the record, that actually could have been desirable, albeit unlikely.

- Congress did not approve the TARP funds for the government to buy stock in banks, but to purchase troubled mortgage-related assets. This is true, but the capital injections did calm the markets, which was the main purpose of the Capital Purchase Program.

- The TARP funds were distributed to the banks without enough strings attached and thus appear to be a bailout for Secretary Paulson's friends on Wall Street. Paulson left himself open to this charge, particularly when senior managers at banks that received bailout funds awarded themselves bonuses.

- The banks didn't lend the TARP funds given to them. True, but the Treasury's intent (although not necessarily Congress's intent) was to shore up the bank's capital positions. Legislators should have *required* that money to be lent if that were their intention. Hoping that added capital or removal of toxic assets would spur lending is merely that—hoping.

- In the TARP legislation, Congress did require the government to provide broad relief to distressed homeowners, which didn't happen.

The EESA didn't stabilize the economy to any significant degree, although it may have helped by stabilizing the banking system. TARP didn't remove many troubled assets from bank balance sheets or provide much actual relief for distressed homeowners. While both programs have helped to stabilize and reassure the financial markets, they didn't achieve their primary stated goals. However, they accomplished a lot by showing that the government would step in to save troubled banks and the auto industry, both of which calmed the markets and saved thousands of jobs.

The Loan Modification Mystery

The difficulties of providing broad-based homeowner relief were in administering a fairly complex and challenging nationwide loan modification program while not rewarding irresponsible borrowers and lenders. The government did not undertake such a program, although the challenges were discussed and substantially addressed in various op-ed pieces and articles. The task didn't appear to be beyond the abilities of our government and financial system.

Indeed, FDIC Chairwoman Sheila Baird and other officials and politicians called for broad relief for distressed homeowners. Section 102 of the EESA *requires* the Treasury secretary to establish a program within TARP to guarantee troubled assets. Yet as of inauguration day in 2009, this had not been done and efforts to provide relief for homeowners remained piecemeal and scattered across several agencies.

The main economic argument in favor of using TARP funds for broad-based loan modification is that it would address the troubled mortgage and MBS problems at their source. The logic goes: fix the at-risk mortgages—or at least a good portion of them—and you restore the income stream that supports the MBSs. Again, Congress intended to give the government a means of buying troubled mortgage assets, not buying preferred stock.

TARP Remains in Place

TARP remained in place throughout the recession and still does as I write this. The program could be folded into another program or linked with financial institution regulatory reform, but keeping a means of support for stressed banks in place probably makes sense, at least for now. Unfortunately, TARP has been characterized by vague goals, little accountability for the funds, and few ways to assess progress. For a $700 billion program, it has been quite slapdash. TARP funds were not really put to their chief intended use—dealing with troubled assets, notably mortgages and MBSs—and accounting for and management of the funds was less than completely businesslike.

Don't Forget the Big Three!

On December 5, 2008, Congress grilled senior executives of General Motors, Ford, and Chrysler (the Big Three), who notoriously flew to Washington in private planes to seek government assistance. Shortly thereafter, Senate Republicans prevented a vote on a rescue bill for the automakers. But on December 19, President Bush provided $13.4 billion in TARP funds to General Motors and Chrysler. (Ford refused any funds.) This basically carried the companies until Obama took office, a wise and useful move on Bush's part.

The Obama Stimulus Plan

In most fiscal policy and legislative initiatives, President Bush left the Obama team to devise its own response. The centerpiece of that response was a large economic stimulus package, and, under TARP, financial assistance for the auto industry. (Chapter 13 covers the auto industry in depth.) The stimulus bill should not be confused with Obama's budget. The stimulus package was passed by Congress, with virtually no Republican support, and signed by Obama in February 2009. The legislation consisted of three major elements:

- Tax cuts, mainly for the middle class and for businesses.

- Financial assistance to states, which are suffering reduced revenues.

- Infrastructure spending, to update transportation and other systems.

Of course, each of these elements has its pros and cons, discussed next.

Tax Cuts—Politics and Economics at Work

The tax cuts were motivated by political as well as by economic policy considerations. Virtually all economists agree that tax cuts provide less economic stimulus than government spending. That's because of the *marginal propensity to spend*, which is higher for someone who receives new income due to increased government spending (for instance, on a new government-funded job) than it is for someone who receives a dollar due to a reduction in her taxes.

 WHAT'S THAT?

The **marginal propensity to spend** is a term that economists use to describe the likelihood of a consumer or household to spend an increase in income. The marginal propensity to save is the likelihood that the consumer or household will save an increase in income. The term *marginal* refers to the increase, which in policy discussions is usually from a tax cut or rebate, but could be from wages or investments. In general, the lower a person's income, the greater the propensity to spend.

Government spending also provides greater economic stimulus because of the *multiplier effect*, which is higher for a dollar of increased government spending than for a dollar of reduced taxes. The multiplier effect (explained in economics texts and *The Complete Idiot's Guide to Economics*) has to do with how much of the "new" dollar is spent as it is "recycled" in the economy. A "new" dollar in the economy is spent, then spent again by the next person who received it, and so on. With each "re-spending," less of the dollar is actually spent, because some is saved and some goes to income and sales taxes. The multiplier measures the total amount spent, and thus the stimulus (the increase to GDP) a policy will produce.

One other thing: a tax cut does no direct good for someone who's unemployed. True, cutting payroll or other business taxes *may* prompt an employer to hire a laid-off worker, but there's no guarantee of that, particularly in a contracting economy.

So why cut taxes as part of the stimulus legislation? The Democrats wanted to deliver on Obama's campaign pledge of "tax cuts for the middle class." Republicans almost always want to cut business taxes because taxes reduce profits and, sometimes, investment. Although tax cuts can be enacted and take effect quickly, this was, to an extent, a case of politics dictating policy.

Federal Assistance to States—Good Idea

States and municipalities have significant budgets, deliver many services, and were financially strapped in the recession. Many remained in financial straits in 2010. When incomes and sales decrease, so do state income and sales tax revenues, and it's hard for states to cut services people depend on. States provide Medicaid, unemployment insurance, law enforcement, courts, corrections, social services, highway maintenance, aid to municipalities, and other essential services. There are also jobs associated with these services, and no state can afford to lose jobs during a downturn.

A similar dynamic holds at the municipal level. Cities and towns raise revenue mainly through property taxes to pay teachers, police, firemen, and so on. Both states and municipalities raise revenue through fees and excise taxes (and—watch out!—traffic tickets), but these also decrease in recessions. Also, towns got used to property tax revenues based on high housing prices. When tax assessments are adjusted downward, municipal property tax revenues decrease.

So this part of the stimulus makes sense from an economic policy perspective *and* (if enough people know about it) a political perspective.

Infrastructure Spending—Do It, but Do It Right

Not everyone was happy with infrastructure spending as part of the stimulus package. Those in favor approved of its "jobs program" element and believed the government should stimulate the economy by creating employment. Also, the stimulus effect would outweigh that of tax cuts, as explained previously. Proponents also worried that the nation's infrastructure has deteriorated, so if we're going to rack up massive deficits, the least we can do is leave future generations with better transportation systems, power grids, and sewage treatment plants.

Opponents disapproved of its "jobs program" element and worried that make-work projects, rather than needed improvements, would result. They were concerned that pork-barrel politics would misdirect funds, that the dollar amounts appeared arbitrary, and that measures of success were missing. They were also concerned that the projects would continue long after the economy recovered. Most opponents also believed that private-sector employment would pull us out of recession, once tax cuts stimulated businesses to hire new workers. In general, opponents tended to trust that the natural course of the business cycle would cause demand to return—which it would, but perhaps a bit too far into the future.

Both sides had logic on their side. Proponents were correct that the stimulus of infrastructure spending would (eventually) outweigh that of tax cuts and that infrastructure improvements give future generations tangible benefits. Opponents were correct about pork-barrel politics, the need for metrics to size the program and measure its success, and the extended time horizon.

The problem with leaving a jobs program out of the stimulus package, even in retrospect, is that no one knew when demand would rebound without one, or when the unassisted private sector would produce significant employment growth. (Chapter 7 will discuss the length of recessions before the Great Depression, which is when the federal government adopted interventionist policies.) Also, we can more or less accurately estimate when infrastructure spending will deliver benefits because we're creating the jobs. Politically, President Obama had to do more than cut taxes, boost aid to states, and ask everyone to hang in there. Finally, infrastructure investment is more than just a political proposition when bridges collapse, brownouts become common, and New Orleans hasn't fully recovered from Katrina.

It Passed, and It Helped

With virtually no Republican support or votes, the Obama stimulus package, the American Recovery and Reinvestment Act of 2009, passed on February 17, 2009. Although originally pegged at $787 billion, a year later the package totaled $862 billion according to the Congressional Budget Office. That latter figure consisted of $626 billion in spending and $236 billion in tax cuts. As part of the package, the legislation extended the time during which workers can file claims for and collect unemployment benefits.

The stimulus package left no one completely happy. Many people on the left believe it was too small and too weighted toward tax cuts. Many on the right believe it was too large and too weighted toward spending. What matters is whether it worked. On February 20, 2010, a *New York Times* editorial noted, "There is virtually no dispute among economists that the stimulus prevented a bad recession from becoming much worse. Among other things, it has preserved or created 1.6 million to 1.8 million jobs, according to various private sector analyses, and it is expected, ultimately, to add a total of roughly 2.5 million jobs." In a recession in which more than 8 million jobs were lost, this was definitely a fiscal policy win.

The Least You Need to Know

- The takeovers of Fannie Mae and Freddie Mac were necessary steps given the money at stake, the importance of those institutions to the U.S. housing market, and the poor quality of management that prevailed in them during the housing bubble. However, their role in the financial crisis has been overstated by opponents of the institutions.

- TARP represents a huge commitment of taxpayer funds, which helped to stabilize the financial markets but failed to address the underlying issue of troubled mortgage-related assets, which was Congress's intent.

- President Obama's stimulus program mainly featured tax cuts, federal aid to states, and infrastructure spending. Although tax cuts do not deliver as much stimulus as spending, they do work faster, and the most controversial part of the program is the infrastructure spending.

Steps Taken by the Federal Reserve

In This Chapter

* The role of banking in the economy
* Why some banks are "too big to fail"
* The Federal Reserve's stress tests for banks
* Reforms and regulations to watch for in banking

U.S. banks helped create the financial crisis that led to the recession, and they will be instrumental in the pace of economic recovery and the longer-term growth of the economy. They have therefore been the focus of much political, regulatory, and media attention. Yet even in 2010, key issues in the U.S. banking system remained unsettled.

More broadly, the financial services industry apparently weathered a potential cataclysm—but barely, and not completely. Investment banking as we knew it is gone. The U.S. government took actual—if temporary—ownership stakes in major banks. The Troubled Asset Relief Program (TARP) funds were used for purposes other than those intended by Congress. And although the soundness of major banks appears more assured than it did at the end of 2008, the condition of some is open to question, even after the stress tests that aimed to restore confidence.

Part 1 of this guide detailed the role of the banks in the crisis and described how banks bought and sold the mortgage-backed securities (MBSs) that led to the credit crisis. Chapter 4 discussed how TARP funds were used to purchase stock in banks rather than to remove toxic assets from their balance sheets.

This chapter examines the role of banks in the economic recovery and their special status as an industry, given the measures that the government under both the Bush and Obama administrations took to ensure their health during the crisis. It also looks at the importance of banks in the economy and why some banks are considered too big to fail. Finally, this chapter looks ahead to banking reforms that we can expect, or at least hope for, in the months ahead.

Why Are Banks So Important?

Someone once asked legendary bank robber Willie Sutton why he robbed banks. He supposedly said, "Because that's where the money is." That's also the answer to the question posed by the title of this section. If money is the lifeblood of the economy, then the banking system is its circulatory system and the Federal Reserve is its heart. (Hopefully, there's a brain somewhere, but that's another matter.)

Today money is different than back in Willie Sutton's heyday (the 1930s and 1940s), when he carried off bags of cash. Nowadays, he'd need a laptop because most money is now exchanged via electronic entries. This makes the banking system vital to the economy, and makes it easy to "create" money in the form of *credit*.

WHAT'S THAT?

Credit refers to money that is loaned to households, businesses, governments, and among banks. It also refers to money that is owed to companies for goods and services that are sold on the understanding that the buyer will pay at a later date. Unlike money that is invested, credit refers to money that is owed to the creditor by the debtor and must be paid under a contractual agreement.

Why Do We Need Credit?

Not long ago someone asked me, "Why do we need credit anyway? Why don't we all just earn money first and then spend it?"

That question goes to the heart of modern economics, and the answer leads to a new appreciation of the role of banking in the economy. Credit began when businesses sold goods to another for future, rather than immediate, payment. Why would the seller do that? Three reasons: First, the seller knows that the buyer—another business person—needs goods to sell in order to make money. Second, the seller realizes he can do more business if he extends payment terms—say, 30 days—to customers instead of demanding immediate payment. Third, the seller trusts that the buyer will pay him as agreed.

By its nature, business is always forward-looking. Business people build or make things in order to sell them and until they sell them, they need financing to buy materials and to pay the rent and the help. When the business sells its goods or services, it pays its creditors and, hopefully, has enough left for profits to finance further growth.

Although businesses finance some of their growth with profits and provide huge amounts of credit to one another, most companies need bank borrowings in order to do business. In fact, bank borrowings usually enable companies to provide payment terms to one anther. Most of those borrowings come from commercial banks, which differ from investment banks in the following ways.

Commercial banks take deposits, make loans, and offer credit cards and other financial services. Deposits take the form of checking accounts, savings accounts, and certificates of deposit (also known as "time deposits"). Major banks and large regional banks are now usually owned by bank holding companies, which may also own insurance, brokerage, and other financial services companies.

Investment banks enable corporations to raise capital in the public stock and bond markets by buying the securities from the issuing companies and then selling them to the public, a process called underwriting. Investment banks also offer advisory, brokerage, and other investment-related services, depending on the scope of their operations.

The Glass-Steagall Act of 1933 separated commercial and investment banking, a division that Congress ended in 1999. Also, only commercial banks are subject to regulation by the Federal Reserve and involved in the Fed's implementation of monetary policy.

What "Too Big to Fail" Means

After the onset of the financial crisis in 2007, we all started hearing that some banks are "too big to fail" and must be saved for the good of the economy, even at significant risk and expense to taxpayers. The government takes that approach because the consequences of a major bank failure can be widespread and severe. Also, *multiple* bank failures—especially of large banks—could generate economic disaster.

A bank operates largely on confidence, which underpins the entire system of credit and of money itself. All of the loans that banks extend to businesses and to consumers express confidence that the debtor will pay those obligations as they become due.

(That's the definition of solvency—the ability to pay obligations as they become due.) Also *fractional reserve banking* dictates that depositors must have confidence in the skill and integrity of their bank's management. Finally, a nation's currency is accepted and its bonds are purchased based on its ability to manage its economy so it can collect enough taxes to pay its obligations as they come due.

WHAT'S THAT?

Fractional reserve banking is the practice of a bank keeping only a portion (a fraction) of total deposits on hand and loaning the rest to borrowers. The bank makes its money by loaning out depositors' money at a higher rate than it pays on the deposits. In practice, over the past 40 years, banks have also developed new ways of acquiring loanable funds—for instance, by issuing commercial paper and other liabilities to parties other than depositors.

Because banking is based on confidence, even the *perceived potential* loss of solvency can lead all or most depositors to withdraw their funds at once, initiating a run on the bank. To prevent runs, the Federal Deposit Insurance Corporation (FDIC) guarantees deposits up to $250,000 per depositor. However, that does not guarantee that depositors won't withdraw their funds, which could still cause the bank to collapse. Also, guaranteeing deposits only covers depositors. It does not guarantee that the bank will remain solvent in other respects, able to pay its bills and its bond holders, nor does it enable the bank to collect loans and other money owed to it.

If a major bank were to fail, several effects would ensue. First, the FDIC would have to honor its commitment to cover any deposits that the bank could not pay. If, for example, a $500 billion bank were to fail and its assets could cover only 80 percent of its deposits and other liabilities, the government would have to pay out $100 billion. The ultimate source of all government funds is the taxpayer, so FDIC payouts are to be avoided. (Citigroup alone had about $1.75 *trillion* in total liabilities as of December 2009.)

Second, the ripple effect on other financial institutions could be substantial, in terms of financial losses and, again, lost confidence. If one major bank were to fail, what is to say that another one wouldn't? Such a question leads to widespread bank runs and potentially triggers bank failures.

Third, the shareholders of the bank would wind up with worthless stock and the bondholders would wind up with a small fraction of what they are owed, if that. Such a development could shake confidence in all bank stocks, igniting a sell-off that could undermine the entire system that provides capital to banks.

Thus, the government cannot let a major bank fail without serious consequences. However, *not* letting a bank fail also has a huge downside that we've now also seen. Billions of dollars in government funds and guarantees have been extended to banks, at the taxpayers' (including unborn taxpayers') risk and expense. Significant *moral hazard* has occurred—and continues—given that bankers, and investors in banks, know that the government will bail them out.

 WHAT'S THAT?

Moral hazard arises when one has been or expects to be buffered from the consequences of one's own risk-taking or foolish behavior, as when you park your car unlocked because you have car insurance. Bankers who know they will be bailed out by taxpayers have little financial incentive to take prudent risks with the loans and investments they make.

In precrisis days, bankers and investors profited in ways that they could not have if they had borne the fully loaded risks and costs of their decisions. Now that those risks have been realized in many ways, many of those bankers and investors have been bailed out. Clearly, that is not a fair situation for taxpayers nor for banks that are "too small to save," yet it characterizes both the Bush and Obama administrations' approach.

Helping the Banks

The government took a two-pronged approach to helping the banks—measures taken by the Treasury and by the Fed.

But first, I want to clarify the role of each of these entities. The Treasury is a department of the administration, headed by the secretary of the Treasury, a cabinet official appointed by the president to a four-year term. The Treasury collects tax revenues (through the IRS), disburses funds to run the government, issues U.S. government securities, and manages the federal debt. It also conducts financial operations as required and directed by the president and Congress, for example the TARP. Incidentally, Treasury Secretary Timothy Geithner's previous position was head of the New York Federal Reserve Bank, the most important of the Fed's 12 regional banks, so he is deeply familiar with Fed operations and well-connected on Wall Street.

The Federal Reserve, the U.S. central bank, supervises the banking system and conducts monetary policy. The Fed chairman is appointed by the president to a *six-year* term. Having the chairman's term overlap presidential terms helps free the Fed of political influence because the Fed is supposed to conduct monetary policy not at the president's orders but independently, with the goals of maintaining low inflation and steady economic growth.

In practice, however, the Fed appears to consider politics and the administration's stake in economic performance. In Chapter 3, I discussed how Fed Chairman Alan Greenspan, who served from mid-1987 to early 2006, kept rates relatively low through the tech stock and housing bubbles. That helped feed the growth—or apparent growth—of the economy under Bill Clinton and George W. Bush, which made Greenspan popular with those presidents. That's partly why some observers now feel that the Fed is currently politicized, implementing policies that may help the banking system but with risk to longer-term economic prospects.

Actions Taken by the Federal Reserve

As noted in Chapter 3, the Fed and the Treasury supported several major institutions in 2008, including Bear Stearns and AIG. As the regulator of the banking system, the Fed took several other steps to address the crisis, the most significant of these being the following.

Lowering the Fed Funds Rate

Between June 2006—when the Fed Funds Rate peaked at 5.25 percent—and December 2008, the Fed lowered the rate in 10 increments to virtually zero (technically, between 0 and 0.25 percent). This was a first in Fed history, and it shows how desperate the central bank was to inject liquidity into the financial system and encourage banks to lend.

Providing Short-Term Loans to Banks

Apart from interest rates, the Fed has other policy tools to achieve its goals and to play its role of *lender of last resort*. A number of these tools of the Fed are called "facilities," a term financial institutions use for lending and other financing arrangements, and which include:

- **Term Asset-Backed Securities Loan Facility,** which helps banks extend credit to households and small businesses by supporting securities collateralized by student, auto, and credit card loans, and loans guaranteed by the Small Business Administration.

- **Term Auction Facility,** under which the Fed auctions funds to banks, as it did aggressively in 2008. These funds must be fully collateralized, and the rates are determined by auctions among the banks.

- **Commercial Paper Funding Facility,** which backs up U.S. issuers of commercial paper (unsecured short-term borrowings among major banks and corporations) by guaranteeing payment in the event of default. The commercial paper market is an essential source of credit for major banks and corporations in the economy, and the subprime crisis threatened the liquidity of this market.

WHAT'S THAT?

The term **lender of last resort** refers to the entity that can supply liquidity—that is, money—to the banking system when the banking system has no money. During one banking crisis in the early 1900s, industrialist JP Morgan acted as the lender of last resort, but that was before the Federal Reserve System was established.

These tools are all designed to put money into the banking system and thus to increase the supply of loanable funds. The Fed has policy tools beyond these and can add others as conditions warrant. Visit www.federalreserve.gov/monetarypolicy and click on "Policy Tools" to stay current.

The Bank Stress Tests

In the *stress tests*, officially the Supervisory Capital Assessment Program, the Fed assessed the potential losses that 19 major banks would suffer under various economic scenarios. Under the "adverse" case, the tests found that the banks could collectively suffer *potential* losses totaling $599 billion. Ten banks required additional capital in order to absorb their potential losses, and nine banks needed no additional capital. The loan losses were deemed possible if in the next two years the U.S. economy performed worse than most economists' "best estimate" forecasts.

WHAT'S THAT?

A **stress test** for a bank is a financial analysis in which regulators or the bank's management determine how much money the bank could lose on its loans and investments before losing enough capital to cause the bank's failure. It's a way of determining the point of failure, similar to the stress tests to which engineers subject a bridge or other weight-bearing structure.

Key results of the stress tests include the following:

- The 10 banks that required additional capital (and the amounts required) were Bank of America ($33.9 billion), Wells Fargo ($13.7 billion), Citigroup ($5.5 billion), Regions Financial ($2.5 billion), SunTrust ($2.5 billion), Morgan Stanley ($1.8 billion), KeyCorp ($1.8 billion), Fifth Third ($1.1 billion), PNC Financial ($0.6 billion), and General Motors Assistance Corp. ($11.5 billion).

- The 9 that required no additional capital were U.S. Bankcorp, JP Morgan Chase, BB&T, Goldman Sachs, MetLife, Capital One, Bank of New York Mellon, American Express, and State Street.

- The amount of additional capital required didn't equal the amount of estimated loan losses. It equaled the amount of additional capital that a bank would require in order to absorb its losses and continue operations.

- Each of the 19 banks tested had at least $100 billion in assets and collectively they held more than 50 percent of the banking industry's total loans, although the nation has some 8,000 banks. While many smaller banks are healthier—and not too big to fail—some of them face potential crisis-related problems, for example in commercial real estate.

- Tested banks that required more capital could raise it through common stock offerings, asset sales, or other methods. They could also request more capital through the Treasury's Capital Assistance Program (a program within and funded by TARP). Banks that did not undergo the stress tests had access to capital on the same terms as the largest banks.

Criticisms of the stress tests include their being a public show and not being stressful enough. A May 8, 2009, *Wall Street Journal* editorial complained about publicizing what regulators usually do more privately, but noted that the banks' stock prices had recovered from January levels. Several commentators complained about the tests being too lenient, and about the banks being able to negotiate over the results of the tests—the latter clearly indicating the extent to which the administration was accommodating the industry, perhaps to the detriment of the economy and taxpayers, although that remains to be seen.

Among the more troubling observations was the International Monetary Fund (IMF) estimate, announced a few weeks before the stress test results, that losses on U.S. loans and securities could total $2.7 trillion. An article by Matthew Richardson and

Nouriel Roubini in the May 5, 2009, *Wall Street Journal* stated that this implies "that the financial system is near insolvency in the aggregate." The article went on to say, "With the U.S. banks and broker-dealers accounting for more than half these losses, there is a huge disconnect between [the IMF's] estimated losses and the regulators' conclusions." If Richardson and Roubini are correct—and Roubini is one of the few economists who warned of the crisis well in advance—then a major bank failure (and bailout) may still lay ahead.

Like most government actions taken to address the banking crisis, the stress tests appear to have been a qualified success—for now. If they were too lenient, which appears quite possible, banks may wind up undercapitalized if the economy remains sluggish and losses mount. On the bright side, there is the market's positive response to the tests. Also, some banks tested are now able to begin repaying TARP funds, which will give the government money to disburse to other financial institutions without asking Congress for more.

The Fed's Expanding Balance Sheet

Many banks availed themselves of the Fed's loan facilities previously described. As a result, the Fed's balance sheet expanded significantly as the crisis unfolded. Like any balance sheet, the Fed's is a snapshot of its assets, liabilities, and net worth on a specific date. Over the course of the crisis, the Fed's balance sheet—generally measured by its total assets—more than doubled. Specifically, from the end of 2007 to the end of 2008, total assets rose from $915 billion to $2.3 trillion, an unprecedented increase.

Concerns about the Fed's balance sheet arise in thoughtful critiques of the government's response to the crisis. However, often left unexplained is the significance of the expansion in the Fed's positions and the potential positive or negative implications.

First, the significance. The goal of the Fed during the crisis was to provide liquidity to the banking system. It does this mainly by extending short-term loans to banks. Ordinarily it does so by creating new reserves—in essence a loan to each bank requiring one, against which the bank can lend to its customers. However, creating those reserves at the high level required in this crisis could have expanded the money supply too much, too fast, and create inflationary pressures. So instead, the Fed started paying interest on reserves, which attracted rather than created reserves. It also sold holdings of Treasury securities and loaned the proceeds, which net-net doesn't change the amount of money in the economy. The Fed created new assets in the form of its various facilities, again with the goal of providing liquidity while minimizing inflationary pressures.

All of these new assets expanded the Fed's balance sheet, with liabilities expanding as well. (Recall that, to a bank, including a central bank, a loan to another entity is an asset—cash to be collected from a borrower—and a deposit is a liability—cash to be paid to a depositor.) For example, on the liability side of the balance sheet, deposits from banks rose from $20 billion at the end of 2007 to $860 billion at the end of 2008. Deposits from the Treasury rose from $16 billion to $106 billion, and a new Treasury Supplementary Financing Account added another nearly $260 billion. Those three liability items funded more than $1.2 trillion of the $1.4 trillion in assets added during 2008.

These moves by the Fed amounted to an unprecedented, extremely strong response to market concerns about bank liquidity. The strength of this response generated strong opinions regarding potential positive and negative implications.

On the positive side, although the strength of the Fed's response "scared" some observers, causing them to see the central bank as trying to ward off a depression, that response by the Fed was apparently called for, given the threat to the U.S. and global financial system. We know this because the Fed kept expanding its balance sheet, creating new facilities, and requesting more assistance from the Treasury over the course of the crisis. Central bankers don't expand their institutions' balance sheets without reason, but in response to demand from the banking system. We can all take solace that the expansion not only ceased after the period of greatest threat to the financial system, but that some contraction in the balance sheet has occurred since then.

Also on the positive side, the Fed can readily "unwind" many of the assets that it created to provide liquidity and thus contract its balance sheet. Most of the asset positions can be unwound—perhaps to precrisis levels—as long as it is done carefully, neither prematurely nor too late. If the Fed's balance sheet were to contract prematurely and credit availability dried up, it could hobble the recovery. If the balance sheet were to expand too much for too long, it could allow credit to expand to the point at which inflation is ignited.

On the negative side, some fear that the Fed *may* have created moral hazard, set the stage for inflation, or assumed inordinate risks in some cases, such as in purchasing MBSs from banks. These fears are real but minor, particularly next to the prospect of the Fed doing too little to address the crisis. So much of what the Fed has done has centered on short-term assets and facilities that it didn't really incur much long-term risk. It also did what it could to minimize inflationary pressures, as explained previously. Finally, the Fed's purchases of risky assets, and specifically MBSs—although they total in the billions—represent a small portion of its total assets.

WHAT TO DO?

Understand that people mean different things when they say "reform"—especially politicians. For example, the "bankruptcy reform" legislation that passed in 2005 made it far more difficult for debtors to declare bankruptcy, while doing nothing to curtail banks' lending to risky parties. The U.S. financial industry reform that is most needed would encourage responsible risk-taking by banks, encourage investment rather than speculation, and protect consumers.

A larger issue related to the troubled banking system, which the administration is only beginning to address, is that of reforming financial institutions to ensure the future safety of the system while retaining its essential nature and functions.

What Needs Reforming?

Ah, where to begin. Given what we know about the causes of the financial crisis and the role of the banks in it, several areas cry out for reform. Those opposed to regulation should consider the results of deregulation, which brought some benefits but at a high price and with huge financial rewards for a small group of people who created little of lasting value. Also, an institution that's "too big to fail" must submit to the regulation that must accompany that status, for the good of the financial system, the economy, and the taxpayer.

Following are seven areas to watch for when judging the policies of the administration in the area of financial institution reform.

Transparency and Disclosure

Transparency and disclosure aim to provide customers and investors with the information they need to make knowledgeable decisions regarding financial institutions and securities. Transparency occurs when people outside the organization can see the financial structure, analyze potential risks and rewards, and understand management's decisions. Disclosure provides transparency, and it occurs not because management decides to provide enough details about the business but because reporting requirements—accounting rules, and regulations from the SEC and other regulatory bodies—force management to provide enough details.

> **WHAT TO DO?**
>
> Bear in mind that most accounting rules and financial reporting requirements involve judging the position and performance of the company or bank in the past. In fact, auditors of U.S. companies and banks actually pass very little judgment on the things that management says about future prospects, performance, and risks. Therefore, it is important to look at financial statements and any other financial information from the past, even the recent past, as just one source of information on a company. It's also important to consider news reports, analyst opinions, and investors' buying and selling activities when considering a company as an investor or current or prospective employee.

In the crisis, trouble arose when people didn't know what they were investing in and who they were doing business with. Off-balance-sheet entities and investments generated undisclosed risks. Depositors didn't know that their bank could become insolvent if subprime mortgages went into delinquency. Derivatives masked risk in ways that didn't allow for its proper pricing. On that subject, in 2000 the Commodity Futures Modernization Act ensured that derivatives would *not* be regulated and thus minimized transparency and disclosure in that area. (Then–Treasury Secretary Lawrence Summers, who became a top economic advisor to Obama, championed that law—not a good sign for the future.)

Regulatory bodies and accounting organizations in the United States and Europe are generally calling for more stringent reporting requirements and higher standards of disclosure in banking. The United States will soon adopt International Financial Reporting Standards (IFRS), which the SEC will allow companies listed on U.S. stock exchanges to use in the next two to three years and will probably mandate by 2014. However, IFRS call for more disclosure in certain areas and less in others. In any case, standards will remain in flux but at least current trends appear to favor greater transparency and disclosure.

A Return to Banking Basics

Some observers, notably Nobel Prize–winning economist and *New York Times* columnist Paul Krugman, have demanded that banking once again become a "boring business." Others have expressed hope that financial institutions will start seeking normal returns resulting from assuming normal risks, rather than extraordinarily high returns achieved at greater risk. Still others call for less speculation and more genuine investment, less making money off money and more investing in new factories and equipment, processes and products, and industries and companies. All are good ideas, whether they come about through regulations, tax policies, or voluntary industry practices.

Separation of Commercial and Investment Banking

The Glass-Steagall Act of 1933 separated commercial and investment banking. That system served the United States well for the next six decades, but that act was repealed in 1999. While the repeal of Glass-Steagall didn't cause the crisis, it was emblematic of the approach to regulation—or rather, deregulation—that contributed to, and to an extent did cause, the crisis. Truly serious regulation of banking would reinstitute the separation of commercial and investment banking, which put money at risk in very different ways. (Former Fed Chairman Paul Volker favors such reinstitution in some form.) Consumer and business lending is a far different matter than putting money into the financial markets, and particularly into exotic financial instruments.

Reform of Securitization

Securitization—packaging auto, credit card, mortgage, or other consumer loans into securities for resale—brings more money to lenders and borrowers, and channels investors' funds into securities that *should* carry a known level of risk. But subprime mortgages were packaged in ways that masked their risk. This happened in part because securitization severs the link between borrower and lender. When a bank resells a loan, it is no longer really the lender and the borrower is no longer really its customer. Also, as we saw, if a loan originator makes money by originating loans, rather than by originating good loans, he has little incentive to care about the quality of the loans.

One way to restore the credibility of securitization would be for the United States to adopt the European practice of using covered bonds. A covered bond is a package of loans combined into a security (the covered bond) which is then sold to investors. The difference is that the loans remain on the balance sheet of the bank that originated them. The bank then sends the interest and principal payments from borrowers upstream to the investors. In this way, investors know what they are buying, and the bank maintains a stake in whether or not the loans are repaid. This differs from securitization, which takes the loan off the bank's balance sheet and severs the relationship between bank and borrower.

Reform of the Bond Rating Agencies

The failings of the *bond rating agencies*, most prominently Standard & Poor's and Moody's, were covered in Part 1 of this guide and elsewhere in the press and media. The rating agencies failed to do their jobs and, because they are paid by the companies whose securities they are rating, they have an incentive to assign high ratings to securities. (A high rating means that the security carries relatively low risk and that the issuing company therefore pays a lower interest rate.)

WHAT'S THAT?

A **bond rating agency** is a company paid by issuers of debt to rate the relative risk of the debt (most often bonds) and thus enable the market to price the debt in terms of the interest the company pays on the bond. The major U.S. rating agencies are Moody's, Standard & Poor's, and Fitch.

Reform of the rating agencies could take any of several paths. Nationalization of the agencies—even combining them into one federal agency—has been suggested, but not widely embraced. Better alternatives might include paying for the ratings out of a public or private pool of funds generated by assessments on the issuers or investors, or both, through a small tax or transaction fee. Some have suggested more competition, but we actually don't need more ratings—just more reliable ones. Toward that end, others have suggested greater disclosure from the agencies, a good idea, but investors will still want a summary rating rather than reams of additional reading. Still others have suggested letting the market set a price without the ratings, as it does with equities. That, however, ignores the fact that investors and issuers have found the ratings to be quite useful in pricing bonds.

However it occurs, reform of the rating agencies will be another way to improve the health of credit markets and the levels of transparency and disclosure for investors in bonds.

Reform of Fannie Mae and Freddie Mac

The government-sponsored enterprises (GSEs) most involved in securitizing mortgages cry out for reform. In addition to shoring up the GSEs' capital, the government must have them return to their mission of providing liquidity to the mortgage markets, while deemphasizing their mission of expanding homeownership to all income groups. Free-market advocates argue for phasing out the GSEs and leaving mortgage lending completely to the private sector. While not a bad idea, that won't happen soon. Also, the private sector created much of the crisis without much help from Fannie and Freddie. Meanwhile, we can hope for serious GSE reforms that result in a reasonable mission, competent management, and honest accounting.

Protection for Borrowers

The financial services industry secured major lobbying and legislative victories in the 1990s, notably bankruptcy "reform" that made it more difficult for individuals to ditch their credit card debt when declaring bankruptcy. This in part led the credit card industry to engage in widespread "bottom feeding"—pitching cards to uncreditworthy prospects—with greater protection from the risks of doing so. The industry also engages in highly questionable, arguably unethical practices, such as raising interest rates on outstanding balances, often without warning, and usurious late fees.

The pendulum appears to be swinging back, with new rules for credit card issuers. These may limit the fine print and confusing legalese in credit card contracts, as well as the practice of raising rates on existing balances. Whether they will limit "predatory" marketing remains to be seen. However, if we're going to have an economy financed in good part by consumer credit, sensible rules only make sense. That means rules that assist the consumer, who, after all, cannot afford the lobbyists and campaign contributions of the type that resulted in so-called bankruptcy reform.

Bank on It?

Reform of the financial services industry is clearly necessary. The concern is how soon it will occur and how effective it will be. Will new rules demand greater transparency and disclosure? Will they limit the incentives for piling up debt and inflating asset prices? Will they do away with off-balance sheet entities and the so-called *shadow banking system?*

WHAT'S THAT?

The **shadow banking system** consists of essentially unregulated, nonbank financial institutions and funds (such as hedge funds, private equity funds, and pension funds) that raise money from investors and channel it into business and other investments. These institutions and funds, because of their number and the huge amounts of money they have raised, have a major effect on the supply and safety of money in the financial system and the degree of risk in the system.

Early signs were not encouraging, given the slow pace and light hand with which the Obama administration proceeded in its first year, with the stress tests and the mortgage relief programs as Exhibits A and B. Clearly, the administration decided not to move too quickly or decisively, but rather to see how things unfolded. The administration may have been counting on a fast economic recovery to help the value of homes and thus mortgage-related assets—and other financial assets—to return to reasonable levels. However, that approach assumes that economic recovery will occur in late 2009 or early 2010—as it has, at least officially—but also that recovery will be strong enough to boost incomes to levels that start to restore asset prices. The latter had yet to occur in early 2010.

These were big bets and not necessarily wise ones. A sluggish—and perhaps "jobless"—recovery may be underway. Incomes (not to mention the flow of credit) will not quickly bounce back to precrisis levels, and may take years to recover enough to significantly boost home prices. In the meanwhile, write-offs of loans at banks will either occur or the assets will be carried in hopes that their values will return, which could undermine the health of the banks as well as lending activity.

The Least You Need to Know

- The banking system is essential to the economy because businesses require credit from when they make and deliver goods to when they collect revenue. Most consumers also require credit, if only to buy homes, automobiles, and durable goods.

- Financial institutions provide credit by taking deposits and invested funds and making loans and facilitating investment in companies. For this reason, the government accords banks special treatment—and regulation—and views major banks as "too big to fail."

- The bank stress tests held in spring 2009 gave some banks a fairly clean bill of health and required others to raise additional capital. Some critics see the tests as understating potential losses at the banks if economic conditions were to deteriorate beyond current forecasts.

- The Federal Reserve acted forcefully to provide liquidity to the financial system through lending facilities and securities purchases. Although this expanded the Fed's balance sheet and created certain dangers, the benefits appear to have outweighed the risks.

- Reform of financial services is necessary to restore full confidence in the banking system and to bolster the role of banks as legitimate lenders rather than (to overstate it a bit) casinos. The question has long been when will reform come and how substantive will it be?

Global Effects of the Crisis

In This Chapter

- How the financial crisis affected other countries
- How Canada avoided the crisis
- The performance of key Asian economies
- Policy responses in other major economies

Although the crisis began with U.S. subprime mortgages, its effects quickly went global through the medium of mortgage-backed securities. When investors lost faith in those securities, and when large banks (which held the securities widely) came to doubt one another's solvency, the credit markets froze and the financial crisis began. Depositors in some European countries started withdrawing their funds, setting off runs on a few banks, a relic of the Great Depression. In mid-2008, several European governments initiated bank-rescue efforts similar to those in the United States.

This chapter looks at how the crisis unfolded in Europe, particularly in the United Kingdom, and at European responses to the crisis. We'll also examine the economic effects of the crisis in key nations and regions.

This chapter also briefly explains the functions of the World Bank and the International Monetary Fund. Before globetrotting, we start with a quick look at the nation to the north of the United States.

Canada: Sensible, as Usual

Canada has five major banks, which operate nationwide and avoided the problems of U.S. banks. There was no subprime crisis in Canada for four main reasons:

1. Any mortgage loan for more than 80 percent of the home's purchase price must be insured, *and* there are strict requirements for obtaining the insurance. Two thirds of mortgage loans are insured by the Canadian Mortgage and Housing Corporation, a quasi-governmental organization.

2. Mortgage interest is not tax-deductible in Canada, so the housing and mortgage industries are not subsidized as they are in the states. Canadians don't want mortgages if they can avoid them.

3. Canadian banks are not only more regulated, but banking practices are relatively conservative, emphasizing depository relationships, greater liquidity, stronger capitalization, and lower leverage.

4. Canada experienced no housing or home-equity bubble and has not adopted America's borrow-and-spend, consumption-driven values at the national or household level.

But Canada was affected because the nation sends about 80 percent of its exports to the United States, which is good when the U.S. economy is growing. However, the U.S. recession and appreciation of the Canadian dollar against the U.S. dollar hurt Canada's exports. The U.S. homebuilding slump hit lumber exports, and prices of other *commodities* that Canada exports fell.

WHAT'S THAT?

Commodities are goods that are pretty much indistinguishable from one another, regardless of which company produces and sells them. The term usually refers to agricultural products and natural resources, such as wheat, corn, and other grains; oil; metals; minerals; and lumber. There are, of course, differences in quality in commodities, but they are usually characterized as "grades" (for instance, of oil or lumber).

Effects on Canada

The International Monetary Fund (explained later in this chapter) forecasted a contraction of 1.6 percent in Canada in 2009 after tepid 0.6 percent growth in 2008. Canadian economists expected the economy to contract by 2 percent (or more among the pessimists) in 2009, and saw unemployment rising from 6.3 percent at the end of 2008 to 8 percent in 2009. Home prices and sales of cars and other big-ticket items were expected to suffer. This outlook was reflected in skidding prices on the Toronto Stock Exchange.

On the bright side, Canada had more room to use monetary and especially fiscal policy than many other nations. Canada had been the only G-7 nation that ran a budget surplus in the years before the crisis and had paid down part of its national debt. Thus Canada could increase government spending, cut taxes, or both without incurring damaging deficits. On the monetary front, Canada's key short-term interest rate stood at 1.5 percent in early 2009. Thus, lowering it to 0.5 percent or—if necessary—lower could produce monetary stimulus.

 WHAT'S THAT?

The **G-7,** or Group of Seven, consists of the chief public finance officials—treasury secretary, minister of finance, or the equivalent—of the United States, Canada, Japan, Germany, the United Kingdom, France, and Italy. They are not a governing body, but rather one that aims to provide a forum for consulting on and coordinating economic policies in the member nations.

It's Contagious: The Crisis in Europe

The financial crisis began with subprime defaults, which caused U.S. home foreclosures to spike to 1.2 million in 2007, almost 80 percent above their 2006 level. The contagion from defaults spread through mortgage-backed securities (MBSs) held around the world. Banks in the United Kingdom were quickly affected, so we'll begin our European tour there.

In the United Kingdom

In February 2007, the global bank HSBC wrote down $10.5 million in MBSs, setting off international concerns about the effect of subprime defaults on banks. In late summer 2007, liquidity concerns rose in the financial markets. U.S. and UK banks experienced stress in 2007, which only increased in 2008.

The crisis exploded after the failure of Lehman Brothers in September 2008 (as described in Chapter 3), which began to ripple out into the global financial system. In response, the Bank of England—the UK's central bank—provided liquidity to the British banking system through low interest rates, coordinated with similar U.S. moves. The UK government also provided loan guarantees and rescue plans (some described next) and required banks to shore up their capital.

UK bank-rescue plans were announced in the summer of 2008 before U.S. efforts to shore up the financial system. In that sense, the UK led by example. UK rescue plans differed from those in the United States in that they generally prohibited rescued banks from paying dividends, required them to increase their capital ratios, and in some cases put voting representatives of the taxpayers on their boards. The UK's stricter plans initially depressed bank-stock prices relative to those of U.S. banks, but strains in the U.S. banking system battered U.S. bank stocks, too.

The British quickly developed an overall rescue plan, perhaps due to less fear of nationalization than in the United States. Yet UK efforts encountered many of the problems of those in the United States: public outrage at the banks, deep concern over the final price of the bailout, growing realization that taxpayers will be stuck with the tab, and the prospect of slow economic growth for years to come.

UK Bank Rescues

Several UK financial institutions were rescued. In September 2007, Northern Rock became the first major UK bank with liquidity problems. Depositors lined up at branches to withdraw their funds, prompting the Bank of England to guarantee deposits and provide a $50 billion bailout. The bank was nationalized, laid off 6,000 people, and shrank its operations in 2008. But it survived, attracted new depositors, and in February 2009 announced it would offer over $20 billion in new mortgages over the next two years.

After the near-death of Northern Rock, the UK stepped up efforts to monitor, support, and rescue stressed banks. Bradford & Bingley, the quaintly named mortgage lender and bank, became distressed by subprime write-offs and the credit crunch in summer 2008. The government facilitated a plan by which, in autumn 2008, it took over the mortgage business and the Spanish bank Grupo Santander bought the banking business.

The more than 280-year-old Royal Bank of Scotland (RBS) saw severe liquidity problems in 2008 due to the subprime crisis and to overextending itself through certain investments and acquisitions. In October 2008, the British government purchased a

58 percent share in RBS, which grew to 70 percent. RBS received some £20 billion in taxpayer funds, at a time when the total market value of its stock hovered at about £5 billion. Clearly, the British considered this bank "too big to fail."

Halifax Bank of Scotland (HBOS) experienced a weakening financial condition due to deterioration in the UK housing market, bad loans, and liquidity problems. In September 2008, the bank agreed to be taken over by Lloyds Bank, a transaction completed in January 2009. Although the banks denied it, the acquisition was widely viewed as a "shotgun wedding."

Lloyds Banking Group stands among the stronger banks in the United Kingdom, but it has received more than £17 billion in government assistance. Lloyds Bank's stock price was not helped by the HBOS acquisition. Previously, Lloyds Bank had considered acquiring Northern Rock, but refused when the government failed to offer the financial support Lloyds wanted.

Developments in UK banks can impact the world financial system. Also, Britain (like New York City) depends heavily on financial services for employment. So the UK banking crisis is a close cousin of the U.S. banking crisis—with similar political and economic fallout.

The UK Political Situation

Prime Minister Gordon Brown faced dilemmas similar to those encountered by Presidents Bush and Obama. These include controversy over the amount of the bail-outs and the uses of the funds. Gordon Brown also had the European Union (EU) to contend with. Rather than adopt the euro, Britain has retained the pound sterling as its currency, and thus controls its monetary system in ways that *eurozone* countries cannot. Britain is one of the four major EU economies (with Germany, France, and Italy), and some EU nations believed that the United Kingdom may have undermined its finances for years to come with its bailout measures.

WHAT'S THAT?

The **eurozone** countries are the 16 nations that have agreed to use the euro as their currency: Austria, Belgium, Cyprus, Finland, France, Germany, Greece, Ireland, Italy, Luxembourg, Malta, the Netherlands, Portugal, Slovakia, Slovenia, and Spain.

The World Bank and the International Monetary Fund

This section briefly describes the World Bank and the International Monetary Fund (IMF). These institutions oversee and coordinate the international banking system, but they do not and cannot regulate the banking system or financial markets. They can only issue research, guidelines, and recommendations. Although not a bank in the traditional sense, the World Bank does extend loans to nations in need of development funds. Those loans can come with guidelines or even conditions, but the World Bank notes that the borrowing nation helps craft them and agrees with them (a subject of debate in some quarters).

Both of these institutions were created in 1944. The World Bank was founded to coordinate financing of rebuilding after World War II. It now promulgates information about world poverty and assists developing nations in improving living standards. The World Bank meets criticism from the right and the left, but no other organization with the support of as many nations (185) engages in such work on the same scale.

The IMF is one of five agencies of the World Bank, and it is funded by its 185 member nations. The IMF aims to promote international monetary cooperation, financial stability, global trade, orderly exchange rates, high employment, economic growth, and reduced poverty. Importantly, the IMF serves as "lender of last resort," a function played by a central bank in a national economy. The IMF is, however, neither a bank nor a central bank, though it does lend money to governments, as it did to Iceland, Hungary, and other nations in the financial crisis.

WHAT TO DO?

Visit the official sites of the World Bank (www.worldbank.org) and the International Monetary Fund (www.imf.org) to get an idea of the issues they concern themselves with and the kind of work they do. These are, of course, imperfect organizations, which, like other organizations, do not announce their flaws on their websites. They are, however, among the few forums we have for systematically studying and assisting the world's developing economies, and for promoting economic cooperation and coordinating policies.

European Economic Effects

As the United States and United Kingdom slashed interest rates and provided loan guarantees to shore up their banking systems, similar problems were occurring else-where and led to a European recession. Like the U.S. economy, European economies saw decreasing demand, increasing unemployment, and falling incomes, which, in a self-reinforcing cycle, led to decreasing demand, increasing unemployment, and falling incomes. Apart from plummeting consumer demand, European producers of *capital goods* suffered decreased demand due to lower business investment.

WHAT'S THAT?

In contrast to consumer goods, **capital goods** are goods that are used to produce other goods. They include equipment used for manufacturing, earthmoving, stamping and cutting metal and wood, extruding and molding metal and plastic, and other factory equipment—as well as the actual factories.

The outlook for European economies was as bad as, or worse than, that of the United States. For example, on February 14, 2009, *The New York Times* reported that in the fourth quarter of 2008, the eurozone nations contracted by 1.5 percent in the fourth quarter, worse than the 1 percent downtick in the United States. This 1.5 percent is actual contraction in output for the quarter, not an annualized rate, which would have been 6 percent. This was the worst economic performance for those nations since 1999, when the euro was adopted. In fact, it was the worst quarter for the major eurozone economies since 1974, according to the *Times* article.

Germany, the United Kingdom, France, and Italy all entered recessions in 2008. In the fourth quarter of 2008, Germany, the largest European economy, contracted by 2.1 percent, France by 1.2 percent, and Italy by 1.8 percent. The European Commission, which oversees the European Union, issued January 2009 forecasts of contractions in the four largest economies that largely turned out to be more optimistic than the actual economic performance. The following table shows the forecast and historical data for GDP growth for Europe's "Big Four" as of autumn 2009.

GDP Growth for the Four Largest European Economies

	2007	2008	2009	2010	2011
Germany	2.5	1.3	-5.0	1.2	1.7
UK	2.6	0.6	-4.6	0.9	1.9
France	2.3	0.4	-2.2	1.2	1.5
Italy	1.6	-1.0	-4.7	0.7	1.4

Source: European Commission, Oct. 2009 Forecast

Each of these nations spent part of 2008 and much of 2009 in recession and will achieve only sluggish growth in 2010. As the following table shows, unemployment rose in 2009 and is expected to increase in 2010. (European unemployment rates are not directly comparable to U.S. rates due to differences in how they are calculated.)

Unemployment Rates for the Four Largest European Economies

	2007	2008	2009	2010
Germany	8.4	7.1	7.7	8.1
UK	5.3	5.7	8.2	8.1
France	8.3	7.8	9.8	10.6
Italy	6.1	6.7	8.2	8.7

Source: European Commission, Oct. 2009 Forecast

WHAT TO DO?

Visit the site of the European Commission at http://ec.europa.eu/ for updates on these forecasts and for other data and information on the European Union and individual European nations.

Differences Across the Pond

Many U.S. officials saw the EU's response to its economic situation as uneven or ineffectual. This is not unfounded criticism, but there's a reason for the problem. While 16 nations have adopted the euro, their economic needs and situations—and thus their preferred policy responses—differ. When they were all growing, things were fine. But in tough times, getting 16 nations to agree on a unified approach to a serious recession has been predictably difficult. (Consider the difficulties in getting the United States to agree on a single approach.) Also, individual countries cannot implement certain measures that they were once able to use, notably, devaluing their currency to boost exports.

Incidentally, the mandated benefits and greater protection for workers in the EU relative to the United States has its pluses and minuses. Among the pluses are less financial damage to individuals and households and reliable support for consumer demand during a downturn. Among the minuses are generally less flexibility for employers trying to respond to their reduced need for labor, and higher taxes.

Although Germany approved a €50 billion fiscal stimulus plan, other nations could also have used more stimulus. Without agreement on a more highly coordinated stimulus plan, the EU more or less aimed to weather its recession without the benefit of closely coordinated fiscal stimulus. In addition, deficits increased across the EU as a result of measures taken to stimulate economies and the lower tax collections that automatically occur during an economic contraction. Some EU countries hoped for domestic and export demand to revive quickly, particularly export demand for capital goods in Asia and for consumer goods in the United States. As it turned out, the former did return in 2009 and benefited some EU economies, such as Germany and France, but the latter did not to any significant degree. In general, exports are not expected to provide the fuel for growth that they did in past recoveries because the global recovery will be weaker than usual.

Meanwhile, the pace of growth in domestic demand in the EU will remain weak relative to past recessions. This is due to factors much like those prevailing in the United States: persistently high unemployment, slow growth in employment, high household debt, sluggish housing markets, and lower lending activity. In addition, the EU faces a challenge that at times has threatened to spill over into the markets and even to test the strength of the union itself.

Greek Tragedy?

One of the major tests of the EU occurred in January and February 2010, when Greece, a eurozone nation, appeared close to defaulting on its bonds. Prices of securities, particularly EU bonds and bank stocks, tumbled, and there were rumors of a potential lack of cohesion in the European monetary union itself. However (and predictably), the stronger EU economies soon announced that they would stand behind Greece—and that the EU would essentially bail out this economically weaker member, if it came to that.

Yet bailouts and potential bailouts come with a cost. During February, the euro lost ground against the dollar (about 4.6 percent in the first five weeks of 2010), and worries rapidly spread regarding the soundness of the *sovereign debt* of other relatively weak EU members, including Portugal, Ireland, and Spain. According to a front-page *Wall Street Journal* article on February 5, 2010, each of these nations, along with Greece, must "finance budget deficits that have ballooned to around 10 percent of gross domestic product. That has sparked fears that Europe's decade-old monetary union could unravel." Indeed, Greece's 2009 budget deficit was nearly 13 percent.

The short-term challenge in Greece's situation was finding a way to guarantee the nation's debt or otherwise bail it out while not insulating the nation from consequences that would enforce greater fiscal discipline. Indeed, the fundamental challenge in all of the economically weaker EU economies is to find ways of reining in public spending while not killing off economic growth. If this sounds familiar, that may be because it's the same challenge facing larger economies in Europe, as well as the U.S. economy. Lack of fiscal discipline is the root cause of these problems, and it stems from people believing politicians who tell them they can have government programs and services while indefinitely deferring payment for them. Sooner or later, bills come due, and when they are due during a recession or other economically challenging conditions, the economy in question can find itself facing difficult choices, all of which are unpleasant.

> **WHAT'S THAT?**
>
> **Sovereign debt** is debt issued by a national government, usually in the form of bonds. These securities are unique in that they are backed by the power of the government issuing them to tax its citizens and businesses. However, taxes must fund many expenses in addition to interest and debt, so even sovereign bonds have risks associated with them.

A Bit About Asia

Generalizing about Asia is impossible given the dozens of economies and their diverse characteristics, ranging from highly advanced Japan, to the large, developing economies of China and India, to smaller developed nations. Here we examine the three largest Asian economies: Japan, China, and India.

The financial crisis didn't bring about any major bank failures in Asia or the need for major bank rescues, mainly because East Asia weathered its own banking crisis in 1997, and most nations there repaired their institutions and put reforms in place that increased banks' stability. Yet Asia felt the effects of the 2008–2009 crisis in the form of slower growth and, in some nations, recession.

Japan: It's Been Tough and It's Getting Tougher

Japan, the economic marvel of the 1980s, has been in various degrees of sluggishness or recession since the 1990s—Japan's so-called Lost Decade—which extended into the early 2000s. During that time, Japan experienced a domestic banking crisis, complete with cratering real estate prices and billions of dollars in bad debt that the banks and government failed to deal with vigorously enough. Rather, the government and banks feared that disclosing the full extent of the losses would worsen the crisis, so banks carried bad loans for years. The government, at times with private-sector as well as public funding, made limited attempts to get the loans off banks' balance sheets and failed.

Japan began recovering in 2002 and 2003 when, according to a *New York Times* article dated February 13, 2009, "the reformist leader Junichiro Koizumi ordered a tough audit of the country's top banks." This disclosed the extent of the bad loans, and the banks stepped up their efforts to charge them off. The *Times* stated that from 1992 to 2005, Japanese banks wrote off the equivalent of 19 percent of the country's annual GDP. However, Koizumi's tough stance restored confidence in the banking system. Unfortunately, soon after Japan got back on its feet, the world financial crisis hit.

The world's second largest economy (although most economists expect China to overtake it in 2010), Japan depends heavily on exports for its growth. That's currently not good, and it is the case for much of Asia. Domestically, Japan's income growth is stagnant and consumer sentiment is poor.

Given this, in January 2010, the Daiwa Institute of Research stated that Japan's GDP fell by 4.2 percent in 2008 and forecasted a decrease of 4.3 percent in 2009 and mild growth of 1 percent in 2010. Japan has taken vigorous steps to address its economic downturn, including a child support subsidy and other measures to stimulate the nation's birth rate, and a major stimulus package. Japan has been buoyed by China's economy, which saw lower growth but did not actually enter recession, and sees its fortunes rising as the U.S. economy recovers.

China: Kept Growing, But Slower

China and the United States have developed a relationship often characterized as "China lending to America so Americans can buy Chinese exports." That's oversimplified, but China does hold about $1 trillion of U.S. debt and consistently runs a trade surplus with the United States. China is also the single largest creditor of the United States.

Moreover, in March 2009, China's Premier Wen Jiabao said, "We have lent a huge amount of money to the United States …. To be honest, I am a little bit worried." He asked the United States "to guarantee the safety of China's assets." The Obama administration issued immediate reassurance, while some observers dismissed the premier's concern as a reaction to a real or imagined snub from Washington. China has since stated that it will continue to purchase U.S. securities.

Meanwhile, China is facing its own internal challenges. After years of rapid expansion, China grew 8.7 percent in 2009. This represents a slowing from 13 percent in 2007 and 9 percent in 2008, but an upward revision of an earlier World Bank forecast. China mounted a $600 billion stimulus program to create jobs and maintain growth during the 2008–2009 global recession. This program focused mainly on infrastructure spending, but also featured measures designed to support consumer demand. China is, of course, a centrally managed socialist economy (under a dictatorship), which has kept the value of its currency artificially low to keep its exports high. However, it has also introduced many market-style reforms, and as a large and developing economy, has attracted billions in foreign investment and remains poised for continued growth.

India: In Relatively Good Shape

After Japan and China, India is Asia's third largest economy, and, like China, it has seen strong growth over the past several years. However, from autumn 2008 to spring 2009, exports, confidence, and domestic demand (notably car sales) all fell. Unlike Japan and China, India depends less on exports for its growth. (Important exports for India include textiles, leather, gems, and jewelry, which were all hurt by the slowdown.)

In October 2009, the IMF forecasted Indian GDP growth of 5.4 percent in 2009, down from 9.4 percent in 2007 and 7.3 percent in 2008. (India's fiscal year ends on March 31 and these figures refer to the fiscal year.) For fiscal 2010, the IMF forecasted 6.4 percent growth. India saw a sharp slowdown in the last calendar quarter of 2008, at 5.3 percent growth—but that was still growth.

In response to the global recession, the Indian government enacted aggressive monetary policy, with the Reserve Bank of India, the nation's central bank, cutting its key interest rate by 400 basis points (that is, by 4 percentage points) from October 2008 to March 2009. On the fiscal front, the government reduced sales and excise taxes and raised spending, and domestic demand has been steadily recovering. Unlike those of many Asian nations, India's economy is far less dependent on exports.

The Crisis' Effects on Developing Economies

The financial crisis reversed many of the forces that had been driving growth in developing economies, which include some of the world's poorest. These nations rely heavily on commodity exports for economic activity and growth, and both volume and prices have fallen.

During the 1990s and 2000s, high global liquidity made large sums available to invest in developing economies. Many "emerging market" bond and equity funds channeled capital from investors in developed nations into developing economies, where potential returns were higher. Those capital flows have been sharply curtailed. Also, in the next several years, developed nations—particularly the United States—will be issuing hundreds of billions of dollars of new debt, which may crowd out some investment in developing nations. Banks building their capital positions, writing off bad debt, and reducing their lending activity may also reduce capital available to developing nations.

Collectively, these factors will curtail growth and deepen poverty in these nations for at least the next few years. In developing economies, in October 2009 the IMF forecasted a drop in growth from 6 percent in 2008 to 1.7 percent in 2009. However, it also forecasted a rebound to 5.1 percent growth in 2010. If that seems strong, bear in mind that it is an average, and these economies depend on strong growth to make any headway.

The World Outlook for 2009 and 2010

In October 2009, the IMF forecasted a global contraction of 1.1 percent for 2009, the lowest rate since World War II. In advanced economies, the IMF forecast was for a 3.4 percent contraction in output for 2009—the first full-year contraction since World War II.

However, the IMF also forecasted a turnaround in the global economy in 2010, with growth for the year of 3.1 percent. This assumed that the advanced economies started to recover in late 2009, which they did, and that they would grow by 1.3 percent for 2010.

WHAT TO DO?

When you read economic forecasts and even historical data on GDP, unemployment, and other measures, always remember that both the forecasts and the historical data are subject to revisions. Revisions occur mainly because of the time lags between the collection of economic data, its release, and ever-unfolding economic events.

At the time of the global forecast, IMF Chief Economist Olivier Blanchard said, "The current numbers should not fool governments into thinking the crisis is over." The forecast noted, "The pace of recovery is slow, and activity remains far below precrisis levels," and went on to say, "The triggers for this rebound are strong public policies across advanced and many emerging economies that have supported demand and all but eliminated fears of a global depression. These fears contributed to the steepest drop in global activity and trade since World War II."

The chief risks to recovery cited by the IMF were weakened financial institutions and governments potentially withdrawing too early from supportive policies. So as I write this, both global economic conditions and the global economic outlook are improving, but with a strong possibility of sluggish growth.

The Least You Need to Know

- As the financial crisis spread through the international banking system, the British government took faster and more decisive action to deal with stress in its banks than the U.S. government did with U.S. banks.
- The European economies generally entered recessions in the last quarter of 2008, even if most achieved growth for the year. They registered contractions in annual GDP growth (that is, recessions) for 2009, but were growing by the end of that year.
- Asian economies were not hit as hard by the banking crisis as the United States and Europe, but they saw recessions or reduced growth in 2009. Even China and India saw moderating growth, although neither registered a contraction (nor did Malaysia, the only other Asian economy that avoided a contraction).
- The outlook was bleak for smaller developing economies, which enjoyed relatively rapid growth in recent years. Capital flowed more freely into these economies and their exports rose as advanced economies grew, but both of those positives faded a bit during the global recession.
- While it may take a while for robust global growth and trade to return, it does appear that quick and aggressive policy action by the government in major economies did head off a deeper and more prolonged global recession, and perhaps even a global depression.

Lessons from Past Recessions and Expansions

Given that the economy follows a cyclical pattern of expansions and contractions, Part 3 offers some useful lessons from a review of economic history. The government's response to the Great Depression under President Franklin D. Roosevelt brought about a long-lasting change in the role of government in the U.S. economy. Before the 1930s, the government created and implemented few economic policies and did little to assist people during downturns. During and after the Great Depression, the government took a more activist role in economic policy and in assisting the system's "losers."

In the 1980s under President Ronald Reagan, the nation moved away from bank regulation and federal assistance programs and the taxes to fund them. (More accurately, the taxes fell out of favor but the programs did not.) Through the 2000s, the nation realigned its policies to favor employers over employees, to deregulate financial institutions, and to increase innovation and decrease taxes. Yet the government did not become smaller, federal deficits skyrocketed twice, and many people found themselves unable to deal with an economic downturn.

Recent Economic Cycles and the S&L Crisis

In This Chapter

- The 1970s stagflation and how it ended
- How the 1980s boomed
- The resolution of the savings and loan crisis
- Comparing today's business cycles to those of the past

A financial crisis typically originates in the stock or credit markets and can create a recession in various ways. In the 2008–2009 financial crisis, loss of confidence in a major class of investments—mortgage-backed securities (MBSs)—generated a credit crisis. Banks didn't know whom they could safely lend to and investors didn't know which banks were safe to invest in. This crisis was accompanied by massive loss of wealth in the housing market and then in the stock market. Those losses left consumers not only "feeling poorer" but with less money to spend and more concern for their futures.

When banks stopped lending and consumers stopped spending, demand plummeted. That led to layoffs and reduced spending by companies, thus putting in motion the self-reinforcing pattern of decreasing demand leading to decreasing supply, which further decreases demand, and so on.

To place this situation in perspective, this chapter examines the major U.S. economic events from the 1970s and into the 1990s. The most significant of these are the recession and stagflation (stagnant growth coupled with inflation) of the 1970s, the severe recession of the early 1980s (which killed off the inflation of the 1970s), and the savings and loan crisis of the late 1980s.

We're not reviewing these crises because "Those who forget history are doomed to repeat it." (We already have that T-shirt.) Rather we want to see what consumers, businesses, banks, and government did in those times, how bad things got, and how we got out of those fixes. (I'll cover the Great Depression in the next chapter.) Indeed, the fact that we came out of these crises is itself encouraging.

The Sluggish '70s

The main concern of people who recall or study the 1970s is that we may see something of a replay of that decade in the 2010s. Few people expect a direct repeat, because the U.S. and global economies and financial systems have changed markedly. Yet the overall impact may come to resemble that of the 1970s in degree if not in kind, and *stagflation* remains a possibility, for reasons explained in this section.

 WHAT'S THAT?

Stagflation describes an economy characterized by stagnant growth in GDP and by inflation. Standard economic theory says this should not occur because in a slow growth or no-growth economy demand should not be strong enough to push up prices and cause inflation. However, in the 1970s, a good part of the inflation was due to the increasing price of oil, which was being set by foreign exporters.

The 1970s brought a long but temporary end to the prosperity of the post–World War II years. In the 1973–1975 recession, GDP decreased by 3.1 percent and years of stagflation followed. Inflation reached 6 percent in 1970 and remained above 4 percent in 1971, leading President Richard Nixon to institute wage and price controls, initially for 90 days but extended in various forms until 1974 when inflation reached *12 percent*. High inflation persisted until the early 1980s recession. The 1970s brought a quadrupling of oil prices from 1972 to 1974—real fuel for inflation—and, in 1975, peak unemployment of 8.7 percent.

A number of events drove these difficulties. In 1971, President Nixon severed the last link to the gold standard by announcing (without consulting trading partners or foreign central bankers) that U.S. dollars would no longer be convertible to gold. Essentially, when a currency is on a gold standard, it is "backed by gold" and the government can print money to the extent that it has amounts of gold equal in some ratio to the amount of currency. At the time of Nixon's decision, other nations could redeem U.S. currency at $35 for an ounce of gold. This was well below the market price of gold, and a number of nations were taking advantage of that by redeeming U.S. dollars for gold, then selling it on the open market. So Nixon "closed the gold window" to put an end to that.

Currency exchange-rate systems are beyond the scope of this guide, but it's enough to know that Nixon aimed to preserve U.S. gold reserves while lowering the value of the dollar to increase U.S. exports and decrease imports. The latter appeared to be a good thing, given that in the early 1970s the United States began running a trade deficit for the first time in the century. However, this measure coupled with the deficits from Vietnam and President Lyndon Johnson's social programs—and rising oil prices—unleashed inflation.

The quadrupling of crude oil prices came about largely through the refusal of Arab oil-exporting states to ship oil to the United States for having supported Israel in the Yom Kippur war, set off when Syria and Egypt attacked Israel in October 1973. (At that point, it became clear that foreign suppliers could control the price of oil, yet U.S. dependence increased over the following three decades.) The price of oil remained fairly stable until the Shah of Iran was overthrown by fundamentalist revolutionaries in 1979, and 66 U.S. hostages were seized and held in Tehran. Moreover, Iraq invaded Iran in 1980, igniting war between those two nations and further reducing oil production.

These developments more than doubled the price of crude oil from $14 in 1978 to $35 per barrel in 1981. Rising oil prices can produce inflation because oil fuels cars, trucks, planes, and ships, and petroleum by-products go into packaging, plastics, fertilizers, and other widely consumed goods.

WHAT TO DO?

Be a student of economic history, if only as you read this part of this book, and understand how the policies of the past have contributed to the problems of the present. After not one, but *two*, oil price increases in the 1970s, which caused economic problems, the United States adopted no lasting policy to end dependence on foreign oil. In fact, that dependence actually increased over the subsequent 25 years.

So what might have been a cyclical 1973–1975 recession morphed into a more extended period of low growth, high unemployment, and high inflation. In October 1974, President Gerald Ford, who became president in August 1974 after Nixon's resignation over Watergate, introduced Whip Inflation Now (WIN). This campaign, complete with WIN lapel buttons, urged the public to curb spending and increase savings, and ultimately failed. During President Jimmy Carter's administration (1976–1980), inflation skyrocketed from almost 6 percent to over 13 percent. GDP growth averaged an anemic 1 percent (versus 3.1 percent in the 1960s), and unemployment remained high. This is the stagflation that many people fear today.

Stagnation + Inflation = Stagflation

Stagflation puzzled policymakers because it contradicted economic theory. Economists had long posited a tradeoff between inflation and unemployment in the business cycle.

During expansions, demand *increases* and starts to outstrip supply, and buyers bid up prices of goods and services, which generates (*demand pull*) inflation. Also or instead, companies hire workers to meet the rising demand, and as the economy approaches full employment, workers demand higher wages, which generates (*wage push*) inflation.

WHAT'S THAT?

The two basic types of inflation are **demand pull inflation,** in which buyers bid up the prices of goods and services, and **cost push inflation,** in which sellers pass their increasing costs on to buyers. Wage push inflation is actually a type of cost push inflation, in which workers demand higher wages, which producers of goods and services then pass on to buyers. An upward inflation spiral occurs when one type of inflationary trend, such as demand pull, reinforces another, such as wage push. In other words, workers see higher prices and then demand higher wages, which pushes up prices, and so on.

During recessions, demand *decreases*, and businesses reduce prices of goods and services and companies lay off workers. Unemployment created by layoffs reduces inflationary pressure and can even cause deflation, a sustained widespread decrease in prices.

But neither of these phenomena occurred in the 1970s. The chief reasons appear to be the decreasing value of the dollar, the increasing price of oil, and Fed policies that raised interest rates to about 9 percent in 1969 and to over 12 percent in 1975. Also, business investment was well below that of the boom years of the 1960s (perhaps prompting thoughts of "supply-side economics," discussed later in this chapter).

More recent fears of stagflation are based on several factors. First, people fear that many jobs—in industries such as financial services, automobiles, and retail, among others—will be permanently lost in this downturn, leading to persistent unemployment. Second, people fear that the U.S. economy may have enough, or too much, productive capacity and that business investment will either sag or move overseas, leading to low demand from the business sector. Third, people fear that low interest rates along with huge federal deficits on top of our towering national debt will cause the value of the dollar to drop (but still fail to boost U.S. exports).

Could stagflation occur again? In a word, yes.

Beyond Disco: Political and Social Effects of the 1970s

The 1970s were socially unsettled. Although things weren't as dramatic or tragic as the assassinations, demonstrations, and social conflicts of the 1960s, stagflation, crime, and a sense of drift persisted. Apart from sociopolitical events like the women's and gay rights movements, and cultural developments such as disco and regrettable hairstyles and haberdashery, the 1970s generated a sense of national ennui, given the loss in Vietnam, the scandal of Watergate, and lingering resentment between the political right and left. The culmination of this sense of drift and a force that increased people's readiness for change came with the seizing of the U.S. hostages in Iran in 1979.

Economic events can have social, political, and psychological effects. They can become turning points that change employment, income, consumption, saving, and investment patterns for years. They can generate new concerns, programs, and priorities and affect the national character for decades, as did the Great Depression and the Reagan Revolution. So while the 1970s had their negative effects, they readied the nation for President Reagan's brand of optimistic, focused leadership. But first, there was a recession to get out of the way.

The 1980s Go Bust, Then Boom

While Ronald Reagan's ascent to the presidency is recalled by many as a breath of fresh air, his first two years in office were difficult economically. Federal Reserve Chairman Paul Volker was determined to wring the staggering levels of inflation out of the economy, and he did. Appointed by Carter in 1979 (and reappointed by Reagan in 1983), Volker raised the Fed Funds rate to an unprecedented *19 percent* in 1980 and 1981. This choked off inflation but also brought on the severe 1982–1983 recession.

Meanwhile, the Republican Congress and administration passed the Economic Recovery Tax Act of 1981, the first of the Reagan tax cuts (another would follow in the Tax Reform Act of 1986), which reduced personal tax rates by 25 percent. A key rationale for this measure was "supply-side economics" (labeled "voodoo economics" by George H. W. Bush before he became Reagan's vice president). Supply-side economics holds that cutting taxes will increase investment in productive capacity and thus increase economic activity and tax receipts.

Like so much in economics, supply-side theory has been "proven" true *and* false. Conservatives believe it worked as predicted. Liberals believe that the resulting deficit spending, often labeled a "liberal" method of economic stimulus, prompted the growth. Moreover, the tax cuts were accompanied by increased defense spending, itself a type of fiscal stimulus.

In any event, the reduced taxes, increased spending, and Volker's recession positioned the nation for its next expansion, and a three-decade era of conspicuous consumption and public fascination with the wealthy. TV shows like *Dallas*, *Dynasty*, and *Lifestyles of the Rich and Famous* hit big, and the workings of business captured the public's imagination. The celebrity CEO emerged, business books rolled off the presses, and corporate raiders like T. Boone Pickens bought companies with borrowed money in a new type of deal called the leveraged buyout.

This first stage of what might be termed America's Second Gilded Age (the first was in the late 1800s) ended with the end of the Reagan administration. President George H. W. Bush ("Bush I") rose from vice president to president in the 1988 election to face the deficits and debt piled up during the Reagan years. When Reagan took office in 1981, the national debt was shy of $1 trillion. When he left office in 1988, it stood at $2.6 trillion. In the same period, GDP had expanded from $2.8 trillion in 1980 to $5.1 trillion in 1987. Perhaps that economic growth could have generated balanced budgets (as supply-siders had claimed) if taxes had been raised sufficiently or had government spending been reduced. Then again, perhaps not, given that increased taxes and reduced spending can reduce growth.

WHAT TO DO?

Stop me if you've heard this one: One economist tells another one about an economic policy that has been a huge success. It spurred investment, created millions of jobs, and tripled economic growth. The second economist listens very politely, and then says, "That's all well and good. But would it work in *theory?*"

Most Americans recall the 1980s as a decade of strong growth, but the decade brought its share of economic turmoil. For instance, high-yield ("junk") bonds made debt financing in the public markets available to many companies, including new companies such as Turner Broadcasting, MCI, and others. But junk bonds also ratcheted up investor expectations regarding "reasonable returns" and ignited a meltdown of sorts when defaults occurred in that class of securities. (Junk or high-yield bonds do not meet the high credit standards of investment-grade bonds and thus pay higher interest.) The major casualty was investment bank Drexel Burnham Lambert, the home of junk bond pioneer Michael Milkin. Other economic difficulties of the decade included the stock market crash of 1987 and the savings and loan crisis of the second half of the decade.

The Crash of 1987 occurred on October 19 of that year, a day known as Black Monday. This echoes Black Thursday, October 24, 1929, the day that initiated the Crash of 1929 and the beginning (though not the cause) of the Great Depression. On Black Monday, the Dow Jones Industrial Average fell by almost 23 percent, or 508 points, from 2,247 to 1,739—the largest one-day percentage decline in history to this day. However, recovery occurred relatively quickly. The Dow finished the year at 1,939 and recovered its previous high of 2,722, reached on August 25, 1987, almost two years later.

Yet this crash ignited worries about the economy and the financial markets and reflected slowing economic growth in 1986 brought about by the Fed's "soft landing" from the strong expansion that followed the 1982–1983 recession. In a soft landing, the Federal Reserve raises interest rates gradually to gently tighten credit conditions to cool off a potentially overheating economy. This aims to reduce inflationary pressures by reducing demand while avoiding an actual recession.

While no single explanation of the Crash of 1987 is widely accepted, they include investors seeing stock prices as overvalued—a view that appears mistaken, given subsequent valuations—trades triggered by computerized programs, which issue "sell signals" when the market reaches certain levels, and lack of liquidity due to the Fed's soft landing policies. Vaguer causes, such as "investor psychology" or "uncertainty," have also been cited. In retrospect, the Crash of 1987 signaled nothing significant, at least in the United States (global equity markets were hit harder in the next few months), and represented a blip during the expansion that lasted until 1991.

The "Bush I" Recession

In our catalogue of contractions, the "Bush I" recession was mild relative to the two previous ones: a dip of 0.2 percent in GDP for 1991 and peak unemployment of 7.5 percent in 1992. Given the excesses of the 1980s—the run-up in the federal debt, the junk bond market, the real estate boom—this recession did what a recession "should" do. It quelled growth, brought some discipline to the markets and the federal budget, and cleared the way for the next expansion. That expansion—under President Bill Clinton—lasted 10 years, from 1991 to 2001, a post–World War II record.

In the Bush-versus-Clinton election of 1992, President Bush was accused of failing to display sympathy for those most affected by the recession on his watch. He had also reluctantly *raised taxes* in the 1990 budget to reduce deficit spending and position the economy for growth. Although Democrats demanded the tax increase (and opposed the Republicans' proposed cuts), it was arguably courageous on Bush's part because he had explicitly said, "Read my lips: no new taxes," and breaking that campaign promise cost him votes.

Wait a minute. Did I just say that when Bush *raised taxes* he positioned the economy for growth? Didn't I say that Reagan *reduced taxes* to produce growth in the 1980s? Which is it?

Whether a tax increase or decrease is called for from a policy standpoint depends on the economy and the financial markets. If the government is running large deficits and the financial markets believe that government borrowing will crowd out private investment and raise interest rates, then a tax increase can calm those fears. Such a tax increase demonstrates responsible fiscal policy, which the financial markets tend to reward.

On balance, George H. W. Bush served as a solid steward of the economy and the Fed's monetary policy was basically fine. There had, however, been problems developing in the real estate market.

The Savings and Loan Crisis

The savings and loan (S&L) crisis of the 1980s is of interest for two reasons. First, it centered on real estate, and second, the federal government successfully addressed the crisis.

S&Ls were mainstays of U.S. banking for much of the past century. They engaged in basic banking—taking deposits and making loans, mainly mortgage loans—and held to conservative practices and growth targets. But things changed in the S&L industry in the 1970s, and not for the better.

Some background on interest rates and inflation is in order. When inflation increases, the "real return"—the inflation-adjusted return—on a loan or bond decreases. For example, if inflation is 3 percent per year and the interest rate on a loan or bond is 5 percent, the real, inflation-adjusted return is 2 percent. That's bad enough, but if inflation reaches, say, 7 percent, then the lender or investor is *losing* 2 percent a year in real terms. (Stocks are generally viewed as a *hedge* against inflation because, unlike fixed interest rates, stock prices and dividends can rise to offset the effects of inflation.)

WHAT'S THAT?

In investing, a **hedge** is generally a margin of safety that the investor creates to protect herself against a risk. The term also refers to a financial tool used to create a hedge. So purchasing an option to buy foreign currency (say euros) at a certain price before you needed the euros would be a hedge against the risk that the dollar would fall against the euro. Purchasing an investment whose value rises with inflation is a hedge against inflation.

The inflation of the 1970s was a disaster for the S&Ls. These banks had made many mortgage loans at rates well below the inflation rates of that decade. Plus, they were legally prohibited from paying more than a certain rate of interest on deposits. So when interest rates rose at other financial institutions to compensate for the high inflation, depositors withdrew their funds from S&Ls *en masse*. This left the S&Ls in money-losing situations, with no funding sources to replace those deposits. For instance in 1981, about 3,300 of the nation's roughly 3,800 S&Ls lost money. This was virtually unavoidable, given the interest rate environment, the S&Ls' portfolios of fixed-rate mortgages, and the ceilings on the rates they could pay on deposits. So Congress passed legislation to make S&Ls more competitive with commercial banks and other lending institutions, but with far from positive results.

The Roots of the Rout

In 1980, Congress passed the Depository Institutions Deregulation and Monetary Control Act. This enabled S&Ls to make commercial loans, open negotiable order of withdrawal (NOW) accounts to compete with commercial bank checking accounts, and offer credit cards. The next year, the Tax Reform Act of 1981 significantly expanded the tax advantages of real estate investment, which helped fuel a real estate boom in the 1980s.

Then in autumn 1982, Congress passed the Garn–St. Germain Depository Institutions Act, which further loosened S&L regulations. Between this act and the 1980 legislation, S&Ls were able to pay higher rates on deposits, borrow from the Federal Reserve, purchase loanable funds, and loan money to businesses. Also, Garn–St. Germain approved adjustable rate mortgages (ARMs) and allowed S&Ls to take ownership stakes in properties on which they made loans.

S&Ls could now compete for deposits, but had to pay more for them than in the past. This was unavoidable given increased competition in banking and new funding sources such as CDs and money-market funds, the latter growing as the commercial paper market grew. Banking became more open, deregulated, and competitive in the 1980s, and S&Ls joined the fray. The only viable alternative would probably have been to somehow maintain the thrifts as "hothouse flowers" by heavily subsidizing them.

Further pressure on the S&Ls came when the Tax Reform Act of 1986 reduced the tax advantages of many real estate investments and thus their attractiveness and real estate prices. Ending these tax shelters made sense in many ways. (Tax shelters are investments that partly or wholly exempt income from taxes.) After all, investments should generally be made on their economic benefits, although encouraging certain investments via tax breaks can be good policy. In any event, phasing out these shelters helped end the mid-1980s real estate boom.

With falling real estate prices and too many bad mortgage loans, S&Ls faced large write-offs, reduced earnings, undercapitalization, slow or no growth, and reluctance of investors to supply funds—just like commercial banks in the crisis of 2008–2009. As a result, large numbers of S&Ls began failing in the 1980s.

The Mop-Up of the S&L Crisis

The real estate bust first brought about the failure of a few large institutions. Home State Savings Bank of Cincinnati failed in 1985, as did several Maryland S&Ls. These bank failures effectively put an end to state insurance funds for S&Ls. Other failures included Silverado Savings and Loan in 1988, which involved George W. Bush's brother Neil Bush, and Lincoln Savings and Loan in 1989, which involved U.S. senators who became known as the Keating Five (and one of whom was Arizona Senator John McCain). Texas, Oklahoma, and Louisiana saw many S&Ls fail, and the nationwide industry shrank significantly.

At the end of the decade, Congress passed the Financial Institutions Reform, Recovery, and Enforcement Act of 1989 (FIRREA), which changed regulation of S&Ls and created the Resolution Trust Corporation to deal with troubled bank assets. FIRREA replaced the Federal Home Loan Bank Board with the Office of Thrift Supervision to regulate S&Ls. It also replaced the Federal Savings and Loan Insurance Corporation (FSLIC) with the Savings Association Insurance Fund to insure S&L deposits.

> **WHAT TO DO?**
>
> Never forget how intertwined banking and politics are in the United States. The S&L industry of the 1980s had its share of corruption and bad management, but it involved elected officials almost solely by making campaign contributions in order to influence policy decisions and legislation. This is exactly the situation that the nation finds itself in 20 years later, and it is why we will probably see little meaningful banking reform.

This legislation also expanded Freddie Mac's and Fannie Mae's role in buying and selling mortgages from low- and moderate-income families. You'll recall from Chapter 2 that from the early 1990s, Fannie and Freddie expanded their activity in subprime mortgages—a contributing factor to, although not the cause of, the subprime crisis.

Resolution Trust Corporation

The Resolution Trust Corporation (RTC) was the "bad bank" referred to in Part 2, a government-created institution that took bad assets off S&Ls' balance sheets to sequester them in one government-owned institution. However, many S&Ls were either too undercapitalized or too compromised to return to profitability. By "too compromised," I mean irreversibly undermined by fraud, poor earnings, or incompetent management.

RTC took the troubled assets off the S&Ls' books and, when necessary, the Office of Thrift Supervision (OTS) took over the insolvent banks. That's right—they were "nationalized," and the shareholders were wiped out (a risk people assume when they buy stock). The OTS turned the bad assets over to the RTC, which set a market clearing price mainly through auctions. RTC retained ownership stakes on assets that they sold for less than face value. That way, when the real estate market recovered, the taxpayers would share in the appreciation realized by the buyers who purchased the mortgages from the RTC. Between 1989 and 1995, the OTS and RTC "resolved" about 750 S&Ls, which were either closed down or broken up and partly or totally sold to other, healthier banks. This was in addition to almost 300 banks resolved by the FSLIC from 1986 to 1989, before formation of the RTC.

Thus, RTC proved that the government can run a major bank rescue, although the situation in 2008–2009 dwarfed the S&L crisis. By mid-2009, the government had already approved (but not distributed) $700 billion for support of banks. In contrast, the General Accounting Office (GAO) puts the cost of the S&L crisis at $160 billion, of which $125 billion came from the federal government. (This does not include state funds and covers only 1986 to 1996.)

Yet the final net loss of the S&L crisis to the taxpayers was about $40 billion—a small price to pay for the unwinding of the thrift industry as we knew it. From 1975 to 1990, the S&Ls' share of the residential mortgage market fell from 53 percent to 30 percent, and it continued to fall in the 1990s. True, certain measures, such as Fannie and Freddie's expansion into subprime loans, contributed to our later troubles. But meanwhile, we have hundreds of billions in TARP funds and hundreds of billions more on the line through various Federal Reserve facilities *with most of the troubled assets still on banks' books.*

A January 24, 2009, *New York Times* article ("First Bailout Formula Had It Right") quotes Tim Ryan, who headed the OTS at the time, as saying that without this system, the cost to taxpayers "would have been triple" the actual cost, pegged by the *Times* at $130 billion. Despite the larger scale of the 2008–2009 crisis, this basic model may represent the best of several unpleasant choices. The Obama administration launched a relatively timid mortgage modification program, but that program, or a more vigorous one, and an RTC-style bank rescue (both funded with TARP money) could have proceeded in tandem. Loans that couldn't be modified could be purchased by the "bad bank," which would sell them, hold them and sell them later, or write them off. If borrowers later defaulted (which frequently happens), the "bad bank" could even hold or sell the foreclosed house. The "bad bank" would also take the devalued mortgage-backed securities off banks' balance sheets, thus restoring a measure of confidence in the banking system.

An RTC-style solution allows the government to take its time selling the assets while waiting until the real estate market improves. One major bar to such a solution in the recent crisis appeared to be resistance to "nationalization," that is, takeover of insolvent banks. But is that so bad? True, shareholders might be wiped out, but they took that risk (and they made money during the boom). Also, current shareholders could be put at the head of the line to buy stock in any banks that were cleaned up and "re-privatized."

The other major bar *may be* that the government (and banks) felt that there were just too many bad mortgages and securities on the books, and they can't or don't want to acknowledge their losses. Estimates of the total problem went beyond $1 trillion and as high as $1.6 trillion and even $2.5 trillion. In any case, many observers (myself included) wondered why the government didn't do more to address this problem, which appeared too large to be solved without the government. The government's inaction may be due to indecision, fear of making matters worse, political gridlock, or a willingness to simply do the bidding of those who created most of this mess (the bankers) in order to help maximize their profits and preserve their institutions and positions.

WHAT TO DO?

Remember that real estate is a cyclical business. The history of increasing housing demand resulting in increasing prices and then overbuilding, which results in falling demand and falling prices and a falloff in building, is extremely well established. It is a great business, but if you work in it or invest in it (or if you own your home), try to get comfortable with its ups and downs, which are one of its chief characteristics.

Past Business Cycles

The Obama stimulus package passed in February 2009, and a mortgage relief plan was approved, all amid much debate. Debate is good, but it's interesting that anyone would argue—as some did—that the government should do little or nothing to try to address the crisis.

History indicates that before the government regularly intervened in the economy, business cycles were more frequent, contractions longer, and expansions shorter (as shown in the table on the next page). The government intervenes through monetary policy, implemented by the Federal Reserve, and fiscal policy, implemented through spending and tax measures. Neither the Fed nor the federal income tax existed in the 1800s, and neither did monetary and fiscal policy as we know it.

As the table indicates, since World War II (1945–2007), the average length of a contraction has fallen to 10 months from 22 months in the era before the 1920s and the Great Depression (1854–1919), and from 18 months during the 1920s and the Depression (1919–1945). Concurrently, the average expansion has increased to 58 months from 27 months in the 65 years before the 1920s and the Depression and from 35 months during the 1920s and the Depression. Similarly, the percent of time that the economy spends in contractions has decreased dramatically.

Historical Patterns in U.S. Business Cycles

Period	Number of Business Cycles in Contractions	Average Length of Contractions	Average Length of Expansions	Percent of Time in Contractions
1854–1919	16	22 months	27 months	45
1919–1945	6	18 months	35 months	34
1945–2007	11*	10 months	58 months	15

* Includes expansion from 2001 to 2007 but not the 2009–2010 recession
Source: National Bureau of Economic Research

While fiscal policy helped improve these patterns, monetary policy has perhaps played a larger role. Monetary policy can be implemented faster (since it operates through the Fed and requires no approval from Congress), and markets respond fairly quickly to changes in interest rates and the money supply. The Fed has engineered softer landings and shorter recessions, controlled inflation during expansions, and "primed the pump" to ignite demand when needed.

It's possible, of course, to argue that these patterns are due to globalization, international trade, technology, or any number of things other than fiscal and monetary policy. Yet the aim of those policies actually was shorter, less severe recessions and longer expansions with low inflation. With a few notable exceptions, those goals were achieved.

The problem in the 2008–2009 crisis was that we cut taxes and spent borrowed money during the expansion of 2001–2007, so our fiscal policy options were limited. With a Fed Funds rate of virtually zero, our monetary policy options were also limited. That may or may not have been by intent, though it arguably was, given that there are people, including many in politics, who are openly dedicated to undermining the effectiveness of the federal government.

In either case, the effect of deficit spending and maintaining low interest rates during the boom (bubble, actually) was to limit the ability of the government to engage in deficit spending and to lower interest rates when the next downturn came. Indeed, that turned out to be the case, and our limited policy options helped to make what might have been a simple downturn a deep and severe recession.

The Least You Need to Know

- The 1970s were a difficult time economically because "stagflation"—the combination of slow economic growth and inflation—proved difficult to address with economic policy.

- The strong medicine of the 1982–1983 recession induced by Fed Chairman Paul Volker's high interest rates provided the cure for stagflation.

- The savings and loan industry suffered in the 1970s, given the nature and regulation of their business. But the early 1980s deregulation of the industry failed to provide a lasting solution.

- The S&L crisis resulted from bad real estate loans, bad management, and a real estate bust. The U.S. government controlled the damage by creating the Resolution Trust Corporation to remove bad assets from S&Ls' balance sheets, a program which by all accounts succeeded.

- Deficit spending, low interest rates, and high government and consumer debt that piled up in years past limited policy options for fighting the recession of 2008–2009. Thus the government could not really end the recession, but it could, and did, help many people to survive it.

The Great Depression and Its Lasting Effects

Chapter

8

In This Chapter

- Life in America before the Depression
- The course of the Great Depression
- Government responses to the Depression
- Long-term shifts in government policy

The Great Depression marks one of two major economic and political turning points of the last century. The other is the less dramatic but also significant events of the 1970s and the new economic and political order that followed. These two points mark major shifts in the U.S. government's role in the economy as well as major cultural shifts.

Two presidents, Franklin Delano Roosevelt (FDR) and Ronald Reagan, spearheaded these shifts and left lasting legacies. Roosevelt's response to the Great Depression brought a new and higher level of government involvement in the nation's economic life, mainly through a host of new social programs and financial market regulations. Reagan's response to the difficulties of the 1970s aimed to shrink both the size of government and its role in the economy. He achieved the former aim but not the latter, although he certainly reduced the amount of regulation and changed the direction of the country, as discussed in the next chapter.

This chapter covers FDR's New Deal and legacy. I'll begin with a look at pre-Depression America, then examine the arc of the Depression itself. Then I'll discuss FDR's response to the Depression and some effects of that response, both positive and negative.

Life Before the Depression

Given the current size of the federal government, it's hard to believe how small it was before FDR expanded its role. There was no Social Security program, no unemployment insurance program, no federally insured bank deposits, and minimal regulation of finance and business. Economic policy tended to focus on creating favorable international trade conditions, maintaining the integrity of the currency, and raising money to finance the occasional war. In those days, the U.S. economy was characterized by family farms and ranches—and frequent booms, busts, and price instability. The unregulated nature of the securities markets made speculation and fraud fairly common.

Regarding the currency, until FDR's administration, the dollar was truly "backed by gold," meaning that anyone could exchange a paper dollar for an equivalent amount of gold. In other words, the value of the currency was tied directly to gold. Such a relationship guarantees the value and, to an extent, the stability of a currency because gold is a rare, durable, and highly valued substance, and therefore has itself long been a medium of exchange. (When President Nixon severed the final link between the dollar and gold, thus making the dollar *fiat currency*, he gave the government far greater license to expand the nation's money supply.)

WHAT'S THAT?

Fiat currency is currency issued by a government as legal tender for the purchase of goods and services and settlement of debts and payment of taxes. It is not tied to gold or another tangible store of value. It has value because the government says it does. The euro is also fiat money, as are most other major currencies.

Until 1913, when the power of the government to tax income was firmly established by the Sixteenth Amendment to the Constitution, federal income taxes were applied only occasionally (usually to finance wartime expenses) and to relatively small segments of the population. The federal government, such as it was, was financed mainly by excise taxes, duties on imports, and estate taxes.

Some observers and economists argue that, although they came along more frequently, panics and economic downturns were shorter and milder than they are under the more actively managed economy of today. That is not true. As pointed out in Chapter 7, before the government put a strong regulatory structure in place and implemented policies to encourage expansions and soften recessions, business cycles were more frequent, expansions shorter, and recessions longer.

The Arc of the Depression

The Great Depression was the prolonged period of economic contraction and slow growth, high unemployment, low investment, dormant lending, decreasing farm and home prices, and overall deflation dating from the stock market crash on Black Thursday, October 24, 1929, until about 1940. Many people think of the end of the Depression as the entry of the United States into World War II after the Japanese bombing of Pearl Harbor in Hawaii on December 7, 1941, but that is a bit late because recovery had started the previous year.

The Crash of 1929 was precipitated by a mass exodus of investors (and speculators) from an overheated stock market. During the six years from 1923 to 1929, the Dow Jones Industrial Average *quintupled*. This was emblematic of the Roaring Twenties, a time of booming economic growth accompanied by conspicuous consumption, widening income inequality, stock market speculation, and widespread borrowing (including borrowing to purchase securities). Housing prices peaked in 1925 and began declining thereafter, but the Dow continued to climb, to a peak of 381.17 on September 3, 1929. Then a month-long sell-off ensued, culminating in Black Thursday, the day most people identify as "the stock market crash" but only one day in a massive four-day sell-off. And the selling continued. On November 13, 1929, the Dow closed at 198.6, having lost almost 50 percent of its value at the September 3 peak.

Consumer spending continued to hold up for the first half of the year following the stock market crash. The Dow climbed back up to 294.07 by April 17, 1930. However, about a year later, in 1931, it began falling until it reached a bottom of 41.22 on July 8, 1932—a decline of almost 90 percent off the September 3, 1929, peak. This left an entire generation (two, actually) extremely wary of the stock market, despite the reforms instituted by FDR.

Things went almost as badly, if not as quickly, in what we now call "the real economy." The Great Depression officially began in the second half of 1930, after a falloff in consumer spending fueled by households' reluctance to take on more debt. In fact, debts had to be repaid, which some economists contend began a period of *deflation* and deflationary spiral, in which people were paying back debts with relatively more expensive dollars while wages and prices (including asset prices) were falling. That set the stage for a general decrease in prices. A cyclical contraction was clearly underway and there are various schools of thought regarding how and why the Great Depression resulted.

WHAT'S THAT?

Deflation is a period of widespread falling prices, which usually occurs because of prolonged, severe decreases in the value of assets (such as real estate) or widespread unemployment. In a deflationary spiral, sellers reduce prices and also production, which means layoffs for workers and lower wages, which further fuels price decreases.

The Role of the Government

There are those who "blame" the private sector and the markets for the Great Depression and those who "blame" the government. Blaming the government seems wrongheaded, given its low level of regulation and high tolerance of speculation before 1933. Some blame the Federal Reserve for *inaction*, for allowing banks to fail and for not expanding the money supply. For free-market fans to take the Fed to task for allowing banks to fail seems disingenuous.

WHAT TO DO?

Consider the criticisms directed toward both the Bush and Obama administrations. If the government allows banks to fail, it is standing idly by while the financial system collapses and isn't doing its job. If the government intervenes, it is practicing "socialism" and not allowing the markets to function properly. In other words, some people are simply in the business of criticizing the government.

Until the Emergency Banking Act of 1933 the government could create credit and expand the money supply only within relatively tight parameters (that is, tight relative to today). The dollar was on the gold standard, with a dollar being redeemable for gold (at $20.67 per ounce at the time, and then, under the Gold Reserve Act of 1933, $35 per ounce). Thus, until 1933, the dollar was tied very directly to the value of gold. Given that, it was impossible for the Fed to expand credit and the money supply to forestall the crisis, as it did in 2008, when it introduced new lending facilities and, in conjunction with the Treasury, acted to rescue the banking system.

FDR ran on the platform of a "New Deal" for working Americans. Measures taken by his administration (described in the second half of this chapter) helped to increase employment, stabilize the markets and prices, and thus revive the economy within the first two years of his presidency.

The first of the two recessions during the Depression ran from 1930 to 1933. In those years, as shown in the following table, GDP contracted in 1930, 1931, and 1932—by a whopping 13.1 percent in the latter year. Contraction moderated significantly in 1933, to a decrease of 1.3 percent, as New Deal policies took hold. Expansion kicked in with a booming 10.9 percent growth rate in 1934 and growth continued until 1938. The year 1938 saw a contraction of 3.4 percent before growth resumed at rates in the very healthy 8 percent range until 1941, when the nation moved to wartime production.

Key Economic Growth Data (Changes from Prior Year, in Real Dollar Terms—1930 to 1940)

	1930	1931	1932	1933
GDP	-8.6	-6.5	-13.1	-1.3
Personal consumption	-5.4	-3.1	-9.0	-2.2
Private investment	-33.3	-37.2	-69.8	47.3
Government spending	10.2	4.2	-3.3	-3.3
	1934	**1935**	**1936**	**1937**
GDP	10.9	8.9	13.0	5.1
Personal consumption	7.1	6.1	10.2	3.7
Private investment	80.6	85.2	28.2	24.9
Government spending	12.8	2.7	16.7	-4.2
	1938	**1939**	**1940**	**1941**
GDP	-3.4	8.1	8.8	17.1
Personal consumption	-1.6	5.6	5.2	7.1
Private investment	-33.9	28.6	39.3	22.1
Government spending	7.7	8.8	2.8	66.2

Source: Bureau of Economic Analysis

As you read the table, consider the formula for the entire economy:

GDP = C + I + G +/– Net Exports

"C" equals personal consumption, "I" equals business investment, and "G" equals government expenditures. (I have omitted net exports from the table, but U.S. trade approximately followed the pattern of GDP. In general, world trade suffered badly during the Depression.)

During the Depression, consumer spending (another term for personal consumption) dropped as GDP dropped and rose when GDP rose, as it does today, because personal consumption makes up the largest share of the economy.

Business investment (another term for private investment) plunged by more than a third in 1930 and in 1931 and by 70 percent in 1932. These decreases were one of the huge effects of the Crash of 1929, not to mention the banking crisis, complete with bank failures and an overall scarcity of credit.

With private investment plummeting and personal consumption decreasing, government expenditures still decreased in 1932 and 1933. However, the government stepped up in 1934 with a 12.8 percent increase in spending followed by a 2.7 percent increase and a major 16.7 increase in 1936. In 1937, FDR was persuaded to pull back on the fiscal throttle, which resulted in the 4.2 percent decrease in government spending in that year and the 3.4 percent decrease in GDP in 1938.

President Herbert Hoover, who preceded FDR, was not the disaster he is often portrayed to be. Although he did leave the markets to function as they may, that was more or less the traditional, accepted policy of the time. Also, government spending increased by 10.2 percent in 1930, the year after the stock market crash, and by 4.2 percent in 1931. Also under Hoover, Congress established the Reconstruction Finance Corporation in 1932, which provided aid to states and cities and made loans to banks and railroads—although its effectiveness was hobbled by bureaucracy and politics. This agency was retained and improved by FDR, and morphed into the Federal Emergency Relief Administration. FDR brought a larger vision and a more activist (and politically liberal) approach to the presidency than Hoover. The populace expected him to take action, and he did.

Measures During the Depression

When FDR took office, about 4,000 banks had collapsed and one in every four workers was unemployed, as a December 19, 2008, *New York Times* article noted. Asset prices had collapsed, foreclosure activity had skyrocketed, and credit had virtually frozen. FDR's immediate goals were to restore people's confidence in the banking and financial system and provide near-term relief to the unemployed. Immediately following his inauguration in March 1933, FDR embarked on what came to be known as his "first 100 days," a phrase still used when a new president takes office.

In those early days of his presidency, FDR enacted a number of measures designed to stabilize the financial system. As he took office, FDR declared a four-day *bank holiday*, and Congress enacted the Emergency Banking Act, which expanded the powers of the U.S. Treasury and the Federal Reserve over the banking system. This legislation enabled the Federal Reserve to make loans to banks at low interest rates. It also calmed depositors, who began to put their money back into the banking system.

WHAT'S THAT?

A **bank holiday** is usually a national holiday in which banks and financial markets are closed. In this case of FDR's declaration, it's a euphemism for the government shutting banks down to forestall a run on them. This extreme measure was deemed necessary to gain time to stabilize the banking system and to restore depositors' faith in its soundness.

As noted, FDR continued Hoover's Reconstruction Finance Corporation as the Federal Emergency Relief Administration, streamlining and expanding the program and using it to bolster banks and businesses and to provide money to states so they could fund their relief programs.

The Agricultural Adjustment Administration, enacted in May 1933, aimed to stabilize and increase the price of crops by decreasing the supply. That was achieved by paying farmers not to plant crops. This measure aimed to restore farm income, forestall further farm foreclosures, and to an extent save the farming system, which had also been battered by severe drought conditions, which gave rise to the term "Dust Bowl" to describe the Midwest's abandoned farms.

The National Industrial Recovery Act, enacted in June 1933, attempted to suspend antitrust laws and thus limit the competition that FDR saw as damaging the U.S. economy and to protect the collective bargaining rights of labor unions. This act was extremely controversial as well as ineffective, and it eroded some support for the New Deal. The act was passed with a sunset provision that let it expire in two years if Congress did not renew it. But it was declared unconstitutional by the Supreme Court in 1935.

The Civilian Conservation Core (CCC) was created in 1933 and lasted until 1942, providing training and jobs in areas directly related to conservation—soil erosion and repair, fire fighting and prevention, flood control, forestry, and wildlife preservation.

The Glass-Steagall Act of 1933 accomplished three major things. First, it established the Federal Deposit Insurance Corporation (FDIC) to insure deposits in commercial banks. Second, it separated depository institutions (commercial banks), which accept deposits and make loans, and investment banks, which accept funds for investment in the financial markets. Third, it empowered the Federal Reserve to regulate the rate of interest that banks could pay on deposits.

The Securities Act of 1933 brought regulation to the investment industry by requiring new levels of disclosure by companies issuing stock to the public. This legislation reflected the then apparently novel idea that investors should be given enough information to make an informed decision. (The act also prohibited misrepresentation and fraud by companies issuing stock.) This act required companies issuing securities for sale to the public to register them with the Federal Trade Commission. Registration was transferred to the Securities and Exchange Commission in 1934, as explained on the following pages.

Also in 1933, FDR signed Executive Order 6012, which made the private ownership of gold illegal and declared all privately held gold the property of the U.S. Treasury. This radical measure aimed mainly to stanch the flow of gold from the vaults of the U.S. Treasury into the private sector. It essentially did away with the ability of private citizens in the United States to redeem dollars for gold and ended the gold standard as it had existed.

Separately, since 1919 the United States had attempted the "noble experiment" of prohibiting alcoholic beverages. FDR had promised to work to repeal *Prohibition*, and he soon issued an Executive Order redefining the allowable content of alcoholic beverages as 3.2 percent (a far cry from the 40 percent in most spirits). This measure paved the way for Congress to pass the Twenty-First Amendment, which repealed the Eighteenth Amendment, which had provided the grounds for Prohibition.

WHAT'S THAT?

Prohibition was the period from 1919 to 1933 in which the United States made the manufacture, sale, and, essentially, consumption of alcoholic beverages illegal. Enacted by the Eighteenth Amendment and repealed by the Twenty-First Amendment, Prohibition encouraged disrespect of the law, cultural upheaval (the Roaring Twenties), and organized crime in the bootlegging (often from Canada, which abstained from this madness) and distillery and brewery business.

Measures Passed in 1934 and 1935

The three most far-reaching measures passed in the second two years of FDR's first term were the Securities Exchange Act of 1934, the Emergency Relief Appropriation Act of 1935, and the Social Security Act of 1935.

Securities Exchange Act

The Securities Exchange Act of 1934 created the Securities and Exchange Commission (SEC) to regulate the secondary market for securities in the United States. The secondary market includes the brokers, dealers, buyers, and sellers who participate in the stock exchanges, such as the New York Stock Exchange and a few regional stock exchanges, and in the over-the-counter market. The SEC regulates aspects of investing and trading such as margin requirements, licensing of brokers, and financial disclosure and audits.

Some people are confused about the nature of the secondary market, which is what most of us think of as "the stock market." In the secondary market, people buy and sell stock that has already been issued by companies (in the primary market). Companies receive money from securities only when they issue them, not when they are traded in the secondary market. Why, then, do companies care about their stock price? Because the higher the stock price, the lower the company's *cost of capital* when it needs to raise more money in the stock market. That is, when a buyer will pay more to own a share in a company, demand for that company's shares is high and it is easier and cheaper for the company to raise capital. Also, the higher the stock price, the happier existing shareholders (that is, owners) are, because they buy stock in anticipation of appreciation. Finally, any shares (or options to purchase shares) that management owns also increase in value as the stock price rises.

 WHAT'S THAT?

A company's **cost of capital** is the rate it must pay on its long-term debt and its equity to lenders and investors. This debt and equity are considered capital, and capital funds a company's long-term growth (that is, new plant and equipment) and enables it to weather difficult business conditions. The cost of capital is usually calculated on a weighted average of the interest and dividends the company pays on debt and stock. In general, the cost depends on general credit and stock market conditions and the degree of risk that lenders and investors associate with the company.

The Securities Act of 1933 and the Securities Exchange Act of 1934 laid the foundation for regulation of the U.S. financial markets and for financial disclosure by companies. These two acts are excellent examples of the way in which regulation can help markets to work more efficiently. A truly efficient market (which really occurs only in theory) is one where buyers and sellers have access to the same information regarding the items being sold. In that way, buyers and sellers determine prices that match supply and demand so the market works in a fair manner and allocates productive resources and goods and services according to people's actual wants and needs.

Regulation of the U.S. financial markets—which requires financial disclosure, audits of financial statements, and licensing of securities brokers and dealers—helped to make U.S. markets among the most trusted in the world. This has helped U.S. companies raise capital more effectively and efficiently than companies in most other nations, including many industrial nations.

Emergency Relief Appropriation Act

The Emergency Relief Appropriation Act of 1935 funded the Works Progress Administration (WPA), the vast public works program that put millions of unemployed workers to work in an array of government-funded jobs. This, the largest of the "alphabet soup" of agencies created by the New Deal (WPA, SEC, and so on), put everyone from construction workers and truck drivers to researchers and writers to work on government projects. Critics charged that the WPA was inefficient and that political considerations often determined where projects were funded (both of which were true to an extent, although every state and most cities and towns benefited). Some critics felt that FDR was simply buying votes. Many people decried it as a "make-work" program, which it clearly was.

Of course, critics meant "make-work" to indicate work for which there was little demand or value. Yet the absence of demand was precisely the problem: people needed work, and the economy needed them to be working, and private industry was not providing that work. Demand had to come from somewhere, and the government provided it. In *An Appalachian New Deal: West Virginia in the Great Depression*, author Jerry Bruce Thomas notes that the WPA not only launched road repaving and rural road-building projects, but also quite a few municipal music projects. "Among the unemployed musicians were many who had played in movie theaters in the era of the silent films and had been left stranded by the coming of the talkies." Thomas goes on to note that WPA municipal bands in Wheeling, Huntington, and Clarksburg, West Virginia, were in place and holding well-attended concerts by 1936. Similar projects across the nation included recordings of oral histories and folk music and the founding of many arts centers.

Such efforts were in addition to the jobs created by investment in highways, dams, bridges, parks, and other elements of national infrastructure and in addition to projects to feed, clothe, and house people hard-hit by the Depression. In 1939 the WPA was renamed the Work Projects Administration; the program was phased out in 1943.

Social Security Act

The Social Security Act of 1935 created the Federal-State Unemployment Compensation Program. This legislation created the unemployment insurance program that exists to this day. The plan provides temporary, partial wage-replacement to involuntarily unemployed workers. Although it cushions workers and their households from the hardships that unemployment brings, that wage-replacement also helps to stabilize the economy during recessions by channeling money to the unemployed and thus supporting demand. The act also established a federal program of grants to states for payments of benefits to people with disabilities, including blindness, and for dependent children.

The act established a board, as stated in the legislation, "to perform the duties imposed upon it by this Act [as well as] studying and making recommendations as to the most effective methods of providing economic security through social insurance, and … old-age pensions, unemployment compensation, accident compensation, and related subjects."

Most consequential was the act's provision for old-age pensions for workers who reach the age of 65 and for a tax to fund that benefit—and our failure as a society to recognize the significance of this and to make adjustments as the population and life expectancies increased. According to Berkeley University, in 1935 the average life expectancy for men was 60 and for women was 64. Thus, at least theoretically, the "average" person was not expected to collect any retirement benefits when the program was created. As explained in Chapter 17, the implications of Social Security for the future are quite serious.

Among the lesser but still important initiatives undertaken in FDR's first term is the establishment of the Rural Electrification Administration (REA), whose name explains its purpose, and the Federal Energy Regulatory Commission (FERC), which expanded the powers of the Federal Power Commission. FERC, an independent regulatory agency run by five commissioners appointed by the president and confirmed by Congress, oversees interstate electricity, natural gas, and other forms of energy.

Those are the major legislative accomplishments of FDR's first term. FDR's policies and his patrician but straightforward and competent leadership style clearly met with voters' approval. The 32nd president won a second term by a landslide. His second term was far less productive, but hardly devoid of important developments.

Second Term Highlights

One of the most consequential pieces of legislation in FDR's second term was the Fair Labor Standards Act, which created the national minimum wage, established "time and a half" as the overtime pay rate, and regulated child labor. The minimum wage was—and is—a case of government price setting in the private-sector labor market. Although similar market interventions occur in other markets (rent control being a notable example), minimum wage legislation is remarkable in its assumption that the government has the right to set a minimum price on one's labor. What if a worker would accept a lower wage in order to obtain the work? Setting an artificial floor on wages distorts the market and may price some workers out of the market who would otherwise be willing and able to participate in it. Such arguments are made by advocates of the free market whenever an increase in the minimum wage is scheduled or considered, and they are valid.

The policy question is whether the minimum wage helps significantly more people than it hurts. It is also market intervention for the government to specify working conditions. For instance, the Occupational Health and Safety Act of 1970 (OSHA) sets a huge array of workplace safety standards, most of which benefit workers without unreasonably burdening employers. Moreover, many employers have found ways around the minimum wage, for example by reclassifying low-wage workers as managers so they will be exempt from the law, and by hiring day workers or illegal immigrants off the books. Overall, however, the minimum wage represents a blow for workplace fairness, especially given today's low rates of union membership in the private sector.

Supreme Court Controversies

FDR got carried away with his popularity and power (and pique) as evidenced by his plan to "pack" the Supreme Court with his own appointees. FDR had seen a few of his New Deal measures struck down as unconstitutional in his first term, most significantly the National Labor Relations Act. A 1935 Supreme Court decision striking down the act held that it gave too much authority to the executive branch and defined interstate commerce too broadly. Also, in 1936 the court effectively struck down the Agricultural Adjustment Act, which aimed to support (or "inflate") crop prices.

To build a more compliant Supreme Court, in 1937, the first year of his second term, FDR proposed the Judiciary Reorganization Bill, which would have the effect of enabling him to appoint an additional five justices to the court. Roosevelt proposed that he be able to appoint another justice for each sitting justice over the age of 70. This would have expanded the court to 14 justices. FDR claimed that this measure would help relieve each individual justice's workload.

This measure met with vigorous and broad opposition, including resistance from FDR's own vice president. Indeed, it was a scheme on FDR's part to expand his power, especially given that the correct way to proceed with this proposal would have been through a constitutional amendment.

However, the matter was soon rendered moot by naturally occurring vacancies on the court. From 1937 to 1942, due to deaths and resignations, FDR had the opportunity to appoint eight justices to the nine-member bench.

FDR's Economic Legacy

The way FDR's legacy is regarded has changed, particularly in recent years as people who were directly affected by the Great Depression die off. Over the past several years, the definition of liberal has come to mean "socialist" to people unable to distinguish between the two approaches to governance. To such people, FDR has always (justifiably) been the founding father of modern American liberalism. However, they also often believe that FDR worsened the Depression, that the Federal Reserve caused the Depression, or that the markets would have soon righted themselves without government intervention. None of those things has been proven true and, in reality, the overall economy generally functioned remarkably well from the 1940s through the 1990s, albeit with stagflation in the 1970s, which a sharp, Fed-induced recession cured.

That record is largely due to what might be termed an economic pact between government and business and households that emerged in the decades after FDR and World War II. One author has labeled this "managed capitalism," and it was probably inevitable that it would end, if for no other reason than U.S. markets would eventually become more open to foreign competition. The demise of that pact is the subject of the next chapter. But before we turn to it, I'll summarize several widely recognized positive and negative effects of FDR's New Deal policies.

WHAT TO DO?

To learn more about FDR and his life and times, read the excellent biography *FDR* by Jean Edward Smith (Random House, 2008). For a closer look at the economy during his presidency and his handling of it, see *The Complete Idiot's Guide to the Great Depression,* by H. Paul Jeffers.

Positive and Negative Effects of the New Deal

Clearly the New Deal and FDR's philosophy of governance shaped much of the next few decades of economic life in the United States. To many people's way of thinking, this was a good thing for several reasons.

Federal programs such as unemployment insurance and Social Security buffered average people from some of the risks inherent in a market economy. In an even more dramatic intervention, the WPA provided government-funded jobs directly to workers when they needed them badly. Not only did this aid individual citizens, it protected the economy from deeper recessionary cycles. Economic policies, particularly deficit spending to boost demand, and the entire notion of government assuring citizens' of some minimal level of economic welfare, gave people a sense that the government was there to serve them and not just to represent the interests of business.

Support of labor unions helped to level the power imbalance that always exists between employers and the employed, given that individual workers cannot match the bargaining power of an employer. Unionizing enabled workers to demand better wages, benefits, and working conditions. And farm policies, such as subsidies for not planting crops and government purchases of agricultural products, saved thousands of farms from failure.

Many Americans would disagree that those are positive developments, even though those policies endured for decades because most voters favored them. However, the policies of the New Deal and FDR hold definite downsides.

People began to look to the federal government to "bail them out" when economic difficulties arose—an attitude that, ironically, prevails in some major corporations (which otherwise favor a free, unregulated market) as well as in some American households.

Homeownership programs and mortgage-market regulation that began during the Depression made homeownership more attractive than renting. This market intervention favored one segment of the population (homeowners, suburbanites, and country dwellers) over another (renters and city dwellers). It also brought about Fannie Mae and other federal programs that support the construction and mortgage industries in far more direct ways than, say, retailers and restaurants are supported.

Unions eventually used their power to demand wages, working conditions, and health-care and retirement benefits far better than those available to nonunion workers. This helped to price American workers out of the global labor market when less expensive foreign labor became more accessible to U.S. companies.

Perhaps worst of all, Social Security was founded as a universal, pay-as-you-go, non-means-tested entitlement program that did not fund its benefits and ultimately permitted Social Security taxes to be used for general, unrelated expenditures. As noted in Chapter 16, Congress and the American people have let this situation go on to the point where the Social Security program depends on a "trust fund" filled with nothing but IOUs from the federal government to the federal government—and on taxpayers who expect their Social Security benefits someday.

One fact about FDR's policies is as close to incontrovertible as is possible for a set of policies—the New Deal and FDR's approach to governance did much to expand and support membership in the U.S. middle class. However, a number of these policies—and many private-sector developments that expanded and supported the middle class from the 1940s to the 1960s—were reversed, beginning in the 1970s and 1980s. At least partly as a result, the middle class has lost ground in the past 40 years. That is the subject of the next chapter.

The Least You Need to Know

- Before the Great Depression, the U.S. economy underwent more frequent and longer recessions and shorter expansions. Recessions and expansions characterize market economies, and workers and investors once faced considerably greater risk during downturns.

- Franklin Delano Roosevelt (FDR) ran on a promise of a "New Deal" for U.S. workers, which appealed to a nation battered by severe unemployment, plummeting demand and production, falling prices, lack of credit, and no safety net of government programs.

- More active government economic policies, federal regulation of banking and the financial markets, and various social programs that originated during the New Deal transformed the U.S. economy into one that presented less risk to average Americans.

- Major components of the New Deal included government-funded programs to generate jobs, support for farm prices, unemployment insurance, support of labor unions, and establishment of Social Security.

- The legacy of government programs had both positive and negative long-term effects on the U.S. economy. From 1980 onward, a strong U.S. conservative movement has attempted, without much success, to make the federal government smaller and, more successfully, to free labor and financial markets from federal regulation.

How the U.S. Middle Class Lost Ground

In This Chapter

- How the U.S. middle class expanded
- Developments that favored the middle class
- What happened to "corporate loyalty"?
- How risk shifted to employees

As Chapter 8 noted, many federal policies of FDR's New Deal focused on helping people to avoid slipping into poverty or to climb up into the middle class. This tradition continued with the G.I. Bill in 1944 and with President Lyndon Johnson's Great Society in the 1960s. Politicians do not pursue such legislation purely out of compassion. They also realize that most voters are middle class and that leaders often stand a better chance of reelection if they appeal to the concerns of the middle class.

This policy orientation shifted in the 1980s, as a reaction to large government pro-grams and the taxes required to fund them, and to the real and perceived failures of some policies. For instance, during the 1970s—the last major economic turning point before the 2008–2009 recession—New York City became something of a national poster child for failed liberal policies. The city was riddled with crime, covered with graffiti, burdened by taxes, inadequately served by its unionized public workforce, and on the brink of bankruptcy. New York had by then also lost a large portion of its white and middle-class population as the suburbs expanded in the 1950s and 1960s.

President Reagan, who began his first term in 1981, shifted the conversation (and policies) toward the conservative end of the political spectrum. Conservative policies, like those of the liberals, were typically well-intentioned but often generated unin-tended outcomes.

This chapter examines the shift that occurred in the political landscape from 1980 through 2007 and the policies that helped to reshape the U.S. economy during that period. The aim of many of these policies was to make government smaller, but they failed to do that, which is arguably their greatest failure. Those policies also had a marked effect on the middle class in that they undercut some factors that contributed to the growth of the middle class in the 1940s, 1950s, and 1960s. However, other forces with similar effects, such as foreign competition and financial innovation, were underway independent of conservative policies. This chapter also examines those forces and their effects on the middle class.

Middle-Class Losers?

The U.S. middle class is still the largest class of U.S. citizens, and is still quite well off compared with the citizens of most nations. Yet the U.S. middle class has lost ground economically over the past 35 years. That fact, and the prospect of sluggish economic growth over the next several years, has led many people to question whether we are at a turning point. It's a question worth asking given the worst recession since the Great Depression, record high levels of federal and household debt, high and widespread unemployment, erosion of the nation's manufacturing base, and the election of Barack Obama, who ran on a platform of change.

It's fairly easy to define the U.S. middle class in terms of income. It can be defined as the middle quintile (the middle 20 percent) of the population when it is divided into five household income quintiles. More broadly and more accurately, we can say that the middle class comprises the middle three *household income* quintiles—the second, third, and fourth. This scheme classifies the bottom quintile as "poor" and the top quintile as "rich."

WHAT'S THAT?

Household income is the measure of income generally used by the U.S. Census Bureau. It includes wages, salaries, tips, Social Security and unemployment insurance payments, and alimony and child support and other regularly received income (so it would exclude gifts and inheritances). Household income is, of course, an average figure, as is per-capita income, which is the income received at the individual (as opposed to household) level.

As Chapter 11 will discuss in greater detail, the *growth* of middle-class income has diminished over the past 30 to 40 years, and as a result so has their share of national income. The incomes of households in the top 20 percent have grown far faster than those of the lower 80 percent. As a result, that top quintile now enjoys a larger share of national income than any of the lower four quintiles. (If the distribution of income growth—not income—were equal, each quintile's income would grow at the same rate and their shares of total income would remain equal over time. That is not the same as "even distribution of income," which no serious individual advocates. If each quintile's income growth were equal over time, the top quintile would still have higher incomes, but their share of total income would remain the same.)

These facts form the premise of this chapter, which is that the middle class (defined here as middle-income households) has lost ground relative to the upper-income households, and that this is a result of certain policies, enacted by both Democrats and Republicans. Another premise of this chapter is that the middle class may lose more ground as the effects of the 2008–2009 recession linger over the next few years.

First, however, let's examine how the middle class came to include so many U.S. citizens.

The Class of the 1900s

By numerical definition, the United States and most industrialized nations have long had a middle class. That is, a good number of people have always fallen into the middle-income brackets. That's in contrast to developing nations, where most people are poor and relatively few are wealthy. Virtually every nation has both rich people and poor people, and many have a middle class or emerging middle class.

The rich are the investor class, the owners of capital, whether they own the railroads, steel, and textile mills of the United States during the Industrial Revolution, or the oil wells of the Middle Eastern nations or the mineral mines of Africa. In capitalist economies, the rich are usually entrepreneurs or descendants of entrepreneurs and business owners. In *Communist* or *Socialist* economies, despite the fact that "the people" theoretically own the capital, the wealthy are usually the political and party officials and the people who manage "the state's" industries.

 WHAT'S THAT?

In **Communist** and **Socialist** economies, the means of production are owned "collectively" by the people or the state, and goods are produced and distributed by government decisions. For that reason, they are sometimes called "command" economies. In traditional Marxist theory, which underpins collectivism, socialism is a stage between capitalism and communism and is characterized by state ownership and unequal distribution of goods and services. In theory, communism is society without state and with equitable distribution of goods and services.

The poor include the unemployed, uneducated, disabled, and others unable (or sometimes unwilling) to work. Many of the poor in the United States work steadily and hard, but at unskilled, minimum-wage, or below minimum-wage jobs in retail or the service sector in agriculture, restaurants, or construction. (Migrant workers and illegal immigrants account for most workers in below minimum-wage jobs.)

The middle class are the working stiffs between the rich and the poor. They are steadily employed at jobs paying well above minimum wage; have high school, vocational, technical, or college educations; and earn enough to afford decent food, housing, transportation, and clothing.

One key characteristic of middle-class life is (or was) its predictability. Middle-class people enjoy a sense of stability and security that is unknown to the poor. They know where their next meal is coming from, know they can pay their bills, know they can survive temporary job loss, and know they can afford health care if they become ill. Most have at least some savings and can someday retire from work and enjoy a few years of leisure with a sense of dignity and financial security. The recession of 2008–2009 unexpectedly did away with this sense of certainty for many people. So by that definition alone, many people have fallen out of the middle class.

After World War II, the U.S. middle class grew to include a huge percentage of citizens. Before the 1930s, people who were not wealthy experienced far more insecure lives. They were more prone to suffer financial reversals or to "lose everything" due to job loss, illness, crop failure (or crop-price declines), bank failure, or bad investments. Much of FDR's New Deal aimed to do away with that insecurity. In that sense, many New Deal programs aimed to buffer people from the risks and effects of the competitive, capitalist U.S. economy. Unemployment insurance buffered people from the effects of job loss in cyclical contractions; federal deposit insurance buffered them from the effects of bank failure; and Social Security buffered them from the financial effects of disability, widowhood, and old age.

Despite strong Republican opposition to the New Deal at the time it was enacted, the middle class came to deeply appreciate its benefits. Those benefits still help many people to remain in the middle class when they otherwise would fall out of it, most recently in the recession of 2008–2009, particularly thanks to unemployment benefits. Of course, as explained next, the private sector also did much to expand the middle class, as major industrial companies grew and provided good jobs for millions of Americans.

Six Drivers of Middle-Class Growth

Essentially, six key factors that emerged in the 1930s and 1940s contributed to the growth of the U.S. middle class:

- Deposit insurance and financial regulation

- Social Security, unemployment benefits, and the minimum wage

- New federal economic policies

- Growth of union membership

- Salaried jobs and corporate benefits

- Expanded access to education

These are listed roughly in the order in which they occurred, not in their order of importance, which is highly debatable. It's even debatable whether these are the six most important drivers of the expansion of the middle class, but they clearly played key roles. Also, as certain of these factors waned, the middle class lost ground financially.

Deposit Insurance and Financial Regulation

Federal regulation of banks and the financial markets largely did away with runs on banks and outright stock fraud, both of which were more common before the 1930s. Lack of faith in the banking and financial system threatened the safety of people's savings and could hobble investment and economic growth. A capitalist economy depends on orderly, transparent, reasonably honest financial markets and reliable *financial intermediaries*—primarily banks, trust companies, and investment funds—to gather money from savers and investors and make those funds available for investment in businesses that produce goods and services.

WHAT'S THAT?

Financial intermediaries include commercial, savings, and investment banks and pensions, employee benefits, and other funds. All of these institutions are in the business of taking money deposited or invested with them and allocating it to loans and investments, based on the perceived returns and the perceived risk associated with those returns.

New Deal–era innovations such as federally insured bank deposits (through the Federal Deposit Insurance Corporation), federal oversight of the stock market (through the Securities and Exchange Commission), and separation of depository institutions and investment banks (through the Glass-Steagall Act) helped to restore faith in the banking and financial system when it was badly needed.

Related New Deal policies encouraged homeownership, which also fueled expansion of the U.S. middle class as we know it. Although homeownership is certainly not necessary to a middle-class lifestyle, in the United States it has become one emblem of membership in the middle class. A home also acts as a repository of long-term savings, more or less forcing people to "save" as they pay their mortgages and increase their equity, and as their homes appreciate in value over the long term. As noted in Part 1, housing itself is a driver of the U.S. economy, providing jobs in construction and many other industries.

Social Security, Unemployment Benefits, and the Minimum Wage

The Social Security and unemployment insurance programs provide a "safety net" that enables workers to survive if they become disabled or lose their jobs. Also the minimum wage, at least theoretically, calls for workers to be paid a living wage.

As of early 2010, the U.S. minimum wage was $7.25, which equals $290 for a 40-hour week and $15,080 for a 52-week year. In 2008, the poverty threshold for a single person was $11,200, so by that definition an individual making $15,000 a year is lower middle class. Note, too, that the minimum wage remained at $5.15 from 1997 to 2007, when it rose to $5.85, with provisions to rise to $6.55 in 2008 and $7.25 in 2009. (In contrast, members of Congress have received automatic annual cost-of-living pay increases since 1989, when they stopped accepting pay for speeches.)

WHAT TO DO?

For an excellent look at the lives of the working poor, a designation that includes tens of millions of U.S. workers, read *Nickel and Dimed: On (Not) Getting By in America* by Barbara Ehrenriech (Holt Paperbacks edition, 2008).

Federal Economic Policy Changes

The 1930s initiated a more activist role for the federal government in economic policy. People argue over the proper aims and tools of those policies, but few argue that the government should do *something* to encourage growth, moderate the business cycle, and maintain a stable currency. The expansions and contractions of a market economy were described by economist Joseph Schumpeter as a process of "creative destruction" in which old technologies and businesses are successively swept aside by new ones. Government policies attempt to moderate the business cycle, to temper expansions (and avoid high inflation), and to generate "soft landings" instead of recessions (and avoid high unemployment).

Here's how the U.S. government became more active in economic policy. British economist John Maynard Keynes formulated his theories of the role of governments in economies before and during the 1920s and further refined them in the 1930s. Keynes theorized that a government can and should stimulate demand and thus economic activity through deficit spending. His theory gained acceptance during the FDR administration, which put it into practice.

Previously, government economic interventions pretty much focused on trade, currency, and wartime finances. In the 1930s, FDR's fiscal policies established to the satisfaction of a majority of people that government economic intervention is legitimate. Keynes's theories also set the stage for the other great twentieth century school of economic thought—monetarism. Monetarism holds that a nation's central bank, such as the U.S. Federal Reserve System, can encourage or moderate economic growth by influencing the nation's money supply. (Increasing the money supply, through low interest rates and reserve requirements, boosts economic growth. Decreasing the money supply, through high interest rates and reserve requirements, moderates economic growth.)

The point is that after FDR, government intervention in the economy, one way or another, for better or worse, became a feature of U.S. political and economic life. That implied that politicians had better be doing something to support economic growth if they wanted to be reelected, and most politicians on both sides of the aisle have taken that implication to heart.

Growth of Union Membership

Most people under 50 have only vague knowledge of the benefits of union membership for workers unless they are among the dwindling number of people in families with union members. Up to a point, unions clearly contributed to the expansion of the U.S. (and European) middle class.

A labor union brings workers together to conduct collective bargaining with employers regarding wages, benefits, and work rules. The latter can include everything from hours and vacation time to the size of work crews and the temperatures in which workers can work. In collective bargaining, workers bargain as a united group and hold over management the threat of a slowdown in production or a strike if their demands are not met. A union recognizes that a worker has little bargaining power relative to an employer and that a united workforce holds considerable power.

Unfortunately, many unions used that power to obtain wages, benefits, and work rules that were unsustainable given the value the workers were creating and the reality of lower-paid foreign workers. This contributed to many companies moving manufacturing operations to right-to-work states, which discourage union membership. Such states make it more difficult for workers to organize, for instance by limiting the power of unions to strike. Worse for U.S. workers, many companies moved their manufacturing to nations with lower labor costs.

The rise of conservatism under President Reagan (who, in August 1981, fired 11,000 unionized federal air traffic controllers who engaged in an illegal strike) may have contributed to the erosion of labor union membership. However, that erosion was already an established trend, at least in the private sector, where union membership peaked in the early 1950s at 36 percent, according to a *Washington Post* article dated March 15, 2009. That same article points out that private-sector union membership now stands at "7.5 percent, a level not seen since 1900."

While they were in their ascendancy, labor unions pushed up wages and retirement benefits. If they pushed them up to artificially high levels, which they almost certainly did in some cases, they also contributed to the ability of hourly workers to earn an income that placed them and their families firmly in the middle class.

Salaried Jobs and Corporate Benefits

After World War II, the return of U.S. troops and subsequent high levels of household formation and birth rates created a growing market for goods and services. U.S. industry rose to meet that demand, initially with very little foreign competition given the damage suffered by European and Asian industries and households in the war. During this time a kind of corporate paternalism prevailed as the ranks of managers and professionals swelled. (By "professionals" I mean technicians, analysts, systems designers, programmers, and other white-collar workers, as well as those in actual *professions* such as accounting, engineering, and law at most Fortune 1000 companies.)

WHAT'S THAT?

Although the term **profession** is used loosely, the traditional professions are medicine, law, accounting, engineering, and architecture. The true professions have educational and training requirements, are overseen by governing bodies, are usually licensed by the state, and have codes of ethics and conduct apart from clients' desires and that even transcend those desires. On the latter point, the customer might always be right, but clients can be wrong and need professionals to tell them when they are.

White-collar workers are generally salaried workers as distinct from hourly workers in production, secretarial, clerical, transportation, maintenance, and similar functions. Thus, white-collar workers are not covered by labor laws or union contracts, nor do they generally form unions. However, from the 1940s through much of the 1980s, at major companies they almost uniformly received good salaries, as well as health, life, and disability insurance and company-paid retirement benefits. These features helped people who had the requisite education to enter (or remain in) the middle class. Also, until the 1990s, as salaried workers they typically were not laid off when business slowed during recessions.

Until the 1980s, a kind of "corporate loyalty" prevailed. This meant that salaried workers tended to work long term in one or two employers and employers considered past accomplishments, personal relationships, and even family obligations in decisions to keep or terminate such employees. (I saw a few bankers long past their days of contributing to the organization kept on staff until retirement because they had brought in major accounts years earlier in their careers and had been stricken by hardships.) This situation changed beginning in the 1980s.

Expanded Access to Education

In the aggregate, higher education translates to higher earnings over a person's working life. That's not to say that a high school dropout running his own contracting business cannot earn more than a teacher or an attorney. It is to say that *in general* higher education usually leads to higher earnings.

At least that was the case for most of the last century. For instance, FDR signed the G.I. Bill (the Servicemen's Readjustment Act of 1944), which, in addition to low-cost mortgages, provided college tuition benefits to members of the armed forces after their wartime service. The G.I. Bill expanded the supply of college graduates in the 1940s and then after the Korean War in the 1950s and during and after Vietnam in the 1960s and 1970s. Most of the graduates found jobs in the expanding U.S. corporations and law firms of the 1940s, 1950s, and 1960s, or in the law, accounting, engineering, and advertising firms that served those companies or in medical or dentistry practices. Virtually all of these individuals and their families joined the burgeoning middle class of the time.

These six factors, among others, contributed to the growth of the U.S. middle class. But beginning in the 1970s, various forces altered the U.S. employment landscape and the fate of many in the middle class.

What Happened?

The middle class lost ground (as did the poor) relative to the top quintile of the five household income brackets from the 1970s through the 2000s. Real (that is, inflation-adjusted) incomes stagnated or diminished for all but the top quintile from the 1970s through the 2000s (as discussed in Chapter 3). If incomes stop growing and prices keep rising—even by a little each year—people lose ground financially.

Room for Argument

Several arguments surround the issue of whether the middle class lost ground over the past few decades. Some have to do with how income is calculated and considered, and some concern other factors.

The first argument states that judging income growth by examining household income is not as valid as judging it by per-capita income. This argument states that the composition of households changed over the past few decades, and that households are now smaller. This is true and it is due to more single and divorced people living alone and to smaller family size. This is a valid argument. However, the following table shows that growth in real per-capita income has also fallen dramatically.

Growth in U.S. Real Per-Capita Income (Total Percentage Growth Over 10-Year Periods, in 2007 Dollars)

1967–1977	34.5
1977–1987	20.0
1988–1997	14.6
1997–2007	8.2

Source: Calculations based on U.S. Census Bureau data

From 1967 to 1977, which includes much of the Stagnant Seventies, real per-capita income grew by 34.5 percent. Four decades later, from 1997 to 2007, which includes two booms and one mild, 11-month recession in 2001, real per-capita income rose by only 8.2 percent. Also, bear in mind that these are national averages. Much of the growth in real per-capita income occurred toward the top of the income distribution, as was the case for households.

The second argument concerns the fact that "returns to education" (higher earnings that go to better-educated workers) rose as demand for educated employees increased. This relates to the makeup of the labor force and the kinds of jobs the economy is creating. In the 1990s and 2000s, millions of manufacturing jobs, which often enable relatively unskilled, less educated workers to generate greater value than they can in service jobs, were shifted to foreign locations. Meanwhile, new U.S. jobs that employ lower-skilled, less-educated workers tended to be in the service sector—in restaurants, retail, maintenance, building trades, and other service-sector positions. So rising returns to education coupled with an expanding service sector and a shrinking manufacturing sector put pressure on the middle class.

Overall, the data (along with copious anecdotal and survey evidence) show that pressure on the middle class (the middle three income quartiles) has increased over the past 40 years. People are working longer hours, the number of people living in poverty continues to rise, as does the number without health insurance. This means that people are falling out of or failing to enter the middle class. The financial crisis and recession of 2008–2009, and the prospect of a sluggish recovery, spell trouble for the middle class (and for the poor).

Some of the broader pressures on the middle class stem from public policies and some from economic changes. Some have to do with the reduced power of the six drivers of middle-class growth cited previously. Others have to do with new factors.

Key Drivers Disappeared

Two key drivers of middle-class expansion lost much of their steam over the past 40 years: union membership and corporate benefits and loyalty. While government policies to an extent hurt unions, they were not the only force working against them. True, union membership peaked a few years after passage of the Taft-Hartley Act in 1947 over President Truman's veto. That legislation weakened the power of unions by instituting more rigorous federal oversight of them, by allowing states to pass "right to work legislation," and by prohibiting certain union tactics.

But unions were also weakened by more workers moving into traditionally nonunion occupations, such as computer programming, and by foreign competition. Abuses of power by unions, exemplified by the sanitation workers' and transit workers' strikes in the 1960s and 1970s in New York City, didn't win unions many fans—but did win them contracts that many nonunion workers consider extremely rich.

Corporate loyalty diminished partly due to policies of deregulation by both Democratic and Republican administrations which made the workforce more flexible. Perhaps more important was the broader restructuring of U.S. industry in the 1980s, due to deregulation and to foreign competition, management buyouts, and corporate takeovers by "raiders" who purchased companies and sold them off in pieces. Investors' increasing demands for short-term profits prompted many companies to cut costs by reducing staff. That left remaining employees less able to push for salary increases and improved benefits, or to protest reduced benefits. Also, in the 1990s and 2000s, companies increasingly used temporary staff and independent contractors for positions they once filled with full-time employees.

Once foreign competitors had the necessary productive capacity to compete with U.S. companies, the size and affluence of the U.S. market made it quite attractive to them. The only policy alternative would have been strong protectionism to support U.S. industries, such as steel, textiles, and garments, among others. Such policies could protect possibly inefficient industries (for awhile) and increase prices paid by U.S. consumers.

Meanwhile, U.S. consumers want low prices. They also want the freedom to change jobs for higher salaries. Thus the notion of loyalty eroded among employees as well as on the employers' side of the desk. Overall, however, over the past 40 years, many of the risks that characterize a capitalist market economy were shifted from employers to employees. That reversed the trend that began with the New Deal and continued through the 1960s, and put the middle class at greater risk and generated greater financial insecurity.

From Production to Consumption

The past two decades saw a cultural shift from production to consumption in the U.S. economy. I am not saying the U.S. economy has not been productive or that GDP has been decreasing, but that there has been a shift from an industrial economy that produces tangible things that people need to a service economy that produces many things that people do not actually need. Of course, education and health care are essential services. But as many observers have asked, how many lawyers and consultants does a nation need? (Even with tangible products, how many applications and features can we really use?)

The shift has been abetted by a banking industry that encourages consumption rather than savings. Credit cards are among the major profit centers in banking. Aggressive marketing of mortgages and home-equity lines of credit helped bring about the financial crisis. Also, the investment side of the financial services industry focused more on speculative investments—the junk bond market of the 1980s, the dot-com IPO market of the 1990s, and the derivatives market of the 2000s being excellent examples.

Financial innovation can be a good thing. Many viable companies were financed with junk bonds and IPOs. However, a shift occurred. Perhaps it was a shift toward a more vibrant form of capitalism, but it was also toward a more risky form of capitalism than that which expanded the middle class in midcentury America.

WHAT'S THAT?

Financial innovation refers broadly to products and services developed by the financial services industry, which includes banks, funds, insurance companies, and others. More narrowly, the term refers to products, such as options, derivatives, swaps, and other tools for managing risk, often for managing it aggressively. Some observers see it as good; others see it as mainly "moving money around" and "making money off money" and doing little to encourage investment or create value. The fact is that it's been a mixed bag, but in the 2000s the innovations caused more harm than good by masking risks and pricing them improperly.

It's all well and good for Americans to want more flexible labor markets and cost-competitive companies. The question is, do they want to have them at the expense of health-care and retirement benefits, savings in the bank, and job security? It's fun to purchase what we want whenever we want it, and to receive high short-term returns in the stock market. The question is, how will we finance future growth?

As it stands, Americans have been choosing labor-market flexibility and low risk for employers over job security and lower risk for employees. They've also chosen short-term priorities over long-term priorities. They've made these choices in the policies they've supported and in their decisions as employees, consumers, employers, and investors.

These policies and behaviors may well have undermined the foundation that made the middle class what it was from the 1940s through the 1960s. They have, however, also produced a very flexible economy and labor force.

The Least You Need to Know

- The U.S. middle class—as defined by steady employment, access to health care, comfortable retirement, education, and homeownership—expanded substantially from the 1940s through the 1960s.

- Government policies that supported the growth of the middle class included New Deal legislation that favored unions and established Social Security, unemployment insurance, and the minimum wage, and broadened access to higher education and homeownership.

- Private-sector developments that contributed to the growth of the middle class included the expansion of U.S. industry in a market largely free of foreign competition and companies that rewarded loyalty and long-term service with pay increases, benefits, and continued employment.

- Pressures on the middle class increased with foreign competition in U.S. markets in the 1970s and with industrial restructuring in the 1980s.

- There is still a large and vital U.S. middle class, but the recession of 2008–2009 and its aftermath put new pressures on the three middle household income quartiles and, by extension, on the U.S. economy as a whole. After all, those three quartiles are 60 percent of households, and the poor have low levels of education and skills and limited ability to pay taxes.

The Impact on Consumers and Households

When consumer spending accounts for about 70 percent of an economy, that sector is going to both determine and be affected by the economic cycle. If consumers spend like crazy and even go into debt, the economy will expand rapidly. If consumers have to pull back suddenly on their spending, the economy will contract rapidly.

When rates rose and a good number of subprime mortgage borrowers could not make their payments, a widespread credit crisis ensued. When the financial markets froze up, businesses realized that more defaults and foreclosures were down the road. This quickly translated into hiring and spending freezes, and then to layoffs and spending cuts.

Recession, high unemployment, and lack of income growth followed. This part explains those phenomena in detail, and places the Great Recession in the context of earlier recessions and the developments that will likely affect consumers in the early 2010s.

Unemployment— Past, Present, and Potential

In This Chapter

- Employment patterns in past recessions
- How high unemployment might rise
- How the unemployed are undercounted
- Unemployment compensation explained

When I was younger and more survivors of the Great Depression were still alive, I would often hear them say, "Jobs! Jobs is everything!" (Forgive the grammar. This was in my native state of New Jersey.) Old-timers would often utter this comment during a rough economic patch, particularly when hearing a speech from a politician talking about something other than jobs.

Back then, I often thought these folks seemed a bit *too* focused on jobs. After all, I'd always had a job, and there were surely other issues on the national agenda. But then I'd recall the old joke, "When your neighbor loses his job, it's a recession. When you lose your job, it's a depression." So unless you're independently wealthy, a job is everything. Without one, most of us soon find ourselves in negative cash flow and relying on our savings or borrowing power, and the latter vanishes fast when you're out of work.

So in this chapter, we look at the issue of jobs and their scarcity during recessions and examine past levels of unemployment. This chapter also summarizes U.S. unemployment insurance programs and looks to where we can expect job growth to occur when it does return.

Unemployment Has Changed

Unemployment is the worst effect of an economic contraction. It not only eliminates people's incomes but can also generate feelings of rejection, uselessness, and despair. Lengthy unemployment fosters uncertainty and usually erodes a household's standard of living. It's also a huge waste of human resources. In addition, *underemployment*— lower-paying work taken to make ends meet, or forced part-time work for workers who want full-time jobs—is another negative consequence of recessions, and we saw all of these in the Great Recession.

Beginning with the recession of 1991, patterns of unemployment started to reflect and to drive changes in the U.S. workforce and in organizations' approaches to layoffs. So while unemployment increases in every recession, unemployment now differs from pre-1990 patterns in the following ways.

 WHAT'S THAT?

The Bureau of Labor Statistics' official "underemployment" rate includes everyone in the official rate plus people who are neither working nor looking for work, but say they want a job and have looked for work recently. More broadly, **underemployment** refers to people who are working part time but would take full-time jobs if such jobs were available, and to people who suffer from "skill underemployment." The latter are people who had or are qualified for more skilled, higher-paying work, but who lost those jobs or cannot find such jobs and have taken lower-skilled, lower-paying work.

"White-Collar" Unemployment Is Common

Before legions of analysts, consultants, programmers, designers, trainers, academics, attorneys, accountants, and media content providers came to populate the U.S. workforce—and before the huge, post–World War II expansion of the management class—layoffs affected mainly hourly employees. Hourly workers were considered a variable expense (a cost that varies with the level of output, such as materials, storage, and fuel), while managers and administrative staff were considered a fixed cost (like the cost of building the factory or the fire insurance premiums). Hourly workers were laid off when sales decreased and companies reduced production, but managerial and professional staff more often stayed put to plan the business's survival if nothing else. Or perhaps managers were just slow to lay off their colleagues.

But since the recession of 1991–1992, white-collar and knowledge workers are regularly laid off due to their increased numbers in today's organizations and because manufacturing represents a smaller part of the labor force. Today, so many U.S. companies are in consulting, programming, sales, engineering, and financial and other services that white-collar and knowledge workers are the new "hourly employees," although they're usually on salary. This means that many of the unemployed tend to be more flexible but not unionized and often less likely to be rehired.

Layoffs Are Not Temporary

Traditionally, a layoff differed from a reduction in force (RIF) in that laid-off employees would, or at least could, be rehired when production increased again. Nowadays, many workers, particularly managers and knowledge workers, are laid off and never rehired. They are not victims of actual layoffs but of periodic "house cleanings" that many companies use to weed out excess, unwanted, or overpaid employees. These workers are often either replaced with cheaper or just newer workers, or simply left behind as the company pursues new strategies.

Companies Adjust Faster to the Business Cycle

Increased use of part-timers, independent contractors, and temporary workers enables companies to maintain smaller staffs and reduce staff faster in recessions. It appears, however, that companies are still slow to rehire workers when the recession appears to be over, as unemployment patterns examined in the next major section will show.

In addition, the goal of using part-timers, contractors, and temps is often to minimize their wages and the cost of their health and pension benefits, which leaves these workers more exposed when they are laid off.

WHAT TO DO?

If you are offered a job as an "independent contractor," you have to make a decision between taking the job, which will provide no benefits, or not. If you take it, neither income taxes nor Social Security taxes will be deducted from your pay. You will therefore have to make quarterly tax payments to the IRS and to your state. On the upside, you will be able to deduct your business expenses from your income.

Safeguards for Workers Have Diminished

The social contract between employer and employee has been shredded by both parties, and loyalty has diminished on both sides. The employer/employee relationship has now typically become a purely economic transaction that must be continually justified. Management may extol "the team," but everyone knows the team is temporary and disposable. Companies evaluate employees based mainly upon current financial considerations rather than past contribution, potential value, or personal relationships.

Also, far fewer private-sector employees are union members, further eroding workers' security. Only about 9 percent of U.S. workers who are not police, firefighters, teachers, or government workers now belong to a union. (Some estimates go as low as 7.5 percent.) Therefore, unions now have little to say about who gets laid off or rehired in terms of seniority or need. In addition, employee benefits once provided voluntarily by many companies, particularly health insurance and retirement income plans, have decreased dramatically. Mandated benefits in the United States stand far below those in the major economies in the European Union.

Interestingly, tens of millions of Americans have supported government policies that diminish union membership and worker safeguards, perhaps in the belief that doing so improves companies' profits or the flexibility of the U.S. workforce. It arguably does, but that improved profitability and flexibility can come at a high price to individual workers.

Past and Future Highs and Lows

During a recession, the key questions regarding unemployment are:

- How high is unemployment?
- How high might unemployment rise?
- What is happening to the unemployed?
- When will the job market turn around?

Let's take these questions one at a time.

How High Did Unemployment Go?

According to the Bureau of Labor Statistics (BLS), which calculates and announces the unemployment rate and other labor statistics, the monthly unemployment rate for the recession of 2008–2009 peaked at 10.1 percent in October 2009. This is above the annual peak rates of 8.7 in 1975 and 9.7 in 1982, and, of course, above the annual peak rates in the milder recessions of 7.5 in 1992 and 6 in 2003. That 10.1 percent national monthly unemployment rate reached in October 2009 was last seen in September 1982. (The peak monthly rate in the early 1980s recession was 10.8, reached in November and December 1982.)

At the end of 2007, unemployment was only 5 percent. At the end of 2008, it was 7.4 percent. By the end of 2009, it had backed off very slightly from the October peak of 10.1 percent to 10 percent, and by January 2010 it had fallen to 9.7 percent. Thus it appears that unemployment, at least as measured by the official rate, peaked at 10.1 percent in October 2009 and then established the downward trajectory that typically follows most recessions.

According to the BLS, from the onset of the recession in December 2007 to January 2010, the United States shed some 8.4 million jobs. During the period of December 2008 and January and February 2009, the economy lost at least 650,000 jobs per month (851,000 in February), the worst three-month decline in percentage terms since 1975. While the economy is always creating and losing jobs, this net figure of jobs lost (technically, a decrease in "payroll employment"—that is, people on payrolls) is staggering.

Even worse, although reported unemployment reached extremely high levels, the official figure almost undoubtedly understates the problem. Indeed, the official unemployment rate always portrays only part of the true unemployment picture, and has several features we should all understand.

First, the unemployment rate leaves a lot of people uncounted. It does not count unemployed people who are "marginally attached to the labor force." These people are defined as those who have looked for work in the past 12 months *but not* in the past four weeks. At the start of 2010, the "marginally attached" totaled about 2.5 million, which is 409,000 higher than a year earlier. The BLS classified 1.1 million of these 2.5 million as "discouraged," meaning they have stopped looking for work because they believe no jobs are available for them. The other 1.4 million or so marginally attached people had not searched for work in the past four weeks. The marginally attached figure does *not* include workers who stopped looking more than 12 months ago—a number that can skyrocket during a prolonged recession. Those people are not counted as part of the labor force.

Second, the unemployment figures do not count people who are working part time but who want to be working full time. In January 2010, there were 8.3 million such workers.

Third, the national unemployment rate can mask significant differences for specific population groups. For instance, when the national rate reached 8.1 percent in February 2009, rates for specific groups were as follows: adult men: 8.1; adult women: 6.7; whites: 7.3; blacks: 13.4; Hispanics: 10.9; Asians: 6.9; teenagers: 21.6.

Fourth, the national unemployment rate can mask wide variations in the rates for individual states. For instance, at the end of 2009, when the national rate was 10 percent, Michigan and Nevada reported the nation's highest rates, 14.6 and 13 percent respectively, while North Dakota reported the lowest rate, at 4.4 percent. South Dakota and Nebraska stood at 4.7 percent.

WHAT TO DO?

Go to the Bureau of Labor Statistics website, www.bls.gov, for the most direct and official source of unemployment and employment data, including data on unemployment in specific states and industries. But do keep the limitations of the official data in mind.

How High Can Unemployment Go?

During a recession, it's almost impossible to know how high unemployment can go. It's also difficult to estimate how long high unemployment will linger after the official end of a recession. Up to a point, jobless rates in the 2008–2009 recession were in line with those of previous severe recessions, although the economy shed jobs quite rapidly. Some observers believe that this was because companies can now react more quickly than in past recessions. This led some to also believe that companies will rehire more quickly. However, the latter did not appear to be occurring at the start of 2010, after two quarters of positive economic growth. How quickly companies rehire—and how many jobs have been permanently lost—remains to be seen.

The following table shows the years of and just before and after recessions since 1970 along with the unemployment rates for those calendar years. The peak unemployment rate in each recession is in bold type and underscored.

Unemployment Rates in Previous Recessions

Years	Unemployment Rate (annual, percent)
1973–1975: Two-year recession	
1973	4.9
1974	5.6
1975	**8.7**
1976	7.7
1977	7.1
1980–1982: Two-year recession	
1980	7.1
1981	7.6
1982	**9.7**
1983	9.6
1984	7.5
1990–1991: Two-year recession	
1990	5.6
1991	6.8
1992	**7.5**
1993	6.9
2001: One-year recession	
2001	4.7
2002	5.8
2003	**6.0**
2004	5.5
2008–????	
2007	4.6
2008	7.2
2009	10.1

Source: Commerce Department and Bureau of Labor Statistics

As the table shows, *peak* annual unemployment during the four previous recessions ranged from a low of 6 percent in the brief and mild recession of 2001 to a high of 9.7 percent in the wrenching recession of the early 1980s, which was engineered by the Fed to wring record-high inflation out of the economy. The Fed accomplished its goal, but with an unemployment rate of over 9.5 percent for two consecutive years.

Why Did Unemployment Go So High in 2009?

Fears of double-digit unemployment in the Great Recession turned out to be well-founded, for several reasons.

As indicated in the table, unemployment does not usually peak until the last year of a recession—or the subsequent year. This is due to the lag between companies recognizing the need for layoffs and their implementation, and because they don't resume hiring until recovery appears certain.

Many record-high poor economic indicators were reached or exceeded in the Great Recession, and unemployment is a driver of certain negative indicators, such as mortgage defaults and foreclosures, and a result of others, such as contraction in GDP and decreased housing starts. Thus either layoffs or (as in this more recent case) mortgage defaults can ignite the vicious cycle that constitutes a severe recession, in which people reduce their expenditures—their demand for goods and services—and companies reduce their production and workforces. This further reduces people's incomes and job security, causing them to further reduce their expenditures, leading companies to further reduce production and their workforces, and so on. This downward spiral can be quite difficult to end, and until it does unemployment tends to rise.

Even in early 2009, a full year into the recession, companies were *still* announcing mass layoffs. An economy that's shedding jobs is well away from hitting peak unemployment. According to the BLS in January 2009, 2,227 employers took mass layoff actions, which involved some 238,000 workers. The BLS defines a mass layoff as involving at least 50 workers at a single employer.

Peak unemployment depends on the length and depth of the recession, and no one can accurately forecast these factors. The 2008–2009 recession could have a long tail, and in early 2010 many observers (myself included) were very concerned about the prospects of a *jobless recovery*, a situation in which economic expansion is either too sluggish or not widespread enough in terms of industry, geography, and workers needed, to fuel significant growth in employment.

WHAT'S THAT?

In a **jobless recovery,** economic growth begins, but not vigorously enough to create enough jobs for everyone who lost theirs during the recession and for all the new entrants into the labor force during and after the recession.

In fact, there were worries about a jobless recovery as early as the summer of 2009—for example, in the July 13, 2009, *Wall Street Journal.* In addition, the June 22, 2009, *Journal* reported that a survey of 179 companies conducted that month by Watson Wyatt Worldwide Inc. found that 52 percent "expect to employ fewer people in three to five years than they did before the recession began."

Without job growth we won't see much growth in household income, and without income growth we won't see much growth in consumption. That will lead to sluggish growth in the overall economy. In a worst-case scenario, high unemployment could continue for two to three years—or more. That scenario appears to be all too likely, given the harshness of this recession and the record-breaking bad news we've seen to date.

What Happens to the Unemployed?

In the recession of 2008–2009, the unemployed generally had a tougher time than in past recessions, for reasons having to do with the previously noted changes in the labor force and in the employer/employee relationship. For instance, increased job mobility since the 1980s has left many workers with little in the way of severance pay, which is usually geared to years of service, and vested benefits from savings plans in which employers match employees' contributions. Indeed, many of these programs are not as generous as they were in past decades.

In this recession, more high-paying jobs have been lost compared to many past recessions. The loss of high-paying jobs in business services, financial services, and auto manufacturing, among other sectors, left many workers with sharply lower incomes. These are the people whom news sources are reporting as "falling out of the middle class." People who lose their jobs when they have no savings and high debt find themselves in a difficult situation—one in which many households found themselves. Such situations drove the record level of foreclosures we saw in this recession.

In addition, the self-employed are left out of unemployment rate calculations (although they are counted in the labor force). However, their loss of income is quite real when companies they'd been selling to cut back on purchases or on independent contractors. Since the 1990s, many white-collar workers who found themselves out of corporate jobs established themselves as self-employed, often in profitable home-based businesses. They, too, saw their incomes fall, although the data are not tracked as well as those of the employed.

Finally, there's the likelihood that many jobs will never return. Three industries—financial services, retail, and automotive—may permanently shed tens of thousands of jobs each. Major investment banks have collapsed, and the brokerage industry and commercial banking remain unsettled. Several major retailers declared bankruptcy, while thousands of others cut back dramatically. Detroit's Big Three are almost certainly shrinking (perhaps even to a Big Two eventually), and the damage will extend to hundreds of manufacturers, distributors, and dealers.

The hardships of unemployment are always difficult, and they end only when economic expansion returns in earnest. In fact, it usually takes two to six quarters after an expansion officially begins for strong employment growth to return, because it takes a while for the expansion to register, both in the economic data and in the public mind. Unfortunately, it's virtually impossible to know when strong employment growth will resume, and the early signs are not encouraging.

When Will Employment Growth Return?

The short answer is, we don't know. It's particularly troubling that long-term unemployment has been so high and persistent as a result of the 2008–2009 recession. During the recession itself, most economists and public officials estimated that a turnaround would begin in 2010. Optimists saw turnaround beginning in the first half of 2010, while pessimists see it beginning in the second half. Pessimists saw the possibility of recession through 2010, and sluggish growth in the range of 0.5 to 1.5 for 2011 and perhaps for a few years beyond. Sluggish growth may arrest growth in unemployment and rises in the rate, but result in slower absorption of new entrants into the labor force after graduation or immigration.

As it turned out, economic growth officially returned in the third quarter of 2009 and continued into the fourth quarter. While the possibility of a "double dip" recession remained, it appeared to be diminishing. But that's small comfort to the millions of unemployed. In situations of no growth or slow growth, new workers find jobs, but it takes longer and they must settle for lower wages and salaries. Workers who have jobs are reluctant to leave them, either for retirement or for new employers, both of which may mean more uncertainty. Nevertheless, younger workers benefit from employers' strategy of controlling labor costs by replacing older, more expensive workers with younger, less expensive ones.

In general, of course, unemployment exerts downward pressure on wages and salaries. When people are worried about their jobs, they can't demand high starting salaries or raises. In addition, during recessions or sluggish growth, most businesses actually have less money to spend on labor. Thus, high unemployment hurts even workers who have jobs.

One of the more difficult aspects of this recession was the duration of unemployment, which reached a post–World War II high of 29 weeks. As of November 2009, 38 percent of the unemployed had been out of work for at least 27 weeks, which is also a post-war record. While Congress has increased unemployment insurance coverage, people's benefits were still running out at unprecedented rates. On February 21, 2010, a front-page *New York Times* article titled "Millions of Unemployed Face Years Without Jobs" detailed the plight of the long-term unemployed in the United States. The piece noted, "6.3 million Americans have been unemployed for six months or longer, the largest number since the government began keeping track in 1948. That is more than double the toll in the next-worst period, in the early 1980s."

Unemployment is bad enough, but when unemployment insurance benefits run out and there are no jobs on the horizon, the situation becomes desperate. In fact, the long-term unemployed may well turn out to be some of the most severe casualties in the erosion of the middle class described in Chapter 9. Capitalism and market economies create winners and losers, and those who lost their jobs and cannot find new ones are among the losers. Without a social safety net, absorbing the risks that are inherent in such an economy is extremely difficult.

Unemployment Compensation: Temporary Safety Net

Unemployment compensation—weekly payments made by the state and federal government to covered workers—originated in the Great Depression. The Social Security Act of 1935 created the Federal-State Unemployment Compensation Program with two main objectives. First, it provides temporary, partial wage replacement to involuntarily unemployed workers. Second, it helps stabilize the economy during recessions by putting spending money into the hands of the recently unemployed.

The Federal Unemployment Tax Act of 1939 (FUTA) provides the framework of the system. FUTA imposes a 6.2 percent tax, collected by the IRS, on the first $7,000 of wage and salary payments to a covered worker, but this is offset by a 5.4 percent federal credit for states with federally approved unemployment compensation programs, which all states maintain. That brings the effective rate to 0.8 percent (6.2–5.4) of the first $7,000 of wages and salaries, or $56 per covered worker per year.

While FUTA generally defines what constitutes "covered employment" (for instance, omitting independent contractors) and imposes certain requirements, the states mainly set the terms of their programs, such as eligibility, qualification, disqualification, weekly benefit amounts, and number of weeks of benefits. States use three major factors in determining eligibility: recent employment and earnings, ability and willingness to seek and accept a new job, and reasons for job loss (for instance, quitting a job without "good cause" usually disqualifies a worker from receiving compensation).

Amount and Weeks of Compensation

To laid-off workers anticipating a long job search, the chief concerns are the weekly amount and the number of weeks of benefits. The maximum is generally set at 26 weeks funded by the state ("state benefits"), but legislation passed in 2008 (and explained in the next section) provided for more weeks of benefits funded by the federal government ("federal benefits").

Unemployment compensation does not aim to restore all of a worker's earnings. Instead, the states set weekly compensation amounts at a fraction of the worker's average weekly wage, up to a state maximum. States use various formulas to determine the level of benefits. All of the formulas are based on the average wages the worker earned in a base period, but states use various base periods. More than half use the calendar quarter in which the worker's wages were highest. Thus the goal is not to let laid-off workers merely scrape by but rather to maintain their financial footing during unemployment, albeit with cutting back on expenses and perhaps borrowing from friends and family and paying creditors (and maybe friends and family) late.

Weekly benefits range from as low as $10 to $258 in Louisiana to as high as $32 to $900 in Massachusetts. It's literally all over the map. To learn more about your state's benefits and its methods of calculating them, see the chapter on "Monetary Entitlement" from the U.S. Department of Labor Employment and Training

Administration's report on state by state unemployment insurance at http://workforcesecurity.doleta.gov/unemploy/uilawcompar/2008/monetary.pdf.

Measures Taken in Response to the Crisis

As of March 2009, the federal government had taken three major steps during the recession to assist jobless workers:

- On June 30, 2008, Congress created the Emergency Unemployment Compensation (EUC) program to make an additional 13 weeks of federally funded unemployment benefits available to people who had exhausted their regular state unemployment benefits.

- On November 21, 2008, the Unemployment Extension Act of 2008 expanded the EUC program to 20 weeks nationwide and created and added another 13 weeks of benefits for unemployed workers in states with high unemployment rates.

- On February 17, 2009, the American Recovery and Reinvestment Act of 2009 (the "stimulus bill") extended the time during which workers can file claims for and collect EUC benefits.

WHAT TO DO?

For more information about how to apply for extended unemployment benefits, go to http://workforcesecurity.doleta.gov/unemploy/supp_act.asp.

Where Will Future Growth Come From?

After a long recession, the primary engine of expansion is pent-up demand. Pent-up demand results from people having postponed major purchases due to unemployment, concern over job security, avoidance of new debt, and increased savings. Rather than spend money on major or discretionary purchases, they pay down debts and reduce spending even on essential items, such as food and clothing, and on small luxuries, such as liquor and lattes. But eventually cars, washers, dryers, and appliances wear out and pent-up demand for these items is released. Of course, people need jobs and incomes in order to make or finance those purchases, so there's a bit of a chicken-and-egg situation, particularly during and after a severe recession, and the turnaround may be gradual.

Another main engine of growth is household formation. Younger, less expensive workers can find jobs (or start companies) even in a tight labor market. When they do, nature takes its course and they think about household formation and starting families. Household formation, driven by population growth due to birth rates and immigration, fuels economic growth.

Other expansionary forces include public works and infrastructure projects such as highways, bridges, tunnels, and sewage treatment plants, as well as new industries, fostered by new technologies or social and cultural developments, as we saw in recent decades with the Internet and the physical fitness boom. More broadly, millions of people now work in jobs that didn't exist, barely existed, or employed small cadres of specialists 40 or 50 years ago. These include software programmer, systems analyst, web designer, webmaster, customer service rep, personal trainer, overnight delivery person, "cable guy," telecommunications consultant, nurse practitioner, and dozens of others.

We have every reason to believe that industries of the future, such as alternative fuels; green technology; and others from the minds of scientists, engineers, and entrepreneurs will fuel job growth just as the personal computer, the Internet (a U.S. government project), telecommunications technology, and others have over the past few decades.

The Least You Need to Know

- Unemployment patterns have changed as the composition of the workforce has changed. Layoffs now affect managerial and other salaried workers rather than only hourly employees, and are now more often permanent.

- Given today's mobile workforce, higher turnover rates, lower personal savings rates, and high household debt, many newly unemployed workers do not have high levels of severance pay, savings, or other financial resources to see them through a period of joblessness.

- The official nationwide unemployment rate fails to reflect often sharply higher rates of unemployment in specific states and population segments, and it does not count as unemployed millions of "discouraged workers" and those who have simply stopped looking for work.

- Unemployment compensation is a federal program created in the Great Depression funded by taxes on workers, administered by the states, and overseen and supplemented by the federal government. Visit the Department of Labor Education and Training Administration site at http://atlas.doleta.gov/unemploy/ for information on unemployment compensation and your state's program.

Income, Wealth, and Savings— Then and Now

In This Chapter

- The national income and wealth picture
- Income distribution patterns over the past three decades
- The wealth effect and wealth destruction
- How household savings could hamper recovery

Often during the crisis and recession we heard that credit is the lifeblood of the economy. While in a sense that's true, it's not as true as the following: *income* is the lifeblood of the economy.

Household income, which mainly comes from employment, interest, and income-producing real estate, enables us to purchase the goods and services that we need and that constitute gross domestic product (GDP), the usual measure of the economy. People also receive income from Social Security, Temporary Assistance for Needy Families ("welfare"), and other transfer payments (that is, government-facilitated transfers of money from one set of people to another). However, the money for transfer payments comes from taxes on others' income.

Companies also produce income, but this chapter focuses on personal income. It looks at the concept of income, and at U.S. income patterns over the past 30 years. This chapter also examines worker productivity and its relationship to wages, and reviews the U.S. savings rate in recent decades—and the effect that renewed savings could have on the recovery.

Many people fail to distinguish between income and wealth, and some even confuse the two. We'll make that distinction and also look at the U.S. distribution of wealth. Wealth and income determine a nation's or household's standard of living, and this chapter explains why much of the population has experienced a lower standard of living over the past few decades even as we thought we were prospering.

We begin with the concept of a standard of living.

Our Standard of Living

Webster's New Collegiate Dictionary defines *standard of living* as "a minimum of necessities, comforts, or luxuries essential to maintaining a person or group in customary or proper status or circumstances." More precisely, the www.allbusiness. com glossary defines it as the "degree of prosperity in a nation, as measured by income levels, quality of housing and food, medical care, educational opportunities, transportation, communications, and other measures." The latter definition is more precise because it calls for a few measurements.

WHAT'S THAT?

A nation's **standard of living** is the level of economic well-being that the average household or individual achieves. It essentially includes the level of income and the amount and quality of goods and services available to people in the nation in categories such as housing, clothing, food, health care, education, and transportation.

One person or nation's standard of living may be another's dream—or nightmare—because in economic terms, everything is relative. For instance, about 2 billion of the world's people live on the equivalent of less than $2 a day, own no refrigerator, and will never ride in a car. Such a "standard of living" borders on the tragic. But this chapter focuses on living standards in the United States and the income required to maintain them.

When commentators noted that during this recession many people were "falling out of the middle class," it meant that some formerly middle-class people could no longer afford that standard of living. Also, in the introduction to this guide, I noted that the United States may face a lower standard of living for several years into the future. The reasons for that go beyond employment and income, and we'll address them in later chapters. In this chapter we're dealing mainly with income.

Recall that GDP is the sum total spent by consumers, businesses, and the government, and that money goes to individuals in the form of personal income. Personal income takes the form of wages, salaries, and tips; interest and dividends paid by banks and businesses; royalties, fees, and residuals; income from rents on real estate or other property (such as a car or equipment); capital gains, gifts, bequests, and alimony; and Social Security payments or tax rebates from the government. Overall, gross domestic product essentially equals personal income, and vice versa.

This is a bit of an oversimplification, but only a bit. Indeed, the National Income and Product Accounts (NIPA) compiled by the Bureau of Economic Analysis recognize that gross domestic product and personal income are one and the same, conceptually and mathematically. The fact that GDP equals personal income (GDP = PI) brings two facts of economic life into sharp focus:

- GDP measures what we collectively produce in a given period.
- Personal income patterns show how we distribute what we produce.

In a sense, on the GDP side of the equation, we produce a big pile of goods and services just by going to work and doing our jobs. Then instead of making one mad dash at that pile and fighting over it, we accept currency in exchange for our work and use it to buy our share of what the nation has collectively produced.

Keep that in mind, but first let's return to standard of living. The more an economy produces, the higher the standard of living of the people in that economy. Granted, this is a rough measure, but it's the best that economists can do. They can't measure "happiness" or "personal fulfillment" as accurately, and they don't want to get into our love lives (these are economists we're talking about). So they measure how much we produce and use that as a measure of well-being—which makes sense, given that, as the philosopher Madonna Ciccone sang, we live in a material world.

 WHAT TO DO?

Visit the World Bank's website at www.worldbank.org for information about living standards in specific nations around the world.

When comparing standards of living among nations, economists typically use per-capita GDP or per-capita income to account for differences in population size. For example, according to the World Bank, per-capita income in 2008 (the most recent year available as I write this) was $87,070 in Norway; $47,580 in the United States; $45,390 in the United Kingdom; $2,940 in China; $1,070 in India; and $280 in Ethiopia. (These figures are calculated by the World Bank atlas method, one of several methods economists use to measure GDP and income in nations using different currencies.)

In countries with higher per-capita GDP and incomes, people are producing more or more valuable goods and services. They may or may not be "working harder" in the usual sense of the term, but they are certainly working more productively. They are also generally producing higher value, higher priced goods and services, such as electronic and medical equipment as opposed to toys and earthenware. For that reason, developed, industrialized nations invariably have higher incomes than developing, nonindustrialized nations.

Many factors determine workers' and nations' productivity. That discussion is beyond the scope of this book, but key among those factors are education, skills, investment, and capital equipment (machinery and factories), along with a stable political and legal system and reliable transportation and communication infrastructure.

With that background and those concepts in mind, we turn to U.S. income patterns.

WHAT TO DO?

Bear in mind that one of the major determinants of economic growth is whether or not a nation has a well-organized and basically honest system of laws, courts, law enforcement, and government. People who believe they could make millions without it should test that belief in an undeveloped third-world nation.

How U.S. Living Standards Have Changed

Today, maintaining what most people think of as a "middle-class lifestyle" in the United States more often than not requires both members of a couple to work outside the home. This represents a decline in living standards, at least by some measures, and certainly against "middle-class" standards of the 1950s and 1960s. In 2007, median household income stood at $50,000. According to 2007 U.S. Census Bureau data, among the 39 million married-couple households making $50,000 and over that year, 26 million—66 percent or two thirds—had both spouses working. If one considers $50,000 the minimum needed for at least a middle-class lifestyle for a couple or family, both members of the couple usually have to work outside the home.

Indeed, the concept of "middle class" is worth taking a moment to define. Americans like to view their society as "classless," and in fact most Americans, regardless of their income, view themselves as middle class. This is not to say they are unaware of differences in income and wealth, but rather that most consider themselves middle class in social and cultural terms. In economic terms, a useful definition of middle class would be households in the middle quintile—the middle 20 percent—of the five income quintiles into which U.S. households can be divided. (Each quintile is 20 percent or one fifth of the population.) These quintiles are shown in the table below, calculated on 2007 income data from the U.S. Census Bureau. This table leaves aside the size of the household, which affects individual earning and spending power, but it is still instructive.

According to U.S. Census Bureau data for 2007, the *upper limit* for the income quintiles for U.S. households and the *lower limits* of the top quintile and top 5 percent are as follows:

Lowest quintile:	$20,300
Second quintile:	$39,100
Third quintile:	$62,000
Fourth quintile:	$100,000
Lower limit of upper quintile:	$100,000
Lower limit of top 5 percent:	$177,000

The data says that in 2007 a "middle class" household (one in the third quintile) earned $39,101 to $62,000. They also say that 40 percent of U.S. households earned $39,100 or less and that 40 percent earned $62,001 or more. Household income of over $100,000 in 2007 put a family in the top 20 percent, and over $177,000 put a household in the top 5 percent. These data are based on a nationwide sample of households and thus ignore regional differences in the cost of living. For instance, an income of $100,000 in Manhattan or Los Angeles purchases far less than it would in Mississippi or Arkansas, where $100,000 a year would provide most families with a very nice lifestyle.

With regard to our discussion of class, it may be useful to think of the income quintiles like this: the lowest quintile is poor, second is lower middle class, third is middle class, fourth is upper middle class, and fifth is upper class. I use the term "upper class" to mean upper *economic* class and to avoid saying "wealthy," because wealth differs from income, as discussed in the next section. When defining class, however, most Americans ignore data—about 90 percent consider themselves to be middle class.

Income Versus Wealth—Bet on Wealth

Many people confuse *income* and *wealth*, and that can impact their thinking and behavior. Income is a flow of money that comes to a person or household over a week, month, year, or other period. It is a flow of money that takes the form of wages, salaries, tips, royalties, interest, and the others noted earlier in this chapter. Wealth consists of the value of the assets an individual or household owns minus the amount of money that it owes. This is net worth, a financial as well as economic term.

WHAT'S THAT?

Income is a flow of money to a person or household during a period as a result of wages, dividends, interest, or other payments. **Wealth** is a given amount of assets, unencumbered by debt, at a given time.

As with standard of living, most economists don't concern themselves with wealth in nonfinancial terms. Yet various experts, including some economists, have pointed out that health, education, relationships, experiences, values, character, reputation, heritage, and faith or spiritual life are also forms of wealth. Sophisticated wealth managers, trust officers, and estate attorneys recognize the value of intellectual, social, spiritual, and familial capital—apart from financial capital—and encourage their clients to do the same. (Though most economists focus on financial wealth, which can be measured, some have done work in "happiness economics," which considers psychological well-being and other nonmonetary factors.)

Many people view households with high incomes as wealthy, but those households are not necessarily wealthy nor do they always accumulate wealth. People living in a $2 million house with a $1.5 million mortgage and another $500,000 in debt are not wealthy, even if they are earning a million a year. They could be spending a million a year—and they still have to pay taxes.

Wealth actually means net worth. Net worth is assets minus liabilities. Thus the household with the $2 million home, the $1.5 million mortgage, and the $500,000 in debt actually has—on the basis of those figures—zero net worth. The $2 million home is an asset, but if they have the mortgage and the debt and nothing in savings and investments, then they would have nothing after selling their home and paying off the mortgage and their debts.

Oddly, more than 10 years after the publication of *The Millionaire Next Door* by Thomas Stanley and William Danko, many people still confuse high income with wealth and think the two are always correlated. They aren't. Obviously, it will be harder to accumulate wealth if you are in the bottom two income quintiles rather than in one of the other three, and perhaps impossible. However, as Stanley and Danko pointed out, becoming a millionaire—someone with at least $1 million in net worth—depends more on living below one's means, saving regularly, investing wisely, and avoiding financial setbacks than on having a large income.

WHAT TO DO?

If you want to become wealthy, forget the "big score" mentality that many people cultivate. Instead, find a line of work that you enjoy or start a business that you care about. Then spend less than you make, save regularly, and invest wisely. Oh, and get a copy of *The Complete Idiot's Guide to Getting Rich, Third Edition*, by Stewart H. Welch III and Larry Waschka (Alpha/Penguin, 2006).

As noted in Chapter 9, as incomes eroded for much of the U.S. population over the past 10 to 15 years, many households borrowed to finance either middle class or more lavish lifestyles. Also, in the early to mid-2000s many people thought they were wealthy because of rising home prices and tapped that "wealth" by refinancing their mortgages or taking home-equity loans and spending it. But people with wealth don't spend or borrow against unrealized paper gains. They can fund a comfortable lifestyle without working, using their savings, or selling off assets, although they may do any of these if it suits their purposes. Thus, "independently wealthy" means able to live comfortably on the earnings from one's investments without dipping into the principal or having to sell off assets.

Then of course, there are the truly wealthy. According to 2004 Internal Revenue Service statistics, 1.45 million Americans had net worth of $2 million or more; 357,000 had net worth of $5 million or more; 126,000 had $10 million or more; and 47,000 had $20 million or more.

The Wealth Effect and Wealth Destruction in the Crisis

The confusion around wealth can be exacerbated by two issues related to the crisis. The first is the so-called *wealth effect*, which occurs when asset values (or at least asset prices) rise and people increase their spending. The other is the so-called wealth destruction that occurs when asset values fall, as they did when the housing bubble burst and the financial crisis ensued.

WHAT'S THAT?

The **wealth effect** is a general increase in consumer spending that occurs as a result of an overall increase in the value of homes or financial assets such as stocks. Economists disagree regarding the magnitude of the effect, but it did seem to occur in the 2000s housing bubble.

The wealth effect occurs when people increase their consumer spending because they feel richer due to the increased value of their assets. Actually, it's not just that they feel richer. In a sense, they *are* richer—*if* they can realize that increased value by selling the assets and converting them to cash or to safe and stable investments. We saw a wealth effect in the 1990s due to rising stock prices, and even more so in the 2000s due to rising home prices.

Economists disagree as to whether the wealth effect actually occurs and whether it is evident in consumer spending data. Zubin Jelveh pointed out in his economics blog on June 17, 2008, that New York University professor David Backus sees no wealth effect but also noted that more economists do see it and that they estimate it to be 2 to 7¢ on the dollar. That is, for a given increase in wealth, consumer spending rises by 2 to 7 percent.

The effect may depend on the assets in question. Stocks, particularly tech stocks, are not as widely held by households as, well, houses. So the wealth effect was less evident in the 1990s, although some economists cited it at the time. But Jelveh notes that between 2001 and 2006 housing wealth grew by $4.8 trillion; consumer spending rose by $2.2 trillion over that period; and, "If consumer spending increased by 2 to 7 cents-on-the-dollar as a result, that would translate into a $96 billion to $336 billion rise." He thus estimates the wealth effect from housing to account for 4 percent to 15 percent of the increase in consumer spending.

Of course, a wealth effect does not necessarily translate to actual wealth, in the net-worth sense of the term. Suppose I own a $300,000 house with no mortgage and its price rises by $100,000. I take a home-equity loan for $50,000, and spend that money—and then the price of my house falls by $75,000 (to $325,000). In that case, my net worth has *decreased* (to $275,000). Note that if I had not taken the home-equity loan, my net worth would have increased by $25,000 in the example.

This raises the topic of wealth destruction.

Who Moved My Wealth?

The crisis prompted much discussion of wealth destruction, with the May 26, 2008, *Newsweek* quoting George Soros, one of the world's wealthiest investors, as saying, "We're in a period of great wealth destruction." Almost a year later, Stephen Schwarzman, CEO of Blackstone Group, a major private equity firm, was quoted by Reuters on March 10, 2009, as saying, "Between 40 and 45 percent of the world's wealth has been destroyed in a little less than a year and a half."

Wealth destruction can be a confusing concept, and one that may vary depending on the wealth being destroyed. If the wealth was created by a bubble in the stock or real estate market, was it really wealth? If it existed only as paper gains, was it really wealth?

The answers to these questions relate to the idea of a "rational" market. In a rational (or "perfect") market, in which everyone has the same information and there is no government intervention (big and theoretical ifs), the price of an asset will reflect its true value because the market price contains all of the relevant information about its value as sifted and considered by hundreds, thousands, or millions of market participants. Unfortunately, markets can be highly irrational and imperfect, and thus can value the stock of the same company at $50 in January and $5 in August, or overvalue real estate in a bubble.

For that reason, real or at least long-lasting wealth will be based on assets valued in relation to some practical measure of their intrinsic value. An established company has earnings and dividend records, and when you buy its stock you buy future earnings and dividends that can be valued. Real estate can be valued in relation to rental rates or incomes in the location. Yes, those earnings and rentals are also results of imperfect, potentially irrational markets, but they are measures from the past and are prices that stand apart from the price of the asset itself. That means they are a lot different from saying that the price will continue to rise because it rose in the past or that it will rise because your broker said it would.

Of course, if you buy a stock or a home at the peak of a market cycle driven by "irrational exuberance" and the price falls by 40 percent in the next year, then you, personally, have seen wealth destroyed. But again, was it really wealth? For example, did you raise the money to buy the stock or house by selling an overvalued stock or home of your own? If not, it's probably accurate to say your wealth was destroyed, but if so, then perhaps it was your speculative gains that were destroyed.

Some of this is semantics and it can be difficult to tell speculative gains from wealth. But that's why wealth is probably best viewed as long-term. Truly wealthy people do not experience major reversals in their lives or lifestyles because the stock or real estate market drops. They generally think long term, invest conservatively, and put only small percentages of their assets—if any—into speculative ventures. True wealth creation occurs when an entrepreneur develops a new way of getting work done or solving problems, or an established company develops new markets or more efficient production methods, or someone builds or produces something that someone can use. By that definition, wealth "created" by finding new ways to increase the market price of assets really doesn't count.

WHAT TO DO?

Always understand whether you are engaged in investing or speculating. Investing usually involves research or relying on someone else's research into the potential risks and rewards. It also usually involves "buying" a share of an income stream from a company's earnings or of interest payments. Speculating usually involves "betting" that the price of an asset will move up or down. Speculating is not necessarily bad, but it should not be the cornerstone of the average person's wealth-building strategy.

Whither Our Incomes?

As noted in Chapters 3 and 9, the top quintile of U.S. households is the only one that saw its percentage share of national income rise in each of the past four decades, while the four lower quintiles saw their share of income decline. The distribution of income favored the top quintile, and the top 5 percent even more, because real income itself grew far more rapidly for the higher quintiles. (By "real" economists mean "adjusted for inflation" so that measures can be compared.) The following table shows the changes in the upper limits of the four lowest income quintiles (with the upper limit of the fourth quintile also being the lower limit of the top quintile) from

1970 to 2005 in the United States. The table also shows the growth of the lower limit of the top 5 percent.

Upper Limits for Lowest Four Quintiles from 1970 to 2005 (in 2007 Dollars)

	Lowest	Second	Third	Fourth	Lower Limit of Top 5%
2005	20,369	38,235	61,240	97,399	176,306
1970	17,574	33,667	48,968	69,863	110,435

These figures show that, for the 35 years from 1970 to 2005, real income grew for each quintile. However, it grew by much greater percentages for households in the upper quintiles. The upper limit of the lowest quintile grew by 16 percent, of the second quintile by 14 percent, of the third quintile by 25 percent, and for the fourth quintile (which is also the lower limit of the fifth quintile) by 39 percent. The top 5 percent of households saw the lower limit of their income grow by a whopping 60 percent.

As noted in Chapter 7, the 1970s were rough for the U.S. economy as a whole. Even the top 5 percent saw only 10 percent growth in their income cutoff point in that decade. But the lower two and middle quartiles fell well behind the top two quintiles and especially the top 5 percent in terms of real income growth. However, this pattern continued even after the 1970s because of the way in which the significant productivity gains of the 1980s and 1990s—that is, the gains in GDP—were distributed.

The Productivity-and-Wage Divide

Productivity is usually measured by the amount of goods and services workers produce per hour. The more that workers produce per hour, the higher their productivity. Productivity can also be measured in overall terms rather than per hour, but that won't account for workers putting in longer workweeks, as they've tended to do in the United States over the past 30 years.

Ideally, as the productivity of labor grows, income in the form of workers' compensation would grow, but that has not occurred consistently in the United States. I say "ideally" because if workers are producing more, they should share in the rewards of doing so, logically and perhaps out of fairness. This will also keep them from engaging in a "workers' revolution" and overthrowing exploitative capitalists—or at least let most voters favor probusiness policies. Another reason is to ensure that workers have enough to spend on the goods and services they are producing. Henry Ford, founder of the car company and nobody's idea of a Socialist, believed in paying a wage that would enable his workers to purchase the cars they were producing.

There are also, however, three compelling arguments for directing increases in income due to productivity gains to investors. (Whether increases in income flow to workers or to investors is influenced by government policies, as well as by market forces.)

First, increasing the rewards for investors makes sense because they'll invest more in the economy (instead of, say, in foreign economies offering higher returns). That will increase the domestic stock of productive capital and thus future productivity.

Second, investors are supplying much of the funding for the equipment and facilities that enable workers to increase their productivity, so it's only fair that they earn a return for doing so. (A company's growth is also funded by its earnings.)

Third, workers are also often investors in the companies that employ them. Many companies promote that ownership through employee stock ownership programs. Even if workers own little or no stock in the company, they often own stock in another company, and thus earn investment income.

The problem, however, is that many workers, particularly the less well off, don't own any stock. Even the vast majority of those that do own stock rely on wage income to pay the bills. Also, the theory that reducing taxes on capital gains or on the wealthy, who own more financial assets, will create "trickle down" gains in income for people less well off—that is, for the lower 60 or 80 percent of households, based on income—has proven false, unless one takes the term "trickle" literally. (The theory, known formally as supply-side economics, holds that reducing capital gains and taxes on the wealthy will encourage business investment enough to boost not only productive capacity but also GDP *and* incomes and thus tax revenues.) Yet as the data clearly show, the top 20 and 5 percent of households have gained far more than the rest of the population.

The following table shows the gains in productivity for selected years—the annual gain for the selected year—and the gain in real (inflation-adjusted) hourly compensation.

Comparison of Productivity and Wage Gains, Annual Percentages for Selected Years

Year	Percent Increase in Output Per Hour (Productivity) for the Year	Percent Increase in Real Hourly Compensation for the Year
1970	1.1	1.3
1975	5.0	2.7
1980	0.4	0.9
1985	3.6	2.1
1990	2.9	-0.2
1995	3.8	-0.3
2000	4.1	3.9

Source: Bureau of Labor Statistics

As the table shows, the increase in real hourly compensation exceeded the gain in productivity in 1970 and 1980, but in no other years shown. In fact, workers lost serious ground in the late 1980s (with actual losses in hourly compensation—not shown—in 1987, 1988, 1989) as well as in 1990. They also lost ground in much of the 1990s. However, these figures oversimplify the situation in that they do not include benefits as part of compensation, although they are part of compensation (and are not taxed). Benefits account for a good part of compensation, and by some data an increasing part, due to the cost of health insurance. That said, employers have also been reducing benefits, through the use of temporary workers and independent contractors. Employers have also kept wages low by offshoring jobs to lower-wage nations, which puts pressure even on wages for jobs that have not been offshored.

The key point is that these data, along with the data on income distribution (and on debt usage and savings, the latter covered later in this chapter) indicate that policies of the past 25 to 30 years have favored the top earners and the wealthy (that is, investors) in the U.S. economy (who tend to have better benefits, such as life insurance and employer-sponsored savings plans based upon their earnings). Indeed, the policies set out to do this—on the theory that increasing the returns on capital would spur investment. And they did! In the 1980s and 1990s, the United States saw tremendous innovation that created new industries and companies in information technology, entertainment, telecommunications, materials, transportation, health care, biotechnology, foods and beverages, financial services, and personal services, among others. So in that sense it worked. However, as the data indicate, "trickle down" did not work.

Productive for Whom?

Income distribution favoring households in the top quintile—and even more those in the top 5 percent and 1 percent—has generated heated debate. While the entire workforce produced gains, the entire workforce did not share in those gains in the historical proportions. I won't pursue that debate here because it has been covered in great depth elsewhere, and people seem to either favor pushing greater rewards toward the top quintile or not.

Yet the result of the trends I've described has been increased financial pressure on the middle class. That pressure increased even more given the unemployment of the 2008–2009 recession. Under the Obama administration, these policies may change, for example, with the expiration of the Bush tax cuts favoring the highest earners. Changes in policies related to education, which heavily influences income, may also lay ahead, as may changes to Social Security and Medicare. These changes pose economic risks, just as the policies of the past did, which we examine in Part 6.

We conclude this chapter on income and wealth with a look at savings.

The U.S. Savings Rate Has Decreased

The United States has been a nation of savers at times, but not in recent times. One of the lessons people learned in the Great Depression was the value of thrift. Starting in the 1980s, Americans began forgetting that lesson and the *savings rate* has been declining ever since.

WHAT'S THAT?

The **savings rate** is the overall percentage of either total or disposable income that the nation is saving rather than using for current consumption. Saving is important not only for individuals and households but for nations, because those with higher savings rates need to attract (and pay for) a lower level of foreign capital to finance a given level of investment.

Why? Some of it had to do with the income distribution patterns established at that time and described previously. Some of it centered on a newfound fascination with the wealthy and a cultural shift to conspicuous consumption. Perhaps it also involved the baby boomers, dubbed the Me Generation by writer Tom Wolfe, feeling entitled to spend all they earned (and then some) or, more charitably, feeling endlessly optimistic about their earnings prospects.

In any event, the pattern of reduced savings is clearly evident in the economic data, as shown in the following table.

Personal Income Data for Selected Years from the National Income and Product Accounts (NIPA) (in Billions of Dollars)

	1980	1985	1990	1995	2000	2005	2008
Personal Income	2,308	3,527	4,879	6,152	8,429	10,270	12,103
Disposable Income[1]	2,009	3,109	4,285	5,408	7,194	9,062	10,642
Personal Outlays[2]	1,808	2,829	3,986	5,157	7,027	9,029	10,451
Personal Saving[3]	201	280	299	250	169	33	191
Savings Rate	10.0%	9.0%	7.0%	4.6%	2.3%	0.4%	1.7%

[1] *Disposable personal income is personal income minus taxes.*
[2] *Personal outlays essentially equal household spending.*
[3] *Savings rate is personal saving as a percentage of disposable income.*
Source: *Bureau of Economic Statistics*

As the table shows, the savings rate went downhill from 1980 to 2005, and jumped in 2008. That recent jump occurred as people reined in their spending and hung on to a few dollars. Incidentally, you may have heard that in certain years the U.S. savings rate has been zero or even negative. That's true, but the actual rate depends on the measure of income being used. For instance, the savings rate in the table is calculated on disposable income, but if calculated on personal income it would, in 2008, round to zero. The two key points are, first, the savings rate is low both in absolute terms and relative to that of most other developed economies (Japan's runs closer to 10 percent), and, second, the *trend* in savings over most of the past three decades has definitely been downward.

The Paradox of Thrift

Economist John Maynard Keynes first identified what he called the paradox of thrift. The phenomenon has to do with the tendency of consumers in a recession to grow tight-fisted, pay down their debt, and increase their savings, out of concern for their financial security. The paradox is that, by saving instead of spending, consumers reduce demand—or at least don't contribute to demand—and thus hamper economic recovery. What they fear can become a self-fulfilling prophecy. This occurred when President George W. Bush, in an attempt to stimulate spending in 2008, sent tax rebate checks to millions of households, only to see much of the money used to pay down debts or build savings.

In the long term, saving benefits an economy by providing domestic funds for businesses to invest, thus increasing productive capacity. But in the short term, during a recession, saving can hinder the chances or the pace of recovery. Although saving is generally a good thing, a recession isn't the best time for a populace to develop the virtue of thrift.

The Least You Need to Know

- Gross domestic product and personal income are two virtually identical measures of an economy. GDP measures what people paid for the goods and services produced, and income measures what people received for producing them.

- Income and wealth are two different economic—and financial—concepts. Income is a flow of money earned by an individual or household in a given period. Wealth is net worth—the assets accumulated by a person or household up to a given point, minus the liabilities.

- The U.S. distribution of income over the past 30 years has resulted in a greater share of income going to the top quintile, and particularly to the top 5 percent and 1 percent, and lower shares going to the other four quintiles.

- Growth in hourly compensation has not kept pace with increases in labor productivity. Some observers believe this is due to workers receiving more in benefits, which are not counted in hourly compensation or taxed (or evenly distributed), while others believe that it is due to policies aimed at rewarding investment, specifically low taxes on capital gains and on high earners, and tamping down wage growth.

- The U.S. savings rate exhibited a declining trend beginning in the 1970s up to the 2008–2009 recession. As a result, U.S. consumers faced the paradox of thrift, in which saving during a recession can contribute to low demand and thus prolong the recession or stunt the rate of recovery.

Consumers and Consumption: A Changing Picture

In This Chapter

- Major trends affecting consumption
- The effects of lower consumption on the economy
- Sectors hit by consumers' cutbacks
- Consumers and the credit card industry

The United States is a consumer society in the truest sense of the term. When the recession hit in December 2007, consumer expenditures were about 70 percent of the U.S. economy. Americans also consume more than they produce, which is why household and government borrowings stood at record highs at the time.

The term "consumer society" also holds strong social connotations in the United States. On one hand, many consumers believe the purchase of ever more sophisticated products—and more of them—defines "the good life," and many tend to define themselves in terms of their possessions. On the other hand, many U.S. businesses depend on Americans' willingness and ability to purchase products and services that are far from essential. These include tens of thousands of advertisers, auto dealers, clothiers, retailers, restaurateurs, hoteliers, and other businesses who count on American consumers' heretofore insatiable need for new, better, faster, and more.

I say "heretofore" because there are signs that consumer spending at the levels of the bubble-driven booms of the 1990s and the 2000s will not return soon. Also, patterns of consumption may change, with a number of key sectors seeing slower growth or decreasing sales in the long term and a few others rising in importance. This chapter examines the trends driving this important development, the evidence of these trends, and their likely effects. It also discusses key sectors that have been affected by consumers' reduced spending and the potential impact of lower credit card usage in the years ahead.

Five Key Trends Affecting Consumption

Five emerging trends will strongly affect consumption. These trends are transitions that took shape during the recession and trace the direction in which consumers have been moving:

- From high employment to high unemployment
- From debt to savings
- From energy gluttony to "green" consumption
- From luxuries to necessities
- From consumption to investment

From High Employment to High Unemployment

By autumn 2009 unemployment reached 10 percent, exceeding the forecasts of the Obama administration and most mainstream economists. As noted in Chapter 11, the possibility of slow job growth amid economic expansion is quite high. This has potentially serious consequences for consumption, and therefore for longer-term economic growth. In fact, the economy could even recover and then relapse into recession.

In the past two recessions, in 1991–1992 and 2001, employment did not recover to its previous peak as quickly as in the previous two recessions, nor as a direct result of rehiring. New jobs had to be created to replace jobs permanently lost. Those recessions affected managers and professionals, creating what the media at the time referred to as "white-collar layoffs," and accelerated the trend toward companies outsourcing formerly full-time staff jobs and using independent contractors. The management ranks had already thinned in the 1980s, the age of leveraged buyouts and takeovers of U.S. companies by their Japanese counterparts.

The Great Recession may well result in the permanent loss of 2 to 3 million jobs—or more. In early 2010, six workers were available for every open job. Those kinds of numbers mean that employers clearly have the upper hand in many, if not most, hiring situations. They can dictate job duties, working conditions, and wages and salaries, and they can reduce vacation time and health care and other benefits because they have the bargaining power to do so. With few benefits mandated by the government and few alternatives for employment, workers will have to accept employers' terms in this "buyer's market" for labor, which means that they may earn less and achieve a lower standard of living than before the recession.

WHAT TO DO?

To survive in a difficult labor market, do all you can to develop multiple skills, multiple careers, and multiple income streams. For guidance on how to do this, get hold of my book *Multipreneuring* (Fireside/Simon & Schuster, 1996). It's out of print, but it's available from online bookstores.

From Debt to Savings

I mentioned a possible increase in household savings and the likely effect on the economy in Chapter 11. The main effect would likely be slower near-term growth as consumers reduce spending and thus demand for goods and services. The larger issue is the potential for a permanent shift from a spending mindset to a savings mindset among households. This could easily occur if consumers shift from using debt to finance purchases, for example, of homes, cars, clothing, and restaurant meals that they cannot afford on their incomes.

A shift from using debt to saving a greater share of income is indeed likely, for several reasons. First, household debt, including credit card debt, stands at an all-time high, and consumers (particularly those facing foreclosure) are realizing that debts eventually come due.

Second, lenders still have billions of dollars worth of bad loans on their books, which they are neither writing off nor selling (given the slow progress of the toxic asset purchase program). Banks will not be in a lending mood for some time, even if consumers return to a borrowing mood, which is also doubtful.

Third, credit card companies have alienated customers by increasing interest rates, late fees, and minimum monthly payments, and limiting credit lines—all without much warning. This erodes *customer loyalty* and generates backlash. Googling "boycott chase"—as in JP Morgan Chase—produces over 400,000 hits (see also www. boycottchase.com).

> **WHAT'S THAT?**
>
> **Customer loyalty** is defined by businesses not as an emotion but as the behavior of continually purchasing a product or service from one, or one or two, providers. There is an emotional dimension to customer loyalty, however, in that truly "loyal" customers will forgive the occasional mistake and will recommend the business to other consumers. Some businesses do far more to cultivate customer loyalty and repeat business than others.

Fourth, interest rates could rise sharply, causing people to borrow less. Interest rates will almost certainly rise when economic growth begins to pick up because the Fed saw how loose money fueled bubbles in tech-stocks in the 1990s and housing in the 2000s. Also, rates will rise if the government continues to borrow heavily, which is also quite likely.

Finally, households that lacked a financial cushion—and had high debt—in this recession will grasp the importance of saving. Baby boomers nearing retirement (or wanting to retire but finding themselves unable to) will save in earnest to make up for excessive spending in the past and for the decreased value of their retirement funds.

That said, if high inflation were to ignite, it could encourage borrowing by making necessities more expensive and by favoring borrowers, who get to pay lenders in "cheaper dollars" down the road. (The higher interest rates lenders charge in inflationary times—known as "the inflation premium"—usually don't fully offset the lower value of the currency.)

From Energy Gluttony to Greenery

Unrest in the Middle East and competition from other nations will keep the price of oil high relative to historical levels. In addition, Americans will almost certainly shun large, heavy vehicles unless they need them due to their work or the weather. U.S. drivers do have short memories, as the return to large vehicles after the two oil shocks of the 1970s showed. However, when combined with other trends discussed here and the memory of unsold SUVs on dealers' lots—and two of Detroit's Big Three going bankrupt—the notion of spending on a gas guzzler for status or fun should hold less appeal than in the past. (See Chapter 13 for an examination of the U.S. auto industry.)

Finally, whether or not one believes in global warming, fossil fuels are not inexhaustible and do produce pollutants. So there are many reasons for developing non–carbon-based sources of energy, such as solar, wind, tidal, and nuclear. The nations that do best in developing those fuel sources and the "green industries" that will power factories, vehicles, and public transportation and heat and cool homes and workplaces will stand to prosper in the future.

From Luxuries to Necessities

Disenchantment with luxury cars could extend to other luxury goods. During the past two booms—in fact, since the mid-1980s—the U.S. public developed a fascination with "lifestyles of the rich and famous." Many people who could not afford luxury homes, cars, clothing, accessories, vacations, and restaurants purchased them on credit or at their companies' expense (it's amazing how many businesses require a Mercedes or BMW).

Widespread public retreat from spending on luxuries would, however, spell trouble for quite a few manufacturers, retailers, and restaurants. Some high-end retailers, such as Abercrombie & Fitch and Neiman Marcus, saw severe decreases in sales volume during the recession. Others, such as leather goods company Coach, guitar manufacturer C. F. Martin, and many exclusive restaurants, introduced more affordable options.

Even some sellers of everyday items, such as kitchen sinks, are having difficulties. For instance Home Depot and Target saw decreasing volume, although the home improvement category usually holds up well or even improves during recessions, and Target positions itself as a "value shopper's" store. Yet, by and large, people continue to spend on true necessities. For example, Wal-Mart, health care (except for elective procedures), and state colleges and universities all held up well or grew.

From Consumption to Investment

As large and productive as the U.S. economy is, Americans have been consuming more than they have been producing. This is reflected in the data, which shows that the United States is a net borrower of capital—borrowing more from foreign nations (including China, an emerging economy!) than it lends—and spending more on imports than it produces in exports.

The world has been partly supporting the lavish U.S. lifestyle and cannot be counted on to do so indefinitely. China and other nations—and their private investors—will not purchase U.S. debt at low interest rates forever. The Middle East, and U.S. and European oil companies, will not sell oil to Americans at lower prices than they can in Asia, where demand is growing rapidly. Other countries have their own economic agendas and their own populations working to achieve better living standards, and they will put their own interests first.

Will the United States do the same? Over the past two decades, U.S. businesses have sent millions of good-paying jobs to foreign economies. That's bad because manufacturing jobs usually a) produce something people need and b) enable semiskilled or skilled workers (without college educations) to produce items of enough value to justify good wages. By "good," I mean at least two times the minimum wage.

Since the 1980s, U.S. companies have invested hundreds of billions of dollars overseas, creating millions of jobs in those economies. This has had a huge effect on the U.S. economy. The United States must now move up the *value chain* and develop industries and jobs that add enough value and provide enough income to sustain something like the historical U.S. lifestyle for future generations. Moving up the value chain means developing industries and jobs that create more value than the old ones. Manufacturing creates more value than crafts. From the 1950s through the 1980s, Japan moved up the value chain by moving from agriculture to manufacturing, and other Asian nations followed suit. The United States need not be number one in the world (nor is it in key areas, such as health care and education), but the U.S. economy must produce goods and services that Americans and the world want and that Americans can produce in return for good wages.

WHAT'S THAT?

The **value chain,** a concept developed by Harvard's Michael Porter, refers to things a business or industry does to produce its goods or services by adding value at each step of production. Turning sheet metal into car bodies and bolting bodies onto frames are value-adding steps. As I use it here, the value chain refers to things an economy does to create value.

A service economy employing millions of people in jobs that add relatively little value—tanning salons, fast-food workers, and similar jobs that grew over the past two decades—do not make for a highly productive and secure economy. Nor, with the exception of certain jobs, do they tend to pay high wages. The only way to address this is to invest more in education, innovation, and manufacturing, which will mean more investment and less consumption for the economy as a whole for at least several years.

Taken together, these trends indicate that the U.S. consumer will not come "roaring back" with high spending to boost the economy to high growth. Indeed, these trends point to the possibility of slow growth for a few years to come.

What Consumers Spend On

Consumer spending data tracks the ways in which households spend their disposable income—that is, their after-tax incomes. Roughly, according to U.S. Census Bureau data the breakdown of expenditures is as follows:

Housing: 32 percent

Transportation: 18 percent

Food: 13 percent

Insurance and Retirement: 11 percent

Medical: 6 percent

Entertainment: 5 percent

Clothing: 4 percent

Other: 11 percent

A few items warrant discussion. First, these are very general percentages, which vary from family to family. People in the highest income brackets spend smaller percentages of their income on certain items because they have a large percentage going into savings and investment (included here in insurance and retirement). Also, food is food and a family can eat only so much. Even if they buy more expensive food, it still accounts for a relatively smaller portion of their total disposable income than housing.

Second, geographical differences can produce differences in spending. For instance, the percentage of income spent on housing typically runs higher for people in high-cost areas such as New York City and Los Angeles. Transportation costs vary with location and factors ranging from access to public transportation to model of car, gas prices, and commuting distance.

Third, there is no percentage assigned to savings because that is subsumed in the category insurance and retirement. Also there's no category for debt retirement, because mortgage payments would go under housing, car payments would go under transportation, and credit card purchases would go under clothing, food (restaurant meals), entertainment (tickets to concerts or sporting events), or other relevant categories of purchase.

The Effects of Consumers' Retreat

In a recession, people reduce their spending for various reasons, with ramifications for specific sectors of the economy. Their reasons depend on their specific plight, the most common ones being job loss, reduced working hours, fear of job loss or reduced hours, reduced salary, delayed salary increases, or reduced access to credit. Any of these happening to a spouse or significant other in the household can also lead to cutbacks.

Obviously people reduce spending on nonessential purchases first. For instance, most people can—and will—postpone major purchases, big ticket items such as cars, appliances, furniture, and carpeting as well as vacations. Major purchases either use up income or savings or must be financed, and in a recession people need a financial cushion and need to avoid taking on debt. Some major purchases are more necessary than others, with vacations and luxuries such as swimming pools getting hard-hit, but, as we've seen, even essentials such as cars and *durable goods* (appliances, furniture, and so on) see significant decreases in sales.

WHAT'S THAT?

Durable goods are manufactured products that serve a function over a period of at least a few years. Examples of consumer durables include cars, furniture, carpeting, appliances, home electronics, and sporting goods. (When businesses purchase durable goods, economists count the purchases as part of business investment in the formula for GDP.) In contrast, food and personal products, such as toothpaste and talcum powder, are consumables; air travel and health care are services.

Household formation slows in a recession. Numerous media reports have noted the trend of recent graduates remaining at home or even returning home after establishing an independent household. Tough times delay marriages as well as plans to have children, which further slows the economy.

The combination of high unemployment, tight credit, and cratering home prices also reduced the ability of Americans to move. The April 23, 2009, *New York Times* reported that the U.S. Census Bureau said that the number of people who changed residences from March 2007 to March 2008 had declined to 35.2 million, the lowest number since 1962, when the nation had 120 million fewer people. This translates to a mobility rate of 11.9 percent in 2008, down from 13.2 percent in 2007 and a new post–World War II record low.

Lack of migration hurts sales of appliances, and the incomes of real estate developers, construction workers, realtors, movers, telephone and cable installers, and anyone else who benefits from moves. It also means fewer people moving to better homes or jobs, given that those are the two major reasons most working people move. (Retirees also move, but usually for better weather or to be closer to their children and grandchildren.) In addition, a move usually generates spending on furniture, decorating, landscaping, tools, and equipment, such as lawn mowers and snowblowers. Given that most people already have homes, most can delay moving to a new one. Unfortunately, in this recession some people were forced to move due to foreclosures, which sent most of them to less expensive housing, relatives, or public housing.

Businesses Hurt by Consumer Cutbacks

Retailers were hurt to the point where the May 22, 2009, *Wall Street Journal* ran a front page story titled "Recession Turns Malls into Ghost Towns." That's a bit of an exaggeration, given that the article stated that sales per square foot at the 1.1 million square foot Eastland Mall in Charlotte, North Carolina, had fallen from $288 to $210 per year—a huge drop, but not one to result in a "ghost town." However, falling sales at malls became a nationwide problem. The article went on to say that "In the 12 months ended March 31, U.S. malls collectively posted a 6.5% decline in tenant's same-store sales."

On July 9, 2009, the *Journal* ran another major story titled "Empty Mall Stores Trigger Rent Cuts," which reported that retailers such as the Gap, Williams Sonoma, and Ann Taylor were reviewing their leases for clauses that would enable them to obtain breaks on rents or to escape the lease entirely. Blockbuster and Starbucks were also attempting to renegotiate leases.

Other companies and industries affected by consumer cutbacks included the following:

- Consumer electronics companies Panasonic and Sony experienced reduced revenues and even losses as consumers avoided malls and pulled back on purchases of televisions and home entertainment units. The first three months of 2009 were at the time the worst quarter in Panasonic's history, with sales falling 30 percent from the same period in 2008.

- Advertising, a major portion of which depends on retailers, automakers, car dealers, and the travel industry, saw severe reductions in volume. This generated job losses at ad agencies, including creative staff, account executives, and media buyers.

- Reduced advertising volume severely hurt magazines and newspapers, both of which rely heavily on advertising and both of which have seen sharply reduced sales and profits. Ad revenue at major newspapers was down about 30 percent in the first quarter of 2009, following declines in 2008.

- Magazines and newspapers are themselves discretionary items, so subscription and newsstand sales were hard-hit. A number of newspapers have (no pun intended) folded, given the downturn and mounting competition from online news and information.

- In mid-summer 2009, retailers and the companies that sell through them expressed anxiety over the back-to-school season. Their concerns were justified. According to the U.S. Census Bureau, U.S. retail sales in September–November 2009 were about 2 percent below those of 2008. The holiday shopping season was also difficult, but retailers had stocked very cautiously and did not have to reduce prices by much.

- Airlines suffered as a result of a reduced volume of business and vacation travel. Revenues were down due to the lower fares airlines had to offer, while profits were down due to higher fuel costs. Delta, Continental, and US Airways all reported lower sales and earnings, although carriers such as Southwest, JetBlue, and AirTran were doing a bit better.

So unemployment, uncertainty, higher savings, lower credit usage, and less mobility hurt housing and home appliances, advertising and media, autos and air travel. The knock-on effects of these difficulties include further job losses, reduced incomes, and lower demand elsewhere in the economy, which creates a vicious cycle and downward spiral of reductions.

Consumers Stop Playing Their Cards

Credit cards helped to create the U.S. consumer culture and its culture of debt. Indeed, credit cards often promote very unwise use of debt. Wise use of debt calls for matching the term of the loan to the life of the asset being financed. Credit cards are the major reason that so many consumers fail to do this, because they enable shoppers to purchase products, diners to buy meals, and vacationers to book flights that will be useless, digested, or over long before they are paid off.

WHAT TO DO?

If you use debt, try to match the term of the loan to the term of the asset you are financing. Car loans and home loans tend to do this automatically, although to minimize your interest costs you should always use the shortest-term loan you can use. Education loans are usually worthwhile because you will have—and will benefit from—your education for the rest of your life. However, using credit cards for restaurants and vacations, unless you pay them off every month, is not matching the loan to the "asset" being financed.

Credit cards are also extremely profitable products for banks and credit card companies. Companies such as MBNA and Capital One have essentially built their businesses on credit cards, with MasterCard and Visa providing the overall branding. American Express began as a travel and entertainment (T&E) card, which by definition and by agreement requires balances incurred during a month to be paid off at the end of that month, but most T&E cards have added credit features and credit cards to their product line (such as American Express Optima). In addition, thousands of retailers created credit cards in order to capture revenue that had been going to the card companies and to enhance their relationship with their customers.

Credit cards are so profitable because the interest rates charged are well above what any sane and creditworthy borrower would pay on a car loan or personal loan. Various membership fees and extremely high late fees—often charged on the basis of "dirty tricks," such as considering a payment late if it was received after 12 noon on the due date—add to the revenue stream. The companies also charge the merchants a small percentage of the transaction and often hold on to money received from consumers and delay payment to merchants in order to invest that money and receive interest on it.

When you pay the balance every month, credit cards and T&E cards can be a convenient way to pay for purchases and keep your records. But as credit products, they are one of the worst deals for consumers. That, unfortunately, is why they are marketed so aggressively—or were until the recession hit. Not only were blanket mailings common, but they often targeted people who could not qualify for other forms of credit or people who were not always financially savvy, such as graduating students. Now the credit risks have grown to the point where cards are not marketed as aggressively, but the product is far too profitable to remain dormant for long.

Consumers tend to spend more when they are using their credit cards rather than cash. This has been proven by studies conducted by the card companies themselves, which they use to encourage merchants to accept their cards. In addition, an academic study conducted by Priya Raghubir and Joydeep Srivastava, published in the September 2008 *Journal of Experimental Psychology* ("Monopoly Money: The Effect of Payment Coupling and Form on Spending Behavior"), showed that "Payment options have a clear effect on consumer spending practices, with forms of payment such as credit cards and gift cards encouraging users to spend more than they do when using cash."

Legislation Affecting Credit Cards

Some changes in the law over the past few decades favored the credit card industry and some did not. An important one that did not was the 1986 law ending the deductibility of interest payments from taxable income for credit card, car, and other consumer loans except mortgages and home-equity loans. This amounted to a tax increase but may have been intended to discourage consumer borrowing. It also helped to generate the massive increase in home-equity loans in the 1990s and early 2000s.

The bankruptcy "reform" legislation of 2004, which had previously failed to pass in various other forms in the late 1990s and 2000, clearly favored card companies, which vigorously supported the bill. This law made it more difficult in general for consumers to file bankruptcy by requiring longer periods of notice, more detailed reporting requirements, credit counseling, and means testing. Even more controversially, the law gave higher priority to the payment of credit card debt than to child support payments. The fact that the law contained no provisions aimed at curbing predatory lending practices, such as unclear contracts, exorbitant fees, and targeting minors in marketing efforts, stirred further controversy and, obviously, favored the industry at the expense of consumers.

Years earlier in 1982, Congress effectively did away with the usury laws that had capped the rates that lenders could charge on loans. This dramatically increased the profitability of card products for banks and credit card companies and set the stage for explosive growth of these products through aggressive marketing.

Credit Card Act of 2009

In May 2009, the U.S. Senate passed and President Obama signed the Credit Card Accountability, Responsibility, and Disclosure Act of 2009. This major piece of legislation had the following major provisions:

- Cardholders must receive 45 days' notice of any interest rate increases.

- Cardholders can pay off their existing balance at the existing rate in the event of an interest rate increase.

- Payments in excess of the minimum must be applied to the balances with the highest interest rates (usually cash advances rather than purchases).

- Rates on existing balances cannot be raised retroactively unless the debtor has been at least 60 days past due.

- Bills must be sent at least 21 days before the due date, and the due date must be the same each month or move to the next business day.

- People under 21 years of age must have a parent or other co-signer who is over 21 in order to obtain a credit card.

The law also forced companies to more clearly disclose the interest being paid and the length of time needed to pay off the balance if only minimum payments are made. Card companies must also provide information on the availability of consumer counseling services.

Needless to say, the industry vigorously opposed this legislation. For instance, intense lobbying did away with a proposal to cap interest rates at 15 percent. Card companies said that the law could hurt consumers by making credit cards less available, by making them less profitable. However, more limited availability of credit cards and lower borrowings may well be part of the intent of the law.

In the nine months between passage of the bill (May 22, 2009) and the date that it took effect (February 22, 2010), banks and card companies did all they could to increase rates, fees, and minimum payments.

WHAT TO DO?

For a summary of the Credit Card Act of 2009, go to www.whitehouse.gov/ the_press_office/Fact-Sheet-Reforms-to-Protect-American-Credit-Card-Holders/.

Likely Effects of the New Law

With $973 billion—or close to $1 trillion—in credit card debt outstanding at the end of 2008, U.S. households probably have had too much access to this form of borrowing. According to a June 10, 2009, report from newjerseynewsroom.com, since the beginning of 2008, "Households that earn upward of $100,000 a year have seen their overdue credit card balances increase by a hefty 40 percent," and those "with more modest incomes—less than $50,000—have seen an increase of just 14 percent." (I would not have said *just* 14 percent, given that the incomes of those households may well have fallen during that period and their jobs certainly became less secure.)

So these facts along with the historically low household savings rate argue for reducing access to consumer credit. But won't that hamper economic growth?

Yes, it will. However, growth based on borrowing created the mess that the U.S. economy found itself in 2008 and 2009. Therefore, building an economy based on savings, investment, productivity, innovation, and growth in good jobs strikes me as the best long-term plan, even if it does slow short-term growth.

The Least You Need to Know

- Consumer spending comprises about 70 percent of the U.S. economy, and consumers were hit hard by high unemployment, increased job insecurity, flat or falling incomes, record high debt, and falling home prices.

- Households have begun a shift from borrowing and spending to debt reduction and saving. This will hamper growth in the near term but position the economy for more solid long-term growth.

- Companies in the retail, restaurant, airline, hotel, auto, and advertising industries have seen dramatic drops in sales and profits in this recession. They have also had to reduce staff, which increases unemployment and further decreases spending.

- Credit card companies have in a sense overplayed their hands, and experienced pressure on profits—and higher delinquencies and write-offs—due to the recession. In addition, the credit card legislation of 2009 could limit the tactics they've used to boost their business, while curtailing card availability and usage among consumers.

- It is unlikely that U.S. consumers will return to their free-spending ways of the 1990s and prerecession 2000s anytime soon. This may signal a shift—or a need for a shift—in the U.S. economy to industries involved more in producing products of value and necessities.

The Impact on Industries and States

Having examined the impact of the financial crisis and the Great Recession on consumers and households, in Part 5 we turn to the impact on specific industries—and industry as a whole—and on the states that make up the nation.

Although the Great Recession affected virtually every sector of the economy, the local impact of a recession can vary widely. Particular industries, such as financial services and autos, and particular locales, such as New York City and Michigan, were particularly hard-hit. In those cases, setbacks and job losses in a key industry affected the local economy quite negatively.

A financial crisis and severe recession will inevitably expose weaknesses in an economy. One such weakness in the U.S. economy has been the loss of manufacturing jobs. Manufacturing jobs pay relatively high wages to relatively unskilled or low-skill workers (that is, relative to unskilled or low-skill workers in service jobs). That's because the machinery enables the workers to create high value items, such as appliances, carpeting, and cars, even though they themselves are relatively low skilled.

With fewer manufacturing jobs than in past decades, as described in Part 3, and a steady decline in real wages, the U.S. middle class has lost ground. It happened slowly over most of the past three decades, but the recession showed how dangerous it has been to allow manufacturing jobs (and household income) to be depleted. So bear that in mind as you look at specific industries and states, and further investigate your own industry and state.

The Auto Industry: In a Ditch or a Turnaround?

In This Chapter

- The economic importance of the U.S. auto industry
- Historical auto sales and future prospects
- Government efforts for the Big Three
- Likely shifts ahead for the auto industry

Many people are shocked that General Motors (GM) and Chrysler ran into trouble during the financial crisis. Others are surprised they didn't run into it sooner. (Ford suffered setbacks but has been relatively unscathed.)

Long-time observers recall the years when the U.S. auto industry ruled the roads, but those days have been gone for awhile. The decline began back in the 1970s, when the first oil shock turned U.S. drivers toward smaller Japanese cars (and Germany's Volkswagen), which featured better gas mileage and steadily improving quality. Panic in Detroit occurred in 1980, when Chrysler survived only thanks to (you guessed it) government-guaranteed loans. In the 1980s, the 1990s, and until the financial crisis, Detroit built its strategy on SUVs and large cars because they were more profitable than smaller vehicles. Dependence on big vehicles, cheap gas, and easy money put Detroit in a ditch when the crisis struck. Then the recession and its aftereffects dealt a near-fatal blow to the U.S. auto industry—and strained the global industry.

This chapter examines the nature and force of that blow, the industry itself, and its predicament. This chapter also looks at the roots of Detroit's problems, government efforts to assist GM and Chrysler, and likely paths forward for the industry.

Autos Not Immune

Over much of its more than 100-year history, the U.S. auto industry focused on convenience and safety, in innovations such as the electric starter, automatic transmission, power steering, power brakes, power windows, air conditioning, and front-wheel drive. But it missed the importance of cost control, build quality, and fuel efficiency. In the 1950s, 1960s, and 1970s, U.S. car companies relied heavily on cosmetic changes to "update" vehicles every year and built their marketing around annual new model introductions.

WHAT TO DO?

Always consider the overall strategy of companies that you work for, invest in, or do business with. You are almost always better off relying on companies that strive to deliver genuine value and make substantive improvements to their products and services rather than those that aim to "game" their customers and increase prices without actual improvements.

The industry failed to improve manufacturing processes in the 1950s and 1960s, even after Japanese automakers did so when rebuilding their industry in the decades after World War II. The U.S. industry also failed to match fuel efficiency, quality, and performance gains that Japanese and German manufacturers achieved in the 1970s and 1980s. These failures combined to steadily erode the Big Three's share of the domestic auto and light truck market, as shown in the following table.

Big Three Share of the Domestic Market

Year	Total Sold (millions)	GM Share	Ford Share	Chrysler Share	Big 3 Share
1950	7.2	45%	25%	17%	87%
1960	7.2	44	27	13	84
1970	9.9	40	28	15	83
1980	11.2	45	20	9	74
1990	13.4	36	24	12	72
2000	17.4	28	23	15	66
2005	17.0	26	17	14	57
2008	13.2	22	15	11	48

Source: Automotive News; www.autonews.com

As the table shows, from 1950 to 2008, U.S. automakers' share of the U.S. market fell from almost 90 percent to below 50 percent. Each of the Big Three lost market share, with GM losing the most. Over that same period, non-U.S. automakers' share grew from a bit over 10 percent to more than 50 percent. Much of that increase resulted from the increasingly higher quality of Japanese cars, which came to dominate the quality rankings issued by J.D. Power and Associates, which tracks auto industry quality data. In the 1980s and 1990s, Toyota in particular won high quality ratings. (In early 2010, Toyota underwent a series of global recalls and bad publicity regarding a problem with unintended acceleration in some models. While this represents a major cost and a potential setback for Toyota, it is likely that the company's reputation for quality and durability and the goodwill it has built will enable it to ride out this problem.)

Over the past 20 years foreign automakers also established U.S. production facilities. These "transplants" were usually built in *right to work* states, such as the Carolinas, Alabama, Tennessee, Kentucky, Georgia, and Texas. These states generally have weaker laws regarding unions' ability to organize workers. Supporters of the transplants believe they create jobs and improve production techniques, while opponents believe they erode U.S. jobs. At least some jobs have been shifted from U.S. factories to transplants. According to the September 13, 2008, *Wall Street Journal*, Michigan lost 83,000 Big Three manufacturing jobs from 1993 to 2008, and states with transplants gained 91,000 new auto manufacturing jobs in that period.

WHAT'S THAT?

In general, **right to work** states tend to limit the ability of workers to unionize or limit the more aggressive tactics that some unions employ to organize workers. Essentially, right to work laws make it illegal for a workplace to have union membership as a condition for employment. As of 2009, 22 U.S. states—mostly in the south and the noncoastal West—had some version of right to work laws.

In addition over the past few decades U.S. energy policy (if one can say there has been one) led to increased reliance on foreign oil while political instability continued in the Middle East. U.S. auto executives not only failed to support a national energy policy but also resisted most fuel efficiency regulation, when such regulation would have encouraged innovation in that area. Also, Congress failed to extend *Corporate Average Fuel Economy (CAFE) standards* to SUVs and light trucks (until 2007); millions of Americans bought gas-guzzlers; and the Fed's easy money policies boosted vehicle purchases and leases. So given that vehicle sales dropped during the recession and the U.S. auto industry continues to struggle, we have several issues to consider regarding this key American industry.

> **WHAT'S THAT?**
>
> **Corporate Average Fuel Economy (CAFE) standards** were laws enacted in 1975 with the aim of improving the fuel economy of passenger vehicles. The regulation sets a standard for each manufacturer's fleet, which allows it to make both high and low miles-per-gallon vehicles. The standards' effectiveness in fuel conservation has been debated. Supporters say they work, or at least contribute to fuel efficiency. Opponents say that higher gas prices (achieved through gas taxes) would be more effective. (Other opponents want neither regulation nor higher gas taxes.) Higher gasoline taxes would almost certainly be more effective.

Four Key Points

As we examine the effects of the crisis on the auto industry, please keep these four points in mind:

The U.S. auto industry is vital to the economy and to national security. The auto industry provides millions of jobs in the plants and in glass and parts factories, dealerships, service stations, parking facilities, car washes, advertising, and advertising-supported media. The Big Three contributed heavily to World War II in manufacturing vehicles and other equipment, and having U.S.-owned vehicle manufacturers may be essential to national security. It's not that auto industry jobs should be saved at all costs, but it makes economic and strategic sense to have a U.S.-owned auto industry, which, incidentally, is quite successful in foreign markets.

The U.S. auto industry has always been politicized. Many people complain that the U.S. government "intervened" in the industry in the crisis. Yet government support of car companies goes way back. Taxpayers funded and continue to fund the roads and highways that made cars useful, as well as bridges, tunnels, parking facilities, state and local policing, and snow removal. Many taxpayers don't drive and thus don't pay gas taxes or tolls, and many others would take public transportation if it were as available as the automobile and the roadway.

The car and oil businesses are interdependent. U.S. foreign policy has long been twisted by the nation's need for foreign oil, which is driven by our dependence on the internal combustion engine. One example of such policy was the U.S. Central Intelligence Agency (CIA)–backed installation of the Shah of Iran and his prime minister as heads of the Iranian government, over the democratically elected President Mohammad Mossadegh, in 1955. The Shah was eventually overthrown in 1979 by Islamic radicals as noted in Chapter 7. Other questionable policies include U.S. friendship with Saddam Hussein in the 1980s, the early 1990s Gulf War against him, the 2003 war to depose him, and U.S. relations with the repressive government of Saudi Arabia. U.S. policies must account for dependence on foreign oil, and the auto industry drives much of that dependence.

Failure to innovate is rampant. No nation's auto industry has developed a commercially viable alternative to the internal combustion engine. Critics have noted that if engine technology had developed at the pace of semiconductor technology, cars would travel more than 100 miles per gallon at speeds in excess of 300 miles per hour. More likely, the internal combustion engine would have been superceded by more efficient technology, or would be fueled by a substance more economical and sustainable than liquefied fossils.

When the Big Three hit the wall in early 2009, many Americans waxed sentimental about muscle cars, tailfins, and "America's love affair with the automobile." I sympathize, as a motorcyclist and former muscle-car owner. But I also recognize that horses gave way to cars, which provided better transportation over longer distances. Horse-lovers can still ride horses. Similarly, when the internal combustion engine gives way to a hydrogen or electric engine, we will all get over it and still be able to drag race.

The Economic Importance of the Auto

Given the number of foreign car manufacturers with U.S. plants, the U.S. auto industry extends beyond the Big Three. It includes many ancillary businesses—including NASCAR!—that collectively employ tens of millions of U.S. workers. (The motor vehicle industry includes trucks and trucking, but we're focusing on passenger vehicles.)

In 2009, the United Auto Workers (UAW) had about 500,000 members, well below its peak of about 1.5 million in 1979. The broader, largely nonunion auto manufacturing and distribution industry directly employed an average of more than 3 million workers in 2008, but by April 2009 that number had dropped toward 2.6 million, as the table on the next page shows.

Motor Vehicle Employment (Number of Workers, Rounded)

	2008 Average	2009 Average	Percent Change
Vehicle and parts manufacturing	876,900	666,400	–24.0
Vehicle and parts wholesaling	338,800	316,200	–6.7
Vehicle and parts dealers	1,844,500	1,640,200	–11.1
Total	3,060,200	2,622,800	–14.3

Source: Bureau of Labor Statistics

These figures do not include the hundreds of thousands of workers in service stations, parking facilities, ad agencies, automotive publications, and similar entities. Nor do they include jobs that benefit from those jobs, for instance in restaurants, grocery stores, hardware stores, and schools. Also, the figures in the preceding table—the most recently available from the Bureau of Labor Statistics as I am writing—do not include many jobs yet to be lost in the U.S. industry due to further restructuring and future dealership closings. Also, the figures in the table are averages for 2008 and 2009. By the end of 2009, the automotive employment picture was even worse.

Skidding Sales Stall the Industry

Auto sales usually decline in a recession, but in the Great Recession they nosedived due to very high unemployment, low job security, high debt, and an overhang of serviceable cars purchased during the 2001–2007 expansion. In the United States, car and light truck sales fell from 16.1 million units in 2007 to 13.2 million in 2008—a 16 percent decrease. Quarter-to-quarter sales deteriorated steadily during 2008. According to Ford's top sales analyst (quoted at Edmund's www.autoobserver.com), sales fell from an annualized rate of 15.6 million units in the first quarter of 2008, to 14.6 million in the second quarter, to 13.1 million in the third quarter, to an agonizing 10.6 million in the fourth quarter. Moreover, many fourth-quarter sales resulted from incentives at double or more than 2007 levels. The industry was paying people to buy cars.

The U.S. government began doing the same in the summer of 2009, with its so-called Cash for Clunkers program (described later in this chapter). The effectiveness of the program was debatable, particularly as U.S. car and light truck sales for 2009 totaled 10.4 million. That's well below the 1990–1999 annual average of 14.6 million vehicles and even further below the 2001–2007 average of 16.7 million.

Although spring 2009 U.S. auto sales stood at a 30-year low, which occurred during the late 1970s, things look better for 2010. However, with sales forecasted at about 11.5 million, it will be a year of recovery but not a huge rebound. In the years ahead we can expect the industry to gradually improve, but the outlook remains somewhat dim (at least in North America, as opposed to Asia, which will see solid expansion in auto sales) because a fundamental restructuring of the industry is underway.

Overcapacity = Too Many Cars

The U.S. and worldwide auto industry had too much manufacturing capacity and too many dealerships. That's one of two main reasons that the auto industry underwent a restructuring rather than a cyclical downturn. The other reason is the severity of the downturn.

Overcapacity in this case is a structural, rather than cyclical, problem, as are high labor costs. There is too much manufacturing capacity—and too many workers and dealers, and perhaps one too many U.S. car companies—given the demand for cars. U.S. automakers had taken steps to address these problems, such as reducing workforces through buyouts of older workers, negotiating lower wages for new workers, and transferring retirees' health-care liabilities to the UAW. But structural problems remained.

WHAT'S THAT?

Overcapacity occurs when a capital-intensive industry—that is, one that requires large factories and heavy machinery—expands to the point where its ability to produce products has significantly outstripped sales and demand for the product. This is problematic because it takes a long time and considerable expense to build or to get rid of productive capacity and it is expensive to maintain.

According to the December 31, 2008, issue of *BusinessWeek*, global automakers had the worldwide capacity to produce 94 million vehicles annually, which is about *34 million too many*. Given (admittedly depressed) demand during the recession, that means that over one third of the industry's global capacity may be overcapacity. North America alone has the capacity to produce about 7 million more vehicles than were demanded during the recession.

A number of analysts see a return to 16.5 million vehicles in annual sales as being years into the future. They see no imminent return of the easy credit and conspicuous consumption of the last two booms, and they expect higher household savings rates. Even without a mad dash to hybrid or electric cars, the days of the SUV, minivan, and muscle car are probably gone, given the price of oil, environmental issues, and Middle East situation. Also, China and India are embracing the automobile, but few drivers there will choose large, gas-guzzling vehicles.

Even with the recession's end, most analysts don't expect a vigorous expansion in sales for several years, although most agree that by 2013 the age of the U.S. fleet will release pent-up demand for new vehicles and solid sales will resume. Meanwhile, companies and particularly U.S. companies must restructure, become leaner and more cost-effective, and develop vehicles that Americans will buy.

During the recession, sales were also down in Europe and in Asia, with China and India quite disappointing. The December 22, 2008, *New York Times* reported that, in its fiscal year 2009 (which ended March 31, 2009), Toyota sold 2.2 million vehicles in North America, down 27 percent from 2008, and 7.5 million vehicles worldwide, down 15.7 percent from 2008. In addition, on March 13, 2009, the *Times* reported that the European Union's bank was lending about $3 billion to German, Italian, French, and Swedish automakers.

The key issue in the United States is how the government, as well as industry and labor, responded to the problems in the auto industry.

Bailouts and Bankruptcies

When the U.S. government assisted the Big Three, it did so with Troubled Asset Relief Program (TARP) funds. In mid-December 2008, the Senate rejected a bill that would have provided $14 billion in non-TARP loans to GM and Chrysler. That left the Bush administration with TARP funds as one of its few options, and it did use those funds. After President Obama took office in late January 2009, he established a task force that handled most of the federal government's interactions with the industry.

Officially titled the Presidential Task Force on the Auto Industry, this 24-member committee is headed by Treasury Secretary Timothy Geithner and White House economic advisor Lawrence Summers. The task force works for Obama (not Congress) and with the auto companies, UAW, and other industry players to oversee plans for GM and Chrysler and other areas of the industry. Key measures undertaken by the task force are described in detail in the following sections on each of the Big Three.

Ford: The First Born

Founded in 1903 by Henry Ford, Ford Motor Company introduced the moving assembly line in 1913 and, with the Model T, transformed the "horseless carriage" into a mass-market product. Henry Ford more than doubled the pay of his workers to a then unheard-of $5 a day, partly so they could buy Ford cars. By the time it was phased out in the late 1920s, the Model T had sold over 15 million units.

Ford shifted to World War II military production for two and a half years starting in 1942. The company maintained mainly family ownership until 1956, when a 22 percent stake was sold to the public. Like GM, Ford offered model lines for various budgets to encourage buyers to graduate (in this case from Ford to Mercury to Lincoln).

Ford created several iconic cars in the years after the Model T, including the Thunderbird, Mustang, Explorer, and the Continental. Best-sellers include the Taurus, which outsold the Honda Accord in the early 1990s, and the F-150 pickup. The company also purchased British luxury car maker Jaguar in the late 1990s. International success came early to Ford in Europe and more recently in China, where it has about 150 factories.

Smaller than GM and larger than Chrysler, Ford achieved higher profits than GM in a number of years. The company often displayed greater focus, perhaps because it is a "family business" and because it had three major brands rather than GM's five original brands (Chevrolet, Pontiac, Oldsmobile, Buick, and Cadillac). In the recession, Ford was able to pass up government assistance and avoid bankruptcy.

Ford, like GM and Chrysler, cut costs aggressively in the years before the recession. For example, National Public Radio reported that Ford and the UAW agreed to put 99¢ per hour of future wage increases into a health-care fund and to increase deductibles by up to one third. Anticipated savings totaled about $650 million a year. The company also reduced its workforce, and as of 2006 planned to end 30,000 jobs and close 14 plants by 2012.

One lingering question is whether Ford will be playing on a level field with its two U.S. competitors being backed by the federal government.

General Motors: Once the Biggest

General Motors (GM), founded in 1908, was once the largest and most powerful U.S company in any industry. GM also took corporate structure and strategy to new levels under Alfred Sloan (for whom the Sloan School of Management at MIT is named). For instance, Sloan made GM some divisions, such as glass and some component makers, independent companies that had to compete with external ones for internal business.

WHAT TO DO?

For an excellent look at the founding of General Motors—and of the modern, multi-division major enterprise—read *Concept of the Corporation,* which was management guru Peter Drucker's first book.

GM prospered throughout the 1950s and 1960s, with the first American sports car, the Corvette; its "gold-standard" Cadillac brand; and muscle cars such as the Pontiac GTO, Oldsmobile Cutlass 442, and Chevrolet Camaro. The company unintentionally launched the career of consumer activist Ralph Nader with the Chevrolet Corvair, a sporty car with a rear-mounted engine described as "unsafe at any speed" in Nadar's 1965 book of the same name. The car was discontinued in 1969.

Like Ford, GM was forward-thinking from the start. A Canadian operation was founded almost simultaneously with the U.S. company, then formally incorporated in 1918. In 1919, GM founded General Motors Acceptance Corporation (GMAC) as the first captive auto financing company, to extend credit to customers needing car loans. In 1929 and 1931, GM expanded to Europe with the purchase of German car maker Opel. GM later purchased stakes in Japanese auto and truck companies, bought Saab in the 1980s (which entered bankruptcy in early 2009 and has been sold to Dutch company Spyker), and in 1990 started Saturn from scratch, complete with its own dealer network. (Saturn was announced to be discontinued by GM by the end of 2010.)

In the 1980s and 1990s, foreign competition in North America increased in the profitable, luxury segments due to Toyota's Lexus, Nissan's Infinity, and BMW and Mercedes Benz, which all hurt Cadillac. Often in the 1990s and early 2000s, the company made virtually all of its annual profits in non-U.S. markets and from GMAC. To trim costs, in 1999 GM spun off Delphi, its auto parts manufacturer, which filed for bankruptcy in 2005. In 2004, GM phased out Oldsmobile, but was still not positioned to withstand the recession.

Like Ford, GM signed earlier agreements with the UAW to shift health-care costs, and in 2007 retirees' health-care liabilities were moved to an independent trust. In 2008, GM developed plans to cut about $10 billion in costs, but by then the financial crisis had hit and car sales were tanking.

Government Intervention in GM

At the end of May 2009, GM went into Chapter 11 bankruptcy, which enabled the company to reorganize rather than liquidate, and then emerged in a slimmed-down form 36 days later. Yes, it was over that quickly, but GM had $50 billion in various forms of government funding and the support of the Auto Task Force. The task force helped the company face the need to shed four of its eight brands and helped the UAW to take responsibility for retirees' health-care insurance and to accept lower compensation for some workers.

In addition, GM did away with debt it couldn't handle and made the U.S. government a 60.8 percent shareholder—a huge stake for the taxpayer—and gave the Canadian government 11.7 percent. Both the U.S. and Canadian governments expect to divest themselves of ownership by 2018. The UAW owns another 17.5 percent and the bondholders got the remaining 10 percent.

The reorganized GM has four divisions: Cadillac, Chevrolet, Buick, and GMC. Saturn was almost purchased by Penske Automotive Group, but the deal fell through, resulting in its demise. Saab was to be purchased by a European consortium, but the deal, which depended on $600 million in financing from the European Investment Bank, did not materialize and has since been sold to Spyker instead. Hummer was to be sold to a Chinese company, but Chinese government approval was denied, and the brand was cancelled. Pontiac will be phased out by the end of 2010. GM will downsize from 47 to 34 U.S. manufacturing plants.

No one expects GM to recapture its former glory—or market share. The intention is to reduce the company's debt (from $176 billion to $48 billion) and labor costs, to reduce its workforce (from 91,000 employees at the end of 2008 to 68,500 by the end of 2009) and flatten its management structure, and to trim the number of dealers (from 5,900 to 3,600) while streamlining marketing. GM also, of course, now intends to build cars that U.S. drivers want to buy, and to launch an initial public offering of common stock in 2010.

Chrysler: Smallest of the Big Three

The last of the Big Three to be founded, Chrysler opened for business in 1925 under Walter Chrysler, a former GM executive. Chrysler started with an affordable high-end car, then introduced Plymouth at the lower end and DeSoto in the midrange. Chrysler also geared up for wartime production in the 1940s. The company did not, however, originate the Jeep trademark, but acquired it when it bought American Motors Corp (AMC) in 1987, then the sole U.S. automaker outside the Big Three.

According to a National Public Radio report on May 14, 2007, Chrysler introduced the Chrysler Airflow in 1934, but its "poor reception helped stifle innovation and marketing at Chrysler for years." Over the years, Chrysler generally remained third among the Big Three in sales and market share. The company entered Europe relatively late, in 1960. However, in 1983 Chrysler originated the minivan and in the 1990s and 2000s became known for its design team, which developed the Dodge Viper, Plymouth Prowler, and Dodge Magnum.

Back in 1980, on the brink of bankruptcy, Chrysler required a government guarantee of $1.5 billion in loans. Legendary Ford executive Lee Iacocca became CEO at a salary of a dollar a year (plus stock options) and quickly enabled the company to pay off its loans seven years early.

The minivan led the company to a market share of 16.2 percent in 1996, according to that NPR report, the highest since 1957. But the Plymouth Voyager and Dodge Caravan faced minivans from Ford, GM, and Toyota, and Chrysler saw continual ups and downs. In 1998, it entered a short-lived merger with Daimler-Benz, which in 2007 sold 80 percent of Chrysler to a *private equity fund*.

WHAT'S THAT?

A **private equity fund** is a group of professional investors who raise money from other investors and use it to purchase stakes or controlling interests in other companies, usually privately held as opposed to publicly traded. They also purchase complete businesses, rather than interests, with the aim of restructuring their finances, improving their operations, or both, and then reselling them at a profit.

Government Intervention in Chrysler

Government intervention in Chrysler was more controversial than the GM intervention. By some accounts the company was "pushed into the arms of Fiat," Italy's major car company and, again by some accounts, Chrysler's bondholders were treated unfairly. In fact, Fiat had explored a deal to purchase a 35 percent stake in Chrysler in January 2009. However, the Auto Task Force did reject a Chrysler restructuring plan and at the end of March gave the company "30 days to complete an alliance with Fiat or risk being cut off from further government funding," according to a Reuters timeline. So while Chrysler was "pushed," the company had already walked up to Fiat.

As to the bondholders, in late April a small group—about 10 percent—of them refused to go along with an administration plan that would have created losses for them. They objected that their debts were senior to obligations owed to other creditors and to union claims. While they were within their rights to protest the government's proposal, and perhaps correct in stating that they would have gained more money in an ordinary bankruptcy proceeding, the administration felt that it was owed—or at least deserved—cooperation. Indeed, the situation was certainly not an ordinary bankruptcy (given that the government does not take stakes in ordinary bankruptcies). Also, 90 percent of the bondholders did not protest the administration's plan.

Although Chrysler is expected to emerge from bankruptcy fairly quickly, its fate remains uncertain. Fiat must live down a reputation for poor quality, established during its brief foray into the U.S. market in the late 1970s, and Chrysler perennially runs third place among U.S. car companies. While the goal of saving U.S. jobs is well-intentioned, if both GM and Chrysler survive, there may still be significant U.S. overcapacity.

Perhaps more to the point, while two of the Big Three required government assistance and underwent bankruptcy, their Japanese and German competitors suffered only the pressure on sales and earnings to be expected in a severe downturn. That may well leave them better positioned to compete with even the reorganized GM and Chrysler.

Cash for Clunkers Program

The Consumer Assistance to Recycle and Save Act (CARS)—informally known as "Cash for Clunkers"—began in July 2009 and helped boost monthly industry-wide sales to the highest level in nearly a year. However, sales in July 2009 still stood at 12 percent below the July 2008 level. The act provided incentives worth $3,500 to $4,500 to car buyers when customers traded in "gas guzzlers" for more fuel-efficient models. This translates to discounts averaging about 15 percent.

In essence, the bill provided government rebates for car buyers, then stuck all taxpayers with the bill. While automakers, dealers, and the UAW favored the deal, conservatives did not. Based on the evidence, the program did boost sales and encouraged buyers to trade up to more fuel-efficient vehicles. In July, traded-in vehicles averaged 15.8 miles per gallon while new vehicles purchased averaged 25.4 mpg. Officially, the program was responsible for the sale of 700,000 new vehicles, and the automakers were certainly happy with it because it did whittle down their inventories of unsold vehicles.

One economic question is whether the program simply shifted demand from the future to the present. It may well have done so, because buyers knew the program was temporary and that they had to buy then or lose the rebate. But the program also tapped current untapped demand. Also, the nation needed the jobs and taxpayers were already assisting the car companies.

However, the program was obviously not a solution to the industry's longer-term problems. In addition, preferable ways to encourage fuel efficiency might be through market mechanisms, such as companies making attractive, well-priced fuel-efficient cars, or policy solutions, such as gradual increases in the gas tax.

The United Auto Workers

Any discussion of the Big Three must include its nemesis, the United Auto Workers (UAW). Founded in Detroit in 1935 and recognized first by GM in 1937, the UAW has about 800 local unions and deals with some 2,000 employers. The UAW—officially, the International Union, United Automobile, Aerospace and Agricultural Implement Workers of America—has the most assets of any U.S. union: $1.2 billion according to the May 21, 2009, *Wall Street Journal*. (To view that in perspective, consider that the average billionaire on the 2009 *Forbes* list of the world's wealthiest people has some $3 billion in net worth, topped by Bill Gates with $40 billion.) UAW membership shrank over the past 30 years as members retired, automakers reduced their U.S. workforces, and foreign companies built "transplants."

When it could, the UAW often used the power to strike as well as *collective bargaining* to extract high wages and benefits from the Big Three. Among the more attractive benefits have been excellent health-care insurance—a huge cost for U.S. car companies—and the "30 and out rule," which enables members to retire with pay and benefits after 30 years of service.

> **WHAT'S THAT?**
>
> In **collective bargaining,** the workers, or at least the unionized workers, in a company or company facility are represented by union leaders who have the power to bargain on their behalf with management. Those union leaders also hold the threat of a strike or work slowdowns over management, which increases their bargaining power.

Many people blame the UAW for the Big Three's demise. The union clearly contributed to high labor costs, and those wages may not be justified by the value the workers add. A comparison of union operations with nonunion U.S. operations reveals that the latter make cars that are as good (or better) for lower compensation. Also, to retire at, say, 50 or 55 with a pension and health care for life is a deal most Americans would like. Yet not enough Americans are willing to fund that deal for UAW members by "buying American." Using strikes to extract high wages and benefits from management will not work forever—as the events of the crisis proved.

By the same token, management failed to tell its story very well, and they did sign the union contracts and attempted to pass the costs on to customers. They also paid themselves beyond the value they were adding and, worse, failed to support a public health-care system of the kind every other industrial nation has. They supported one energy strategy—buy imported oil—and by some accounts squelched efforts to develop an electric car. So as always in this financial crisis, there's plenty of blame to go around.

Political Views of the Bailouts

The auto industry bailout generated ample criticism, much of it from the right and—in my opinion—hard to understand, although more criticism from the left would have been welcome. Cries of socialism seem hysterical to me, given that most free marketers don't appear ready to allow GM or Chrysler to fail. With unemployment approaching 10 percent, did we have time for the car companies to proceed into bankruptcy without assistance? Does the right want most vehicle manufacturing capacity to be foreign-owned? Did it want the U.S. taxpayer to extend aid with no strings attached?

All of that said, critics on the right made some strong points:

- The bondholders got far smaller stakes in the reorganized companies than the unions, which means that they shouldered a disproportionate share of the burden. Of course, they're still creditors, and the idea was to save jobs and the industry. Yet the fact remains that the bondholders were not treated by the government the way creditors should be treated.

- On June 1, 2009, a *Wall Street Journal* editorial pointed out that the UAW extracted measures to bar GM small-car imports made in its overseas plants. This move to protect UAW jobs creates retooling costs. The editorial also noted that GM must sell Opel and that the new owners must "stay out of the U.S., and even China, where GM's business is strong."

- That same editorial pointed out that GM could be favored by the government over Ford, the one U.S. car company that did not require assistance.

- If the government decides to push "green cars," it may encourage manufacturing of cars the market rejects.

I doubt that most liberals outside the auto industry, though they are generally pro-union, feel that the UAW members deserve outsized pay and benefits. Indeed, many have lost sympathy for the UAW, given union rules that limit work, abuses of disability pay, and excessive overtime. Yet liberals, with the exception of a few economists, stayed silent on the protectionism just cited, when they should understand that market mechanisms are generally far preferable.

People on the right and on the left—and in government—must understand that excess industry capacity cannot be sustained and that trying to counter market-driven contraction will be costly and contrary to sound economic policy. The United States must always have the capacity to manufacture military vehicles and material, but not at the expense of supporting an inefficient industry and overcompensated workers.

The Least You Need to Know

- The auto industry received federal assistance because of its importance in terms of employment and potential military production, and for cultural reasons, but also because the United States needs every manufacturing job it can hold onto.

- The auto industry directly employs about 3 million people and less directly employs millions more in service stations, parking facilities, and car washes—and in restaurants, retail stores, and other businesses.

- Government at all levels has supported the auto industry by funding road and highway construction, snow removal, and similar activities. Government charges drivers' fees, taxes, and fines, but people who don't drive have supported the auto industry and have suffered from the government's lack of commitment to public transportation.

- Each of the Big Three automakers has a great history behind it, but they failed to keep pace with advances in manufacturing processes and quality that other companies, particularly in Japan and Germany, achieved. That, coupled with lagging fuel efficiency, led to deep losses in market share for the U.S. auto industry.

- While most policies aim to soften the effects of the recession and the industry's restructuring, some aspects—particularly pro-UAW features—appear at least partly politically motivated.

U.S. Industrial Problems and Potential

In This Chapter

- The altered composition of the U.S. economy
- How services differ from manufactured goods
- Why exports won't rescue the U.S. economy

Even after two quarters of positive growth in the second half of 2009, in early 2010 most people felt any U.S recovery would be tentative at best. Consumers, businesses, and banks remained cautious, as did the U.S. government. Despite the Obama stimulus package receiving widespread credit for preventing worse economic performance and for boosting third- and fourth-quarter growth, the federal government did not appear ready to approve more stimulus spending. So for a variety of reasons, people remained cautious. In this chapter we examine some reasons for this in terms of the composition of the U.S. economy.

We have in previous chapters examined specific industries, such as housing, finance, and autos. However, we have not actually examined the composition of the economy and how it has changed over the past few decades and years. This chapter will examine the composition of the U.S. economy, in terms of what economists call sectors, how those sectors have changed, and what those changes imply for the next few years. (Chapter 18 will examine even more basic and longer-term issues of U.S. economic sustainability.)

As you read this chapter, bear in mind that business investment in new equipment, vehicles, and productive capacity is a lagging indicator in any recovery. That's because after a recession, businesses first expand workers' hours, then rehire, and then finally, when demand clearly picks up and they are fairly certain recovery is underway, they begin expanding operations and adding to productive and distribution capacity.

The Importance of Business Investment

Business investment is a relatively small part of GDP compared with consumer spending, but it is extremely important to economic growth because it expands productive capacity—the ability of the economy to produce goods and services. In fact, in many other nations, business investment, or more accurately *business fixed investment*, is a significantly higher percentage of GDP, as it once was in the United States. In fact, in 2008, according to the U.S. Central Intelligence Agency World Factbook, the United States ranked 135th among the world's nations in business fixed investment as a percentage of GDP, at 14.6 percent. (The world average was 21.9, or a bit more than one fifth of GDP, as it was in the United States during much of the 1950s and 1960s.)

WHAT'S THAT?

Business fixed investment is the amount that a business spends in a year on capital goods, such as factories, machinery, buildings, raw material, and other goods used to produce goods. Business fixed investment increases a nation's productive capacity and expands an economy's industrial base, thus laying a foundation for future growth. It also includes replacement of worn-out capacity.

Now many nations that spend more on fixed investment as a percentage of GDP are much poorer than the United States. These include Guyana (40.5 percent of GDP), China (40.2 percent), India (39 percent), and Bulgaria (38.3 percent), all in the top 10. With a lower GDP, a smaller industrial base, and a smaller consumer sector, when those developing nation's invest to expand their productive capacity, it will naturally represent a larger share of their GDP.

But the United States also lagged in business fixed investment when compared with other developed nations, such as Japan (22.5 percent, ranked 77), France (21 percent, ranked 91), Italy (20.5 percent, ranked 98), Germany (18.9 percent, ranked 117), and the United Kingdom (16.7 percent, ranked 131). Of course, U.S. companies do invest, but they do a lot of their investment in productive capacity in foreign nations.

While it's true that service sectors use a lot of real estate and invest heavily in information and communications technology, they do not build factories that produce tangible goods. That is another reason that business investment has fallen as a percentage of GDP over the past 30 to 40 years.

WHAT TO DO?

Check out the CIA World Factbook yourself when you want to get a broader view of the world or data on a specific nation or economy. It's located at https://www.cia.gov/library/publications/the-world-factbook/ and is updated regularly.

Structural Economic Fundamentals

The composition of the U.S. economy has changed considerably over the past several decades. These changes have occurred as people, enterprises, and government have responded to changing needs, technologies, and developments in the global economy. For example, when large-scale farming became possible with the development of new planting, harvesting, and pest control techniques and technologies, farming became more efficient and the family farm went into decline. Similarly, when the post–World War II expansion of the suburbs occurred, durable goods manufacturing expanded. However, after foreign competitors entered the U.S. economy in the 1970s and exporting of manufacturing jobs began in the 1980s, durable goods' share of GDP contracted.

The latter factor is one that I want to focus on in this chapter. While the nature and causes of the economic cycle remain fundamentally the same, the composition of an economy can make a difference in both areas. For instance, the nature and causes of the economic cycle in an agricultural economy or one that depends heavily on exports of one or two commodities, such as oil or coffee, will differ from those in a more industrial economy.

A High-Level, Historic View

The Bureau of Economic Analysis (BEA) has compiled historical data on the composition of the U.S. economy and labor force since the middle part of the last century. These data can be compiled, viewed, and analyzed in various ways. Here, I want to examine the composition of the economy at a fairly high level and how it has changed over time.

These changes, along with our knowledge of the financial crisis and the Great Recession, and of changes in the global economy, will enable us to draw some conclusions (or at least some useful inferences) about how the U.S. economy will fare in the years ahead. I am particularly interested in how the U.S. economy has changed over the past few decades and in where growth will come from in the next few years. I am particularly concerned about growth that will enable the U.S. economy to expand at a reasonable, sustainable average annual real (inflation-adjusted) rate of 3 percent.

WHAT TO DO?

Visit www.bea.gov to have a look at the labor market data yourself, particularly if you are interested in examining a specific segment or aspect of the economy.

Industries' Shares of GDP

The BEA has compiled data on the percentage of the economy that various sectors account for, and presented it in tables at www.bea.gov. Those BEA tables are titled "Value Added by Industry as a Percentage of Gross Domestic Product (GDP)" and are compiled for the years 1947 through 2008. In the following table, I have pulled from the BEA tables data for every 10 years from 1950 to 2000, plus 2008, for 15 major industry sectors (including government).

These shares may not add up exactly to 100 percent due to rounding errors.

Share of GDP by Industry: Selected Years, 1950–2008

	1950	1960	1970	1980	1990	2000	2008
Farming and fishing	6.8	3.8	2.6	2.2	1.7	1.0	1.1
Oil, gas, and mining	2.6	1.9	1.4	3.3	1.5	1.2	2.3
Utilities	1.6	2.2	2.0	2.2	2.5	1.9	2.1
Construction	4.4	4.4	4.8	4.7	4.3	4.4	4.1
Manufacturing	27.0	25.3	22.7	20.0	16.3	14.5	11.5
Wholesaling	6.3	6.6	6.5	6.8	6.0	6.0	5.7
Retailing	8.8	7.9	8.0	7.2	6.9	6.7	6.2
Transportation and warehousing	5.9	4.5	3.9	3.7	2.9	3.1	2.9
Information	2.7	3.1	3.4	3.5	3.9	4.7	4.4
Finance and insurance	2.7	3.6	4.1	4.9	5.9	7.5	7.5
Real estate and leasing	8.7	10.5	10.5	11.0	12.1	12.1	12.5
Professional and business services	3.9	4.7	5.4	6.7	9.8	11.6	12.7
Education and health care	2.0	2.7	3.9	5.0	6.7	6.9	8.1
Arts and entertainment	3.0	2.8	2.8	3.0	3.4	3.6	3.8
Federal, state, and local government	10.8	13.2	15.2	13.8	13.9	12.3	12.9

Source: Bureau of Economic Analysis

Here are a few general points about this important table before I comment on it in detail:

The BEA measure "value added" consists of three components: an industry group's compensation paid to employees, its taxes paid on production and imports minus any subsidies it receives, and its gross operating surplus (a measure of its *return on investment*). This measure of value added expresses an industry's financial contribution to the total economy, and it works well as long as it is applied consistently to all industry sectors. Private industry has generally accounted for 85 to 89 percent of the value added in the U.S. economy, and the government for 11 to 15 percent, over the past six decades. The largest government share occurred in the early 1970s.

WHAT'S THAT?

Return on investment is the amount or percentage that a company or individual earns annually on a sum of money invested in a project, venture, or security. When expressed as a percentage—which it usually is—it is also known as the rate of return.

I did not break out federal from state and local government in this table, but in recent years state and local governments have accounted for about two thirds of value added to GDP by government. This represents a change from the 1940s, when the federal government accounted for half or more of government's share of value added.

In general, the value added figures in this table may not match certain other available measures of various sectors' "share of the economy" because activities can be measured or classified in different ways. For instance, health care is often cited as 16 percent of the economy and government as 25 or 30 percent. However, health care includes many activities classified here as "finance and insurance" and "professional and business services." Similarly, the government at all levels delivers many services through private-sector contractors, which would account for government being only 11 to 15 percent of the economy in this table.

This table shows how the makeup of the U.S. economy has changed over the past 60 years, and it certainly mirrors the changes that most of us have heard about. The major trend is certainly the lower share of GDP accounted for by manufacturing. In 1950, manufacturing accounted for 27 percent of U.S. GDP. That figure rose to a peak of 28.3 percent in 1953, but then began declining. Manufacturing continued to account for more than one fifth of GDP through the 1970s, until 1980 when it hit 20 percent. From that point onward, manufacturing's share of GDP continued to decline steadily, falling to a mere 11.7 percent in 2008.

This means that in the nearly 60 years, from 1950 to 2008, about 15 percent of the value added to GDP by U.S. workers and other productive resources shifted out of manufacturing industries and into other activities. Where did those workers and resources go?

As the table shows, they didn't move to farming, forestry, and fishing. That industry sector's share of GDP fell from 6.8 percent in 1950 to only 1.1 percent in 2008. Where did the more than 5 percent of productive resources once devoted to farming and fishing go? That question actually leaves us wondering about a shift of about 20 percent of the economy: the 15 percent gone from manufacturing and the 5 percent gone from farming and fishing between 1950 and 2008.

Mining and the other extractive industries, mainly oil and gas, have remained substantially the same, in the 1.5 to 2.5 percent range, with 1980 a bit of an aberration at 3.3 percent. Utilities, at about 2 percent, and construction, at about 4 to 5 percent, have both maintained level contributions to GDP, both being correlated to the size of the population and of the overall economy. (Bear in mind that we are discussing percentages of overall economic activity as measured by GDP.)

Wholesaling and retailing each declined a bit, as did transportation and warehousing, so they haven't made up for manufacturing and farming's declining share of GDP. Nor have the arts and entertainment, which increased its share from 3 percent in 1950 to 3.8 percent in 2008.

The major gains in share of GDP have occurred in professional and business services, which rose from 3.9 percent in 1950 to 12.7 percent in 2008 (an 8.8 percent increase); education and health care, which rose from 2 percent to 8.1 percent (a 6.1 percent increase); finance and insurance, which rose from 2.7 percent to 7.5 percent (a 4.8 percent increase); and real estate and leasing, which rose from 8.7 percent to 12.5 percent.

Consider that in 1950, professional and business services and real estate and leasing *together* accounted for only 12.6 percent of the economy, while manufacturing accounted for 27 percent. Now *each* of those service sectors separately accounts for a larger share of GDP than manufacturing. Truly, the composition of the U.S. economy has changed, and that raises an important question for the years ahead.

What Does the Decline in Manufacturing Mean?

I realize that many observers and analysts have lamented the decline of manufacturing in America. I, too, have pointed out (in Chapter 9) that manufacturing jobs enable relatively uneducated workers to generate high value, because they operate machinery (designed by highly educated people) that produces high-value products, such as vehicles, engines, and machinery. When U.S. companies export jobs and build factories in foreign locations, as they have done, then U.S. workers must find other ways to add high value and thus move up the value chain.

Many of us have, and have in fact gone into high-value-adding areas of the economy. Business services includes legal services, accounting, systems design, and scientific, technical, and engineering services. Finance and insurance includes "Wall Street" and the life, health, auto, and property and casualty insurance industries. Real estate and leasing includes real estate brokerage, rentals, and leasing (as distinct from real estate development, which comes under "construction").

This is what people mean when they say that the United States has shifted to a *service economy*. It's not just personal services, such as tanning salons and shopping services, but major organizations, for example, in banking, law, accounting, and consulting, that mainly sell knowledge and expertise.

WHAT'S THAT?

A **service economy** is an economy based more on services than on manufacturing. As U.S. workers have found themselves "priced out of the labor market" by lower-cost foreign workers, manufacturing has moved to foreign locations. Some service jobs, particularly in personal services, cannot move overseas, but some—such as data entry and customer service—can, and have. High-value service jobs—such as those in law, engineering, and medicine—require a lot of education, and even some of those jobs can be moved to foreign locations.

The chief implications of this are that, first, an economy that relies heavily on professional and business services, and on finance, insurance, and real estate *requires* an educated workforce. Clerical jobs, such as data entry, can be—and have been—easily sent overseas. Many paper-handling functions, such as file clerk, have been largely eliminated. High-value-added jobs, such as attorney, paralegal, financial analyst, and insurance and real estate sales, require education, licenses, and other professional certifications, and (usually) well-developed social skills.

Unfortunately, the United States has underinvested in education. Observers who argue that our public schools are falling apart are partly right. They are falling apart in poorer areas. Teachers are underpaid in many locations, and equipment and even books are in short supply. Teachers' unions often make it extremely difficult to rid schools of incompetent, uncaring teachers. In some inner city locations high school dropout rates top 20 and even 25 percent—or higher.

These problems come directly from the fact that most K–12 education is funded by local property taxes. This means that people in relatively affluent cities and towns have better schools because they have more money and higher property values, so they pay more in taxes. This, however, leaves children in less affluent (not to mention poor) cities and towns at a tremendous disadvantage. In fact, it perpetuates a system in which the rich get richer and the poor get poorer.

Services are more labor intensive. They tend to require more labor than manufacturing does to create a given level of value. Certain aspects of service industries can be automated and performed by or with the assistance of computer programs. This is the case in computer-assisted design and in financial analysis. However, sophisticated, high-value-added services generally require human knowledge, expertise, and interpersonal skills. A computer cannot represent you in front of a mediator, negotiate a lease, or soothe a client's nerves.

The production of services does not generate the same *economies of scale* as those of manufactured products. Economies of scale occur when the fixed costs of a factory and equipment are allocated to higher volumes of product. In other words, if you're making thousands of widgets, the marginal (or additional) cost of each widget falls for two reasons. First, the factory and equipment are paid for at a (hopefully) relatively low (break-even) point of production volume, and, second, you are getting a volume discount on the materials for each widget. Economies of scale are more difficult to achieve in service industries, because, for example, attorneys or consultants are needed to deliver "the product," and they cannot be cloned and must be paid every week.

WHAT'S THAT?

Economies of scale occur in a business operation when the fixed costs of doing business are amortized over a larger volume of production. When that occurs, the cost of each additional (or marginal) unit produced decreases, which is more economical. It is cheaper, on a per-unit basis, to produce more units of a product because the factory and other fixed costs are paid for anyway. Variable costs, such as material and labor, still rise as more units are produced, but the savings achieved by having fixed costs amortized over more units can be high. This is why producers can offer "volume discounts" to customers who purchase greater quantities of a product.

Services do not generate the same export volume or value as exported goods. Services can be exported, despite the oft-cited example of haircuts. However, the people delivering the services will usually have to get on a plane or be located in a foreign office. It's not like making thousands of widgets by machine and shipping them to an export market.

Together all of these things—along with several other factors—mean that the U.S. economy could have a difficult time regaining steady, sustainable 3 percent average real annual growth in GDP. Consider the formula for the U.S. economy: C + I + G +/– Net Exports. "C" equals consumer spending, "I" equals business investment, "G" equals government spending, and net exports are positive if exports exceed imports and negative if they do not.

Here's how the postrecession prospects for the U.S. economy break down as of early 2010. Consumers are overextended in terms of credit, wary about their jobs, and suffering lackluster income growth. So a vigorous, consumer-led recovery is probably not in the offing. Business investment may pick up, but not until the recovery is underway, which leads to a chicken-and-egg situation in which business won't invest until recovery comes, but recovery depends somewhat on businesses investing. Government spending has been tried, successfully, in terms of the Obama stimulus package. However, given the levels of deficit spending and political opposition to it, government spending won't occur at a level that can be counted upon to pull the United States into strong growth.

Exports, Currencies, and Recoveries

What about exports? They provide some hope but, given the composition of the economy—the kinds of things the United States produces—not a lot. Some economies, such as Japan at one time and China today, can to an extent export their way out of a recession. By that I mean that a nation can at times devalue its currency by printing money or buying up foreign currencies (which bids up the price of foreign currencies and puts more of its currency into circulation). Devaluing a currency lowers the price of that nation's goods on world markets relative to the domestic products of other nations and relative to their exports. For example, before the euro was established, if Italy experienced a recession, it could devalue the lira to reduce the price of its exports, and thus increase its domestic production, put people back to work, and get the manufacturing sector and the overall economy moving again.

Of course, it is not quite this simple or surefire; if it were, every nation would do it. First, there's a downside to a nation devaluing its currency in that it can discourage lenders and investors, who fear putting money into a nation with a falling currency. Second, it assumes that there is a ready market for the nation's exports, which may not be the case. Third, it assumes that foreign markets will welcome the nation's imports and not respond with import quotas, high tariffs, and other trade barriers and forms of *protectionism*.

WHAT'S THAT?

Protectionism is a set of practices designed to limit competition of imports in a domestic market. The most common protectionist practices are high tariffs and import duties, quotas on how much volume can be imported, and barriers such as regulations that specify certain ingredients or procedures that foreign producers would find difficult because they lack the resources that would enable them to provide those ingredients or perform those procedures.

However, exports can buffer economic contractions and help a nation's economy recover. For example, China's exports have been rising over the past decade, and the Chinese economy suffered lower growth as the economies of its trading partners experienced recession. The sheer level of China's exports and its low costs relative to other nations helped it to weather the global downturn without actual contraction. (Of course, a roughly $600 billion stimulus program also helped.) On the other hand, Japan could not in the 1990s export its way out of a decade of sluggishness. The economic sluggishness caused by its domestic real estate and banking problems, along with the foreign competition Japan's exports faced by then, prevented that.

The United States is in a position similar to Japan's at that time, but for somewhat different reasons. The U.S. recession was also related to real estate, banking, and credit problems, but the U.S. dollar differs markedly from the Japanese yen. From April through September 2009, the U.S. dollar fell by 11.5 percent on a trade-weighted basis (that is, the dollar fell in proportion to the currencies of its main trading partners). Some observers believed this was good, or at least not bad, because it brought the value of the dollar back to its 2007 levels against other currencies and could help boost U.S. exports. Others believe that a strong dollar is important because it helps ensure that the dollar remains the world's main reserve currency and it helps attract foreign investment to the United States. (In mid-October 2009, the dollar neared $1.50 against the euro, compared with $1.25 in March of that year, but the dollar gained ground against the euro as EU debt problems mounted in early 2010.)

Opponents of Obama cited the weak dollar as a failing of the administration, while supporters can say it doesn't matter. Perhaps a more objective view comes from Harvard professor and former International Monetary Fund chief economist Ken Rogoff, quoted at FT.com (the website of the *Financial Times*, which is one of the world's two major business and financial newspapers, the other being *The Wall Street Journal*) on October 7, 2009. "The first-order reason for the decline in the dollar has been the normalisation of markets," said Rogoff. "The financial crisis probably has brought forward the day when the dollar is no longer dominant—but maybe from 75 years to 40 years." Indeed, the October 19, 2009, *New York Times* quoted C. Fred Bergsten, director of the Peterson Institute for International Economics as saying, "The dollar went up 40 percent between 1995 and 2002, so this is a necessary rebalancing."

A near-term question, however, is whether the declining value of the dollar will boost exports to the point where the U.S. economy benefits. The answer is that it probably won't, at least not to the point where growth is ignited. That's mainly because an "export-led" recovery is difficult to achieve when the economies of key U.S. trading partners—Canada, Mexico, China, Japan, and Germany—are also sluggish. Also, the United States can allow the dollar to depreciate only so much against foreign currencies.

Because the United States is a debtor nation and depends on foreign lenders and investors for financing, it cannot afford to allow the dollar to decline by a large amount or indefinitely. Also, as the dollar declines, the price of imports to the United States—notably huge quantities of foreign oil—increases, and rising fuel costs won't help the U.S. economy. The October 19, 2009, *New York Times* also said, "The dollar's drop is a central factor in oil's recent rise back above $75 a barrel, which means higher gasoline prices." That same article pointed out that David Malpass, a Wall Street economist and critic of the dollar's decline, said, "As the dollar devalues, we have less capital and purchasing power compared to the rest of the world, and there is an increasing risk of higher interest rates and inflation." But again, a devalued dollar could help to increase U.S. export volume.

About U.S. Export and Trade Volume

As I've pointed out, the United States consistently runs international trade deficits, with imports exceeding exports virtually every year since the mid-1970s. Leaving foreign investment aside and considering only trade in goods and services, in 2008 U.S. exports grew by 12 percent to $1.8 trillion, while imports increased 7.4 percent to $2.5 trillion. In the first half of 2009, U.S. exports of goods and services *declined* by 19.3 percent, to $746 billion relative to the same period in 2008, when they totaled $925 billion. Imports fell even faster, by 28.8 percent in the first half of 2009 versus that of 2008. (These figures are from the U.S. Department of Commerce International Trade Administration.)

The good news is that the decline in U.S. exports slowed over successive quarters in 2009 because of the declining dollar and, perhaps more important, improving economic conditions among trading partners. For instance, between the first and second quarters of 2009, U.S. exports of goods and services fell by only 1.3 percent, which was quite an improvement over the decline of 11.5 percent between the last quarter of 2008 and the first quarter of 2009. Exports improved steadily in the second half of 2009 as well. According to the BEA, "Real exports of goods and services increased 17.8 percent in the third quarter and 22.4 percent in the fourth quarter." Moreover, in each of those quarters exports outpaced imports, if only barely in the fourth quarter.

Incidentally, while the U.S. manufacturing sector accounts for only 11.5 percent of the U.S. economy, U.S. products fare well in international markets. Indeed, capital goods (goods used to make other goods) are the largest goods export category for the United States, with volume of $470 billion in 2008. The United States ran a trade surplus in capital goods of almost $16 billion in 2008, with the fastest-growing categories being medicinal equipment, materials handling equipment, industrial and aircraft engines, and telecommunications equipment.

However, while manufacturing is not dead in the United States, it is certainly not as healthy as it once was. More to the point, it is not going to provide the engine of growth that the U.S. economy will require to create well over 10 million jobs in the next few years.

The Least You Need to Know

- Business investment is important to an economy because it not only represents current spending (as does consumer spending) but also expands productive capacity and thus the economy's future growth potential.
- Manufacturing has come to play a far smaller role in the U.S. economy than it did in the middle of the last century. In 1950, manufacturing accounted for 27 percent of the U.S. economy. In 2008, it accounted for 11.5 percent.
- In place of manufacturing (and farming, forestry, and fishing) the U.S. economy now relies more on business services, finance, insurance, and real estate. These industries require an educated workforce, and do not offer either the economies of scale or the export potential of manufactured goods.

- The dollar declined against the euro during much of 2009, but regained value against the EU currency as problems with debt in Greece and other European nations came to light in early 2010.

- With consumers tapped out, businesses wary, government mired in deficits, and exports unlikely to rise sharply, the U.S. economy may face several quarters, if not years, of sluggish growth.

Chapter 15

The State of the States

In This Chapter

- Dynamics of state budgets and policies
- How a few populous states have been faring
- U.S. regional economic performance
- State unemployment rates and rankings

Given the size and diversity of the U.S. economy, it's a wonder we all spend so much time discussing aggregate measures of nationwide economic activity. After all, although national growth, unemployment, income, housing, and other data are widely reported, the real action for most of us is closer to home, in our cities and states. Every city and state has its own growth, unemployment, income, housing, and other issues, which have more impact on us than national trends.

Of course national trends are important. They simultaneously represent a roll-up of the economic performance of all the individual states *and* exert influence on the states. National aggregated numbers are used to set economic policies which then play out at the state level. Also, senior corporate executives in the United States and in other nations, foreign-policy makers, and the global financial markets to varying degrees all view the U.S. economy as a whole, which affects the decisions of major companies, foreign finance ministers, and investors everywhere. Yet states and regions within the nation often differ in their economic performance, which can have a huge impact on us as individuals.

This chapter explores economic phenomena at the state level and the impact of the financial crisis and recession on specific regions of the United States, and on specific states' economic performance. We'll also examine state budget realities and the economic situations of a few key states, as well as the employment picture in the states.

Fifty Different Economies

Within the United States are 50 states with often wildly diverse industries, employment pictures, income levels, education levels, living standards, and tax and budgetary policies. Also, each member of Congress represents his or her state's interests, which often makes consensus and even progress on national economic policy difficult.

Meanwhile, each state sets economic policies of its own. The states lack the economic and policy-making power of the federal government and, of course, they have no monetary policy. However, each state sets its own income, property, and sales taxes and a huge range of fees, all of which have economic consequences, especially during a downturn.

In fact, most of the economic power of the states—at least from the standpoint of policy—resides in their taxing power and budget priorities. In general, states can generally be characterized as low-tax states (often described as *"pro-business"*) or high-tax states, the latter typically providing higher levels of government services (often educational and social services). Of course, taxes play a huge role in determining the amounts of spending the state does in areas such as police and corrections; education and social services; and roads, water treatment, and other public works.

WHAT'S THAT?

States are characterized as **pro-business,** or not, based on more than taxes. Taxes, particularly on business property and income, are part of the picture. But an equally large part is the level of regulation in areas such as working conditions, waste disposal, and required health care and other forms of insurance. In general, business people want a low-tax environment, but they also want a low-regulation environment.

The states—and the regions of the United States—have their individual demographic and industrial compositions, all of which affect households and businesses in the state and regional economies. Areas with significant employment concentrated in industries that were particularly hard-hit by the recession saw high unemployment in those sectors as well as in related, and even unrelated, industries. For instance, New York City's concentration in financial services created unemployment in that industry, which spilled over to other industries, most significantly retail, real estate, and restaurants. The troubles in the auto industry generated extremely high unemployment in Michigan, and not only in the auto industry.

In addition, states that had relatively high tax rates before the recession had difficulty raising them to close budget shortfalls during the recession, as was the case in California, which I'll discuss in this chapter.

State Budgetary Dynamics

In all but four states (Alabama, Michigan, New York, and Texas) the fiscal year begins on July 1 and ends on June 30. As of June 30, 2009, around the beginning of the end of the recession, no state could be described as being in good shape.

The effect of the crisis on state governments has been dramatic—when unemployment rises and economic activity decreases, revenue from income taxes and various fees, such as those associated with vehicle registrations and real estate transactions, also decreases. When spending by households and businesses falls, so does revenue from sales taxes. Meanwhile, in tough times state expenditures for health care, unemployment benefits, services for the needy, such as housing for the homeless, and enrollments at state colleges all increase.

All states must balance their budgets every year and, by federal law, they are not permitted to file for bankruptcy. So to balance their budgets in times of decreased economic activity they must either increase taxes and fees to maintain revenues or they must reduce expenditures. Failing either of these solutions, they must sell bonds to make up the shortfall. That's what the federal government does, but the federal government has nationwide taxing authority as well as the ability to print money, both of which the states lack.

States and municipalities compete with one another on an economic level in two ways. Some, such as Texas, try to attract businesses and residents by keeping taxes (and regulation of business) low. However, this also limits the amount of money such states can spend on services. So while Texas is generally rated among the best states to do business in, it also rates among the highest in poverty, high school dropout rates, and people without health insurance. Other states, such as California, try to attract businesses and residents by providing high levels of state services.

However, this generally translates to high taxes, as in the case of California, a state that is generally rated among the worst to do business in (at least by conservatives and quite a few business people). California has also experienced widely reported budgetary problems including a huge deficit, as discussed later in this chapter. In 1978, the state's high taxes gave rise to what became a widespread *tax revolt* movement with the passage of a ballot initiative called Proposition 13. That revolt may in turn have contributed to the election of Ronald Reagan to the presidency the following year. To this day, many groups and individuals in California are understandably resisting increases in the state's already high taxes during a towering budget deficit.

WHAT'S THAT?

The **tax revolt** movement uses public relations and campaign contributions to encourage the election of candidates who support low taxes. The movement also favors a flat tax—one tax rate for everyone—as opposed to a graduated income tax, which levies higher tax rates on higher incomes. The problem with resistance to taxes is that it has not been matched with resistance to government services and entitlement programs. Resistance to health insurance reform is one exception, but there the market has created expensive inefficiencies. Also, few tax resisters above 65 seem ready to give up their Medicare.

So when a state or city increases its taxes it can erode the tax base because businesses and households prefer low taxes. If taxes are too high, people can move out of, or avoid moving into, the state or city. However, people also prefer safe streets, public trash pickup, pure water, prompt snow removal, paid firefighters, and good schools. So there is constant tension at the state and local levels between low taxes—including property taxes, which is how most municipalities fund their expenditures—and high levels of public service.

Specific Problems at the State Level

The key problems the states face in a downturn, particularly one as severe as that of 2008–2009, include the following:

- If they raise tax rates they might discourage people from moving into the state, encourage people to move out, or hamper business formation or the sales of taxed goods.

- If they reduce expenditures, they may create new and perhaps more expensive problems. For example, reducing police or corrections expenditures can increase crime. Reducing health and housing services can increase serious illness and homelessness. Reducing education can discourage families from populating the state with children, which reduces future tax revenues.

- If the state reduces its public labor force through layoffs or early retirement, it may increase unemployment, which can increase other costs and usually reduces tax revenues.

WHAT TO DO?

Please understand that this is a broad discussion of state-level economics. For a more detailed picture, visit the left-leaning but highly analytical and well-documented site of the Center on Budget and Policy Priorities at www.cbpp.org and click on the State Budget and Tax link.

During a severe downturn, there is a risk of a continuing downward spiral of decreasing state revenues, jobs, and services, and increasing debt and interest costs. As states reduce their labor expenditures by laying off employees, instituting voluntary or involuntary furloughs, or reducing wages or benefits, they also take money away from households in the state, which further reduces spending and thus economic activity. To finance the shortfalls, the state may have to issue more debt in the form of bonds sold in the public bond markets. But doing so can reduce the state's creditworthiness and increase the interest rates it must pay on its bonds. That in turn may mean it must raise taxes or further reduce services.

The Obama stimulus package (the American Recovery and Reinvestment Act of 2009, or ARRA) contained about $135 to $145 billion in aid to the states. This helped but left most states struggling. Indeed, that amount covered only about 40 percent of the estimated aggregate state budget shortfalls of $350 billion from July 1, 2009, to December 31, 2011. Thus, as of July 1, 2009, 23 states had enacted tax increases, and another 13 had proposed increases in the works. In addition, ARRA funds were generally made available to the states only until their 2011 fiscal years end. Unless the U.S. economy were to recover to fairly robust growth by then—or Congress were to authorize additional aid and funding of this type—difficulties at the state levels will continue.

In general, states try to enact taxes and fees in ways that do not hurt those already suffering the most economic hardship, but that is not always possible. Many, if not most, of those who use state and municipal social services are children, elderly people, or ill or impoverished people (or elderly, ill, *and* impoverished). Many social services are delivered at the municipal (city or town) level and as a practical matter most municipalities have limited ability to tax residents, and do so mainly in the form of property taxes. Municipal services not covered by municipal taxes and by revenue from various fees and fines are generally covered by the states, which channel money from state taxes and, often, from the federal government to cities and towns. In general, only large cities, and major public works agencies, such as the Port Authority of New York, can issue bonds in the public financial markets.

In the Great Recession, states and some cities took various measures to increase revenues. These include increasing rates of income, sales, business, tobacco, alcohol, and motor vehicle taxes and increasing motor vehicle related fees, such as registrations and title transfers, and fees related to such things as court hearings, fines, state parks, and hunting and fishing licenses. Some states employed increases in more than one of these. Other so-called revenue enhancement measures already taken by states include reducing state income tax credits or deductions. In some cases, tax increases and other measures are temporary but certainly not in all cases.

While the increases are both more widespread and higher than in recent recessions, typically at least some states raise taxes and fees when they face budget shortfalls in a downturn. The problem is that this downturn was unusually severe—the longest since World War II.

Regions of Recession

The U.S. recession, unlike some in the past, hit the entire nation hard. Given that the housing bubble was nationwide and affected the global financial markets, the entire nation was affected. Not every region or state has suffered equally, but this is not a downturn that affects a few states and creates a very uneven recession, like the early 1990s recession, which hit the "oil patch" states of Texas and Oklahoma extremely hard. Similarly, the so-called "rust belt" states of the Midwest lost millions of jobs when manufacturing started leaving the nation in the 1980s and 1990s. Yet even in this broad-based recession, certain housing markets were hit harder than others, mainly those that saw the highest appreciation and the most new construction, such as Miami, Phoenix, Las Vegas, and California.

Regional differences and situations in specific states warrant coverage, but rather than attempt to cover 50 states in one chapter, I'll first discuss regional economic developments in this section and then, in the next section, examine a few key states. The regions we'll use are the Federal Reserve's 12 districts, which correspond to the areas served by each of the Federal Reserve Banks. Those banks and the areas they cover are the following, listed in order of the Fed's numbering system (that is, District 1 is Boston, District 2 is New York, etc.):

Boston: CT (excluding Fairfield County), MA, ME, NH, RI, and VT

New York: NY, 12 counties in northern NJ, Fairfield County in CT, Puerto Rico, and the Virgin Islands

Philadelphia: Eastern PA, southern NJ, and all of DE

Cleveland: OH, western PA, eastern KY, and northern WV

Richmond: MD, VA, NC, SC, and most of WV

Atlanta: AL, FL, GA, and parts of LA, MS, and TN

Chicago: IA and most of IL, IN, MI, and WI

St. Louis: AR and portions of MO, MS, TN, KY, IN, and IL

Minneapolis: MN, MT, ND, SD, 26 counties in northwestern WI, and MI's Upper Peninsula

Kansas City: CO, KS, NE, OK, WY, northern NM, and western MO

Dallas: TX, northern LA, and southern NM

San Francisco: AK, AZ, CA, HI, ID, NV, OR, UT, and WA, and American Samoa, Guam, and the Northern Mariana Islands

WHAT TO DO?

For more information on the Federal Reserve system and its structure, visit www.federalreserve.gov and download the first chapter of the publication *The Federal Reserve System: Purposes and Functions.*

Regional Differences

The Federal Reserve Beige Book is published eight times per year, based on information on economic conditions gathered from the regional banks and from economists, market experts, and other sources in the regions. The comments here are based on the June 2009 Beige Book, released toward the end of the recession.

Overall, although recessionary conditions persisted in mid-2009, 5 of the 12 districts reported at the time that downward trends were moderating. This had been a theme in various media reports on several areas of economic activity, such as auto sales, housing activity, and even job losses (although the overall unemployment rate continued to rise in June).

The economies of specific regions and that of the nation may have been stabilizing, at least in some respects. Where they were not, the negative trends generally appeared to be decreasing at a decreasing rate. This did not necessarily signal the end of the recession at the regional level. Also, it's quite possible for conditions to stabilize and then to improve very slowly, or for the economy to actually expand and then revert to recession. However, at that point any good news—or even less-bad news—was welcome.

Boston: In New England, manufacturing remained weak, although high tech saw some increase in orders but not employment. Spending by business was being reduced, and vacancy rates for commercial properties were still rising. Retailers saw flat (but not falling) sales and stable employment.

New York: The labor market in the tri-state area (the five boroughs of New York City and the surrounding counties) remained weak. The financial-services sector was a long way from recovery, although manufacturing had stabilized. Consumer spending rose modestly but tight credit hampered auto sales. Tourism and hotels saw no increases and new commercial construction dropped substantially. Realtors reported an uptick in new home sales.

Philadelphia: Economic activity remained slow, with declining manufacturing orders, declining demand for commercial and industrial loans, and mixed retail sales activity. New commercial construction dropped substantially. However, real estate agents saw an uptick in residential sales and a working off of some unsold existing home inventory.

Cleveland: Manufacturing orders declined while steel shipments remained at depressed levels, and weakness in automotive related industries and capital spending persisted. Shipping volume remained low, but the steep drop from earlier in the year abated. Also, home sales increased slightly and this district reported stable retail employment amid weak consumer sales.

Richmond: New orders and shipments of manufactured goods rose across a number of industries and demand for IT workers started to rise. However, commercial property vacancies continued to increase, putting downward pressure on rents. Demand for commercial loans declined. Bookings in resort areas started to pick up but were weaker than a year ago. Home sales rose slightly.

Atlanta: The pace of the decline in manufacturing moderated but hiring freezes or job cuts in the government sector were reported. New commercial construction projects had been postponed or cancelled. Soft consumer sales were expected to persist and promotions and discounts played a large role in keeping theme park and cruise bookings stable.

Chicago: Manufacturing activity declined, with the district noting that export demand was weak, except from Asia, and that auto-related manufacturing activity remained weak. Commercial vacancy rates rose and hurt overall loan demand. Home construction had stabilized at low levels and residential inventories remained elevated, but there was an uptick in home sales. New car sales rose slightly as did sales of used cars.

St. Louis: Manufacturing declined and automotive-related manufacturing remained particularly weak. Commercial real estate remained weak, with new commercial construction projects often postponed or canceled. Consumer retail sales remained soft.

Minneapolis: Manufacturing declined, but consumer spending rose slightly. Summer activity and sales at campgrounds and resorts were strong. Commercial construction dropped substantially, but residential construction stabilized at low levels.

Kansas City: Manufacturing declined but the pace of decline slowed. Consumer spending remained flat and was expected to remain that way for months. Tight credit conditions hampered new vehicle sales, although sales of used vehicles rose. Home construction saw an uptick.

Dallas: Manufacturing generally declined except in high technology. Cargo and container shipments remained at low levels, but there were encouraging signs in import and export activity. Weakness continued in construction-related manufacturing and petrochemicals. However, home sales and residential construction saw increased activity.

San Francisco: Manufacturing held steady but at continuing low levels, except in high technology, which saw an increase. The wood products industry remained depressed, and metal fabrication was extremely weak. Demand for commercial and industrial loans decreased. Residential home construction stabilized, but at low levels.

Clearly, when you break down the country into 12 regions, economic activity shows differences. Major themes definitely emerge, however, with weak or weakening manufacturing activity in most districts and commercial real estate continuing to decrease across the nation, the picture in mid-2009 remained fairly bleak. On the bright side, new home construction was stabilizing, albeit at low levels, and home sales were increasing in a number of districts. However, reasons for these increases included seasonal factors, low interest rates, declining home prices, and tax credits for first-time buyers—and most of the sales increase occurred in the lower-priced end of the market. So this did not herald a broad turnaround in the housing market. Despite increased mortgage activity in districts where residential real estate was strengthening, credit conditions generally remained tight.

As the preceding reports showed, the regional story was a mixed bag with few spots of good news and few trends signaling improvement. The mixed picture will continue until strong nationwide growth has been reestablished. In fact, even in January 2010, the Fed reported that "Reports from the twelve Federal Reserve Districts indicated that while economic activity remains at a low level, conditions have improved modestly …." That's not exactly a rave review, and it indicates how sluggish the recovery remained "on the ground" (the level at which the Fed districts make their observations), even in the fourth quarter of 2009.

Some State Stories

A few states experienced particularly dramatic changes as a result of the crisis and recession. Here are some highlights.

California

With a population of some 37 million people and, with GDP of about $1.9 trillion, the largest state economy (and the world's ninth largest), California has the biggest state budget—totaling about $110 billion for FY (fiscal year) 2010. It also has the biggest budgetary problems, with a FY 2010 budget deficit that was projected at $24 billion as of July 1, 2009, but was finally closed by the agreed-upon budget at the end of the month.

The state's Republicans and Governor Schwarzenegger held the line on tax increases, which resulted in cuts to the state budget. While cuts make almost no one happy, a state can raise taxes only so much and can deliver services at only a certain level, and it appears that California has—at least under the pressure of the recession—reached the limits on both counts. In early summer 2009 the state actually began issuing IOUs rather than checks, surely a tipping point in its finances. Shortly thereafter the budget compromise, which included heavy cuts in education and social services, was reached.

New York (Tri-State Area)

The New York City tri-state area includes the five boroughs of New York and the locales within about a 50-mile radius. The economy of this area is still heavily driven by New York City (that is, Manhattan) and, to important degrees, Brooklyn, northern New Jersey, and Queens. In recent decades key industries have been financial services, real estate, retail, media and publishing, restaurants, health care, hospitality, tourism, and personal services.

Toward the end of the bubble in 2007, financial services—and the jobs that industry supported in other industries—accounted for about 30 percent of New York City's GDP. In the recession, job losses in that industry depressed retail and restaurant activity, decreased real estate prices (which remain high by national standards), and increased commercial real estate vacancies. However, the city has often proven its resiliency (particularly after near bankruptcy in the late 1970s) and the state is in better shape than California, although the state government may be in even greater disarray.

Michigan

As the home of the Big Three automakers, Michigan is ground zero for the fallout from the restructuring of the auto industry. That was reflected in its mid-2009 unemployment rate of 15.2 percent, the highest in the nation and the highest in any state since 1984, when West Virginia exceeded 15 percent. Again, it's not only jobs lost in the auto industry, but the way those losses ripple through the state economy and affect consumer and business spending across the board. In fact, the unofficial rate has almost certainly topped 20 percent, which amounts to Depression-level unemployment. One could only hope that U.S. auto industry restructuring proceeds quickly and that consumer spending on autos and other durables picks up in earnest.

Other states were also hard-hit, as revealed by a look at state-level unemployment statistics.

State-by-State Employment Stats

As of mid-July 2009, official unemployment rates ranged from a low of 4.2 percent in North Dakota to Michigan's high of 15.2 percent. Fifteen states and Washington, D.C., had unemployment rates over the national rate of 9.5—and their rates all exceeded 10 percent.

The following states' June 2009 unemployment rates represented new records since January 1976, when the Bureau of Labor Statistics began compiling these data in this manner: Georgia, Florida, California, Nevada, Oregon, and Rhode Island. Michigan hit its record high of 16.9 percent in November 1982. All of the other states' records were established in either 1982 or 1983—the years of the worst post–World War II recession until the current one.

Sixteen Highest Unemployment States (June 30, 2009)

State	Unemployment Rate	State	Unemployment Rate
Alabama	10.1	North Carolina	11.0
Georgia	10.1	Ohio	11.1
Illinois	10.3	California	11.6
Florida	10.6	Nevada	12.0
Indiana	10.7	South Carolina	12.1
Tennessee	10.8	Oregon	12.2
District of Columbia	10.9	Rhode Island	12.4
Kentucky	10.9	Michigan	15.2

Source: Bureau of Labor Statistics

The 16 states with the lowest unemployment rates in June 2009 are shown in the following table.

Sixteen Lowest Unemployment States (June 30, 2009)

State	Unemployment Rate	State	Unemployment Rate
North Dakota	4.4	Louisiana	6.8
Nebraska	5.0	New Hampshire	6.8
South Dakota	5.1	New Mexico	6.8
Utah	5.7	Kansas	7.0
Wyoming	5.9	Vermont	7.1
Iowa	6.2	Arkansas	7.2
Oklahoma	6.3	Virginia	7.2
Montana	6.4	Maryland	7.3

Source: Bureau of Labor Statistics

You'll notice that the low unemployment states tend to be somewhat more rural relative to states with higher unemployment. Those states also tend to have economies a bit more focused on agriculture and less concentrated in a single nonagricultural industry, such as gaming and tourism in Nevada and autos in Michigan. Note that I am not implying that unemployment above 6 is "low," but rather that these 16 states were well below the national average of 9.5 percent in June 2009.

At that time the other 19 states' unemployment rates ranged from 7.4 percent in Hawaii to 9.3 percent in Washington. Bear in mind that 4 percent is considered the *national* "full employment rate," which accounts for the *frictional unemployment*. Although that does represent a national average, when you consider that in June 2009 only one state had an unemployment rate under 5 percent, you gain a new appreciation of the severity of the recession.

 WHAT'S THAT?

Frictional unemployment is the percentage of unemployment caused by people who are between jobs, essentially because they voluntarily left their jobs (but not the workforce) or are moving from one job to another. The unemployment figures measure the percentage of people who are involuntarily unemployed due to layoffs and cutbacks.

All Economics Isn't Local

Late Speaker of the House Thomas "Tip" O'Neil was fond of saying, "All politics is local." While a lot of economics is local—especially our jobs, incomes, spending, and a good portion of our taxes—the financial crisis highlighted the interconnectedness of the various sectors of the economy. That interconnectedness linked home prices, mortgage activity, financial markets, and the international banking system with manufacturing, retail, restaurant, and city and state jobs. That linkage helped generate a global financial crisis and a severe national recession with often outsized state-level effects.

We live our economic lives in our communities, cities, and states, and, given sunken home prices, few of us were moving during the recession. That means that, given that U.S. economic policies could not in practice end the recession, people were stuck with tough economic conditions and could not move to places with better employment prospects. Even in early 2010, the U.S. economy still had much debt to work off, had to adjust capacity (not just in the auto business, but also in retail and in commercial real estate), and had to come to terms with new, lower levels of consumer spending. And the major wild card remained job growth, both in specific states and regions and nationwide.

The Least You Need to Know

* States vary significantly in the effects they've experienced in the recession, depending mainly on the concentration of their industries and the size of their state budgets. However, many states were hit hard and most required federal assistance from the Obama stimulus package.

* States must by law balance their budgets and cannot declare bankruptcy. When they experience decreasing revenues due to lower tax receipts, they have three basic choices: raise tax rates (and fees), reduce services and state employment, or issue more debt (or some combination of these choices).

* States compete with one another to attract businesses and households by providing some balance between low, or at least reasonable, taxes and high, or at least reasonable, levels of state and city services. In practice, states tend to be either low-tax, pro-business states with relatively low levels of public services, or high-tax states with higher levels of public services and a bit more difficultly as business environments.

- States issue debt in the financial markets and must keep their financial houses in order or their bonds will be rated lower and they will have to pay higher interest and thus incur yet more expense.

- The United States contains regional and state economies that have their own budgetary policies and problems, industrial bases, and unemployment rates and varying abilities to deal with economic downturns.

Structural Problems in the U.S. Economy

Many economists and other observers believe that the Great Recession may represent a real turning point for the U.S. economy and the nation, rather than just a dip in the business cycle. This is because of certain structural problems in the U.S. economy. Overcapacity in the auto industry, lack of other manufacturing jobs, and high levels of public debt can worsen cyclical problems related to temporary mismatches between supply and demand. That is what occurred in the Great Recession. What could have been a mild or even a normal recession became a severe downturn that cost millions of people their jobs and hundreds of thousands of people their homes.

Part 6 examines three of the most important structural problems in the U.S. economy: public finances related to federal deficits and spending on Social Security and Medicare, the U.S. system of financing health care, and barriers to achieving sustainable economic growth. There are a few other structural problems, but these are the most pressing and appear to be the most difficult to resolve.

Taxes, Deficits, and Social Security

Chapter

16

In This Chapter

- Major elements of the federal budget
- The size of and reasons for deficits
- Is Social Security headed for crisis?
- Policy options for averting potential disaster

Much concern was voiced over the deficits in President Obama's first proposed budget, which the Democratic Congress adopted (with no Republican support) in a nonbinding resolution at the end of April 2009, and which ultimately was adopted substantially in its proposed form.

That Republican opposition raises an issue. Discussions of the federal budget and deficit spending are—there's no getting around it—political, and often devoid of meaningful content even compared with most other political discussions. Specifically, Democrats are often portrayed as not minding deficit spending, yet the lowest run-up in the national debt since 1980 occurred during the Clinton administration. Republicans voice strong dislike of deficits, yet can't seem to stop running them up. Meanwhile, the majority of U.S. voters claim to hate deficit spending, but will punish any politician who seriously wants to reduce spending or raise taxes, and they reward (at times with second terms) presidents who run up the highest deficits.

This chapter examines U.S. budget issues, particularly deficit spending, in the context of the current recession. On the subject of deficits, this chapter also examines Social Security and touches on Medicare, which together are the largest federal expenditure and which may be headed for a crisis. The extent and timing of that crisis have a lot to do with policies in effect well before the Great Recession, yet a sluggish economy will only make matters worse. We begin with a brief look at U.S. tax policy.

A Taxing Situation

Taxes and budgeting are divisive topics. Those on the political right complain about how high taxes are, although U.S. taxes are relatively low. The most comparable measure of taxes is their percent of GDP, and by that measure U.S. taxes are significantly lower than those of most other countries in the Organization for Economic Cooperation and Development (OECD). According to the OECD, total U.S. taxes—including those at the state level—average about 28 to 30 percent of GDP, compared with about 34 percent in the rest of the OECD. Opponents of taxes compare metrics such as corporate tax rates, but what matters is what those rates are applied to. Definitions of financial terms, such as income, vary wildly among nations, and corporations have many ways of lowering the taxable income.

Meanwhile, the political left complains about how much social spending the government should be doing, although social programs (Social Security and Medicare) are the largest federal budget item. They also point out that the highest earners should pay the highest share of taxes, but omit the fact that the top 20 percent of earners already pay 80 percent to, more recently, *86 percent* of total income taxes. Income taxes for the lowest 40 percent of earners are actually negative, because "refundable credits" such as the Child Tax Credit result in IRS payments to some of those households.

WHAT TO DO?

Try to view tax policies through an economic as well as a political lens. Government services are not free, and public goods (such as defense, policing, courts, and roads) make the production and enjoyment of private goods possible. The problem is not that the U.S. government is unresponsive to voters, but that it is responding to voters who largely fail to understand economic, and particularly tax, policy.

The United States does raise a larger portion of federal revenue through income taxes than other OECD nations. Those nations use higher taxes on goods and services, mainly the *value added tax* (*VAT*) and national sales taxes. That the United States favors income taxes should please the political left because those taxes are "progressive," meaning that higher earners pay a greater percentage of their incomes in taxes. Taxes on goods and services are "regressive," in that everyone pays the same rate, but the tax consumes a larger percentage of lower earners' incomes.

> **WHAT'S THAT?**
>
> The **value added tax (VAT),** which is widely used in European nations, levies a tax on a product or service as it is being produced. Thus, at each stage of production as a product moves from raw material to manufacturer to distributor, a tax is levied. The VAT is levied only on the value added (that is, the increase in the value of the product or service at that stage). In contrast, a sales tax is levied on the entire value of a product.

Despite complaints all around, most Americans seem happy with current tax policy (if not with paying taxes). Few want cutbacks on programs that benefit them, and most programs benefit them or someone they know. Politicians won't admit (at least not publicly) that cutting programs is the price of lower taxes—and they make very few substantive cuts. They talk about balancing the budget, but it's mostly just talk. Moreover, a balanced budget would not be very useful during a recession because deficit spending provides economic stimulus.

Past U.S. deficits have generated a $10 trillion national debt, on which the nation must pay interest. That interest represented 4 percent of the 2009 budget, but is expected to rise to *11 percent* in 2013. Given this, some budget surpluses in the future would be a good idea, but only after the economy recovers. Yet until then, and even beyond then, the United States faces the prospect of "deficits as far as the eye can see," as commentators often point out.

The U.S. Federal Budget

The key issues in the federal budget, as in any budget, are where the money comes from and where it goes.

Where It Goes: Composition of Federal Outlays

In most fiscal years, 53 to 56 percent of the federal budget consists of mandated expenditures—specifically, Social Security, Medicare, and Medicaid. U.S. federal fiscal years end on September 30, so that fiscal year (FY) 2011 ends on September 30, 2011. Another 4 to 10 percent of the budget consists of interest payments on the debt. They, too, are "mandated," because the Treasury cannot default on interest payments. So mandated expenditures plus interest amount to about 60 to 63 percent of total expenditures, and any administration, of either party, is stuck with that at least for now.

Social Security, Medicare, and Medicaid are the "entitlement programs" we often hear about. Many people seem to believe these are "entitlements" in the sense that the recipients *think* they're entitled to something they're not. In fact, they are entitled to the benefits because they paid into the Social Security and Medicare systems through payroll taxes. This is not to say entitlement programs can't be "reformed" by changing the eligibility or benefits, or both. But Congress would have to vote to do so, and that would anger many voters—particularly the beneficiaries, who numbered almost 51 million in 2008. Still, reform of some sort will almost certainly occur, as we'll discuss later in this chapter.

The remaining roughly 40 percent of budgeted outlays are "discretionary" programs—the budgets of the departments of Defense, Agriculture, Education, Health and Human Services, Homeland Security, Housing and Urban Development, and the others that make up the federal government. They are discretionary because Congress must approve their budgets in the appropriations process. In that process, Congress increases or decreases the president's proposed expenditures and then the budget is reconciled to resolve those differences.

How much money are we talking about? Here are the budgeted outlays for 2009 through 2013, as reflected in the documents for President Obama's 2011 budget.

Projected Budgeted Outlays for 2009 to 2013 (in Billions of Dollars)

	2010	2011	2012	2013	2014
Discretionary:					
Defense/Security	855	895	827	811	825
All Others	553	520	475	456	457
Subtotal Discretionary[1]	1,408	1,415	1,301	1,267	1,283
Mandatory:					
Soc. Security	715	730	762	801	845
Medicare and Medicaid	726	788	775	848	936
Other	682	648	571	547	584
Subtotal Mandatory[1]	2,123	2,165	2,107	2,208	2,364
Net Interest	188	251	343	436	571
Disaster Costs[2]	1	3	4	4	4
Total Outlays	3,721	3,834	3,755	3,915	3,386

1 Subtotals and totals may be off by one due to rounding differences.

2 Budgeted for payments in case of federally declared disasters.

WHAT TO DO?

Visit the Office of Management and the Budget at www.whitehouse.gov/omb for full documentation of the administration's budget.

Most of the budget is set in stone, or at least wet concrete. Mandated payments have to be funded unless Congress changes the laws governing the entitlement programs. Add in Defense, Homeland Security, Agriculture, and the other departments, and you've got a huge budget that's extremely difficult to reduce.

Thus, most budget arguments amount to political posturing, as is the case with the much-reviled "earmarks" associated with pork-barrel spending. Earmarks don't affect the budget. They are just the way legislators direct certain *already appropriated* funds to local officials or campaign donors in their districts or states. Earmarks are evidence of politicians' financial fecklessness and the system of "legal graft" that funds their campaigns. But total annual earmarked spending averages less than $10 billion and less than 2 percent of the appropriations bill. In a federal budget that's over $3 trillion, that's not even a rounding error.

The president and legislators—and lobbyists—do argue over allocations for certain programs within the departments, such as specific weapons systems, or housing or education initiatives (such as No Child Left Behind). And the president and Congress do reallocate priorities, as when President Reagan called for significantly increased defense spending. Yet nothing or no one seems capable of stopping the growth in the federal budget.

That's actually not necessarily a bad thing, given that, as noted previously, government in the United States amounts to a lower percentage of GDP than in most other OECD nations. Recall that GDP = C + I + G + (Ex − Im). Government is a key part of the economy. Government also includes state and city expenditures (not discussed here), but many state expenditures are funded partly by federal tax dollars. In fact, most Americans agree—even if they think they don't—that government at various levels should represent about 30 percent of the economy, which it does in most years.

Thus, the major question is, how do we pay for it?

Where It Comes From: Composition of Receipts

Individual income taxes are the largest single source of federal funding. Add in Social Security and Medicare payroll taxes, and you've got about 80 percent of the funding. Of total receipts, 44 to 48 percent come from income taxes, and another

25 to 28 percent from Social Security taxes in most years. However, as discussed next, money collected from Social Security is being used, and has been used for decades, to fund general government expenditures as well as Social Security benefits.

Corporate taxes account for 8 to 10 percent of receipts, and the other 10 to 12 percent—which is 100 percent less the 80 percent from individuals and payroll taxes less the 8 to 10 percent from corporate taxes—comes from federal excise and estate taxes, customs duties, and the like.

Whether the current system is "fair" is debatable. It may be a bit too progressive given that about 40 percent of the populace pays no income taxes. Those people are thus not technically "taxpayers" and may therefore have less motivation to monitor the government and to vote. Some people see corporate taxes as a deterrent to business activity, while others note that corporations benefit from government services and should therefore pay taxes. The owners—the shareholders—pay taxes, but pay less on capital gains when they sell the stock than they do on dividends. So there are many ways to view and argue about the current system.

The key issues in funding the government, particularly during this difficult economic time, concern deficit spending and the future of Social Security and Medicare.

The Ballooning Federal Deficit

The Obama budget called for spending to exceed receipts by $1.6 trillion in FY 2010. This follows the deficit of $1.4 trillion in FY 2009 (George W. Bush's final budget), or about 10 percent of GDP. Most economists consider deficits of 3 percent of GDP acceptable, and over 5 percent as high. The 2011 Obama budget projected a $1.3 trillion deficit in 2011, followed by $828 billion in 2012, $727 billion in 2013, and $706 billion in 2014. As a percent of GDP, these deficits amount to 8.3 percent in 2011, 5.1 percent in 2012, 4.2 percent in 2013, and 3.9 percent in 2014. For the five years 2010 through 2014, deficits are projected to total $5.8 trillion. That's in addition to the $10 trillion in debt already on the books.

Those projections also may be based on spending projections and economic assumptions that may be too optimistic. Indeed, as the March 23, 2009, *Wall Street Journal* reported, the Congressional Budget Office (CBO) states that Obama's proposals will cost considerably more than projected. Some of the overage was due to the CBO's higher projected expenditures on entitlements and to the CBO's lower projections for economic growth.

In any event, the deficits are going to be substantial. And they will have to be funded by adding to the already towering national debt.

The Effect of the Obama Budgets

Deficit spending claims a portion of future generations' taxes, generates financial laxity in both government and society, and leads people to believe there's a free lunch. It may also create more U.S. debt securities than the world may be willing to purchase (at least at affordable interest rates), and high federal borrowing may suck up some capital that would have been put into business investment.

The Obama budgets have two policy goals. In the near term, they are meant to stimulate the economy, a goal whose necessity has been well documented and widely (although not completely) accepted by the populace. In the long term, they are meant to reverse what the budget statement called "a legacy of misplaced priorities."

Anyone who has not been living in a tree knows that President Bush's priorities included lower taxes on the highest earners, wars in Iraq and Afghanistan, and expanded spending on homeland security (and the creation of that department) and on prescription drug benefits. Which (if any) of these priorities was misplaced has been extensively argued elsewhere. What is not arguable is that cutting taxes while increasing spending generated extraordinarily high deficits, which Obama inherited and which limited the government's fiscal policy options during the recession. (The war in Iraq is the only war in U.S. history during which taxes were reduced.)

Moreover, the extraordinarily high deficits under George W. Bush occurred during a six-year economic expansion. However, in a recession, deficit spending represents the only fiscal policy option. When investors stop investing, businesses stop hiring, and consumers stop spending, economic stimulus has to come from somewhere. President Reagan realized this in his first term, and Obama realized it in his.

Thus, the Obama budget has pluses and minuses. On the plus side, it provided stimulus and may start to reverse the income-distribution patterns that eroded the lower four quintiles' share of national income over the past 35 years (as described in Chapter 11). It will also shuffle spending priorities to a degree, more in favor of social programs but without cutting back on much else. On the minus side, it will generate large deficits, add to the national debt, potentially crowd out private investment, and perhaps erode the value of the dollar. Whether or not the more ambitious goals of expanding health insurance to the uninsured and bolstering education come to pass remain to be seen. And whether those goals are pluses or minuses depends on your political views.

Your view of Social Security also depends on those views, although from a practical standpoint, no one seems to be refusing to cash their Social Security checks.

The Biggies: Social Security and Medicare

As previously noted, Social Security and Medicare (and Medicaid, which I'll lump in with "Medicare" in this discussion) account for about 52 to 56 percent of federal expenditures. Clearly, Republicans have a point when they say that social programs have bloated the federal budget. But there are other, even larger, issues around Social Security.

Social Security tax payments go into the general revenue fund and can be—and are—used to fund programs other than Social Security. For the past several decades, the workforce has been larger than the retiree population, and payments into the system have exceeded benefits paid out, creating a "Social Security surplus." That surplus is the amount in a given fiscal year by which the amount collected in Social Security taxes exceeds the payments to beneficiaries. This raises the subject of the *Social Security Trust Fund*, a topic of great confusion and controversy.

WHAT'S THAT?

The **Social Security Trust Fund,** created in 1983, is an accounting convention used to track the money collected as Social Security taxes but spent on other programs. The "fund" holds U.S. bonds, which are essentially IOUs written by the U.S. government to itself. It is not a "trust fund" in the usual sense of the term, with money invested in marketable securities.

The Social Security Trust Fund

Social Security has always been a pay-as-you-go program. Right from the start, taxes on workers were used to pay the benefits of the retirees, surviving spouses, and people with disabilities collecting them. That works as long as there are enough workers paying enough Social Security taxes to fund the current retirees' benefits. But in the early 1980s, officials foresaw the day when there would not be enough workers to support the retirees. (The birth of the 76 million baby boomers from 1946 to 1965 and their delayed entry into parenthood were the tip-offs.)

The National Commission on Social Security Reform was created in 1983 to examine Social Security funding. This commission was headed by future Federal Reserve Chairman (and future opponent of taxes) Alan Greenspan and is known as the Greenspan Commission. This commission recommended raising the Social Security tax, with the provision that the "surplus funds" go into a trust fund to secure the benefits for those paying into the Social Security system, which, by the way, is mandatory, just like paying income taxes.

The Social Security Trust Fund is, depending on whom you believe, either a fund in the true sense of the term, or a mere means of accounting for future beneficiaries' claims against future taxes. Everything in my financial background tells me it is the latter (and I support the program, though definitely not the way it has been handled).

It is a trust fund in the sense that it does have assets: Treasury bonds in the amount that the Social Security program has "loaned" to the federal government each year, the Social Security surplus. In other words, the Social Security surplus funds go into general revenue with the rest of your taxes and is *spent by the federal government every year.* In return, the government issues special, non-negotiable Treasury bonds to the trust fund. In the years since the fund was created, it has accumulated over $2 trillion in government bonds.

In the world of finance—not government finance, but private-sector finance—a trust fund consists of money invested in real assets, such as income-producing property, or, more often, financial assets that yield interest or dividends. The Treasury bonds in the trust fund do pay about 5.5 percent. But make no mistake: this is simply the government selling its own bonds to itself and then paying itself interest, all by means of accounting entries.

Thus the "trust fund" does not fit the usual, financial definition of the term. A genuine trust is a legally binding agreement in which one party (the trustee) holds assets for the benefit of another party (the beneficiary), usually at the direction of the party that originally owned the assets (the trustor). The Social Security Trust Fund does not fund anything. It is simply a claim maintained by a federal program against future revenues or against future debt sold to the public. Those who believe in the financial viability of the trust fund point out that the features of the Social Security program— the terms of eligibility and the benefits—are set by law, and that is true. However, that law can—by law—be changed by Congress. Future beneficiaries have no truly binding, permanent claim to the future benefits because Congress can legally change the features of the program.

Those who see the Treasury bonds in the trust fund as real assets are correct—they *are* U.S. government bonds. But—and this point is critical—those bonds do not represent actual money saved and invested, as securities in a private pension fund or a true trust fund would. (Ironically, they represent actual money that has been *spent on other programs*.) The bonds are backed by the full faith and credit of the U.S. government, meaning its power to levy taxes, issue debt, and, if necessary, print money.

All of this gives rise to one of the largest questions in public finance: Is Social Security headed for a crisis?

> **WHAT TO DO?**
>
> Please familiarize yourself with the workings of the Social Security program, in particular the "trust fund." It is, in my opinion, the worst financial scam ever perpetrated by the U.S. government on the nation's taxpayers. The actual problem is that the age of eligibility for retirement benefits was not increased as the life span of U.S. citizens increased. Money paid into the program has funded participants' benefits, but it has also funded hundreds of billions of dollars of other, totally unrelated expenditures.

Social Security Crisis—Coming or Not?

First, what do we mean by "Social Security crisis"? A relatively few people define it as the point at which the Social Security program starts collecting less in taxes than it pays out in benefits. That's the year when Social Security no longer operates completely on a pay-as-you-go basis. In its annual Performance and Accountability Report for 2009, the Social Security Administration (SSA) puts that date at 2016, one year sooner than the estimate in its 2008 report. Thus, in 2016 the Social Security program will need to redeem bonds—the government will have to start paying them back—to make up the shortfall between Social Security taxes collected and benefits to be paid. (What occurs at that point might be termed the Social Security deficit.)

Other people define the crisis as the point at which the Social Security Trust Fund itself runs out of Treasury bonds to redeem. This is the point at which the program is insolvent—when it is unable to pay its obligations as they come due. The same 2009 SSA report projected that the trust fund will be exhausted in 2037, four years sooner than the estimate in its 2008 report. That means that at *current* tax rates and *current* benefit levels, the fund would be completely depleted in 2037 and, of course, the Social Security taxes collected at the time would fall well short of the level of benefit payments to be funded.

The estimated dates—when Social Security must redeem bonds, and when it will run out of bonds—were brought forward, from 2017 to 2016 and from 2041 to 2037, respectively, because of the recession. During the Great Recession, more than 8 million people lost their jobs, resulting in lower payroll tax collections for Social Security and Medicare. The SSA does not calculate that economic recovery will enable the fund to recover those lost taxes in the reported time periods.

That 2009 report also points out that the projected 75-year shortfall (which would take us out to the year 2083) is $5.3 trillion (up from $4.3 trillion in the 2008 report). You will hear that figure thrown about at times in discussions, as in—"The Social Security Administration itself projects a $5.3 trillion shortfall"—and it's true. It's a huge number, which over that 75-year period equals 2 percent of the payrolls to which taxes can be applied and about 0.7 percent of GDP. It's most likely that any actual crisis, to the extent that we can date it, would occur somewhere between 2025 and 2037.

However, it's largely an issue of demographics, as well as one's definition of crisis. Baby boomers retiring at the age of 66 in 2016 will have been born in 1950. (For Social Security purposes, retirement age for people born 1943–1954 is 66.) Given that the boomers were born from 1946 to 1965, that leaves tens of millions of them in the workforce, paying Social Security taxes, which minimizes the amount of bonds that must be redeemed. In fact, if all baby boomers were to retire at 66, the last one would hang up his (or her) spikes in 2031.

But millions of baby boomers plan to continue working past the age of 66—in many cases well past it. Many of them are self-employed. Many lack the pension programs that their parents enjoyed. Many haven't saved enough for retirement, and many others lost ground in the financial crisis and realize that they cannot live on that money and Social Security anyway. Many simply don't want to retire, at least not at 66, which is a lot younger than it used to be.

The actual ages at which baby boomers retire and start drawing benefits are the wild cards in this scenario. Senior citizens are by and large healthier, more active, and more involved in work-as-fulfillment than prior generations. That means that the boomers may well start drawing benefits after the age of eligibility. The bad news (in a sense) is that they will live longer and thus draw down benefits longer than previous generations, but that has been considered in the calculations of current "crisis" dates.

Potential Responses to the Potential Crisis

The bonds in the trust fund can be redeemed only with money collected from tax-payers or raised from investors purchasing Treasury securities. Thus the actual crisis represented by Social Security occurs if or when increased taxes or debt become a drag on the economy, or when investors start demanding onerous interest rates on Treasury securities.

No one can accurately forecast those dates, because they largely depend on the growth and performance of the U.S. economy over the period in question and on baby boomers' retirement decisions. The financial crisis and the recession caused many people to question the prospects for economic growth and performance in the years ahead and, like it or not, a good portion of the boomers will begin claiming their benefits in the late 2010s and the 2020s. The people running the SSA and the Treasury realize that benefits can be paid only by redeeming the bonds, and that the trust fund is, again, essentially an accounting convention used to track the money collected as Social Security taxes but spent on other programs. So "reform" of the program is almost a certainty in the not-too-distant future.

Indeed, the 2008 SSA Performance and Accountability Report said, "Possible reform alternatives being discussed—singularly or in combination—are: 1) increasing payroll taxes, 2) slowing the growth in benefits, or 3) increasing expected returns by investing" in private securities in various ways. The second approach—slowing growth in benefits—means raising the age for some or all beneficiaries, lowering the level of benefits, or *means-testing eligibility*. Any of these measures would require a change to the current law governing Social Security.

WHAT'S THAT?

Means-testing eligibility is the process of applying guidelines for income, assets, or other measures of financial well-being to determine whether a person or household is eligible for the benefits of a government program. As it stands now, both Social Security and Medicare are entitlement programs, meaning that all citizens who paid taxes to fund the programs become eligible for benefits regardless of their income or assets. Means-testing these programs is extremely controversial, because people paid into them on the understanding that they would receive the benefits.

The SSA itself has expressed concerns, yet concerns do not necessarily equal a "crisis" in Social Security. Indeed, those who see no crisis point out that:

- The government cannot default on the Treasury bonds held in the Social Security Trust Fund anymore than it can default on its bonds held by other parties, so program viability until 2037 is assured.

- Our elected officials will honor the understanding under which voters paid their Social Security taxes, even if it means raising taxes or selling more debt to the public.

- Economic growth and increasing productivity—and perhaps additions to the workforce through immigration—will increase tax revenues and fund more of the benefits than currently estimated.

No one seriously posits that the U.S. government will default on its Treasury obligations, let alone "go broke." During George W. Bush's administration, there was talk about Social Security "going broke" as he and other Republicans promoted their plan to partially "privatize" the program, allowing citizens to put their money in their own investment accounts. But it's difficult to tell how much they believed it and how much was simply an effort to sell the plan. On the surface, partial privatization—investing some of the trust fund in publicly traded securities rather than non-negotiable Treasury bonds—is not a bad idea. But we would need many safeguards regarding the quality of the securities invested in and market fluctuations in their value. The fact remains, however, that the U.S. government will continue to honor its Treasury obligations.

Therefore, viability, of a sort, until 2037 is more or less assured—"more or less" because the date could again be adjusted for economic sluggishness. But those who say there's no need for reform either do not understand the nature of the trust fund or are unaware of the fact that benefits must be paid in cash, not in non-negotiable Treasury bonds. In truth, the 1983 Social Security solution proposed by the Greenspan Commission and implemented during Reagan's first term did nothing to "shore up" Social Security. Instead, it was a tax increase, plain and simple, and the proceeds went into the general revenue fund in exchange for Treasury bonds.

The tax increase was perhaps necessary to justify the accounting entries that constitute the "trust fund" and thus the amount of the future claims of the people in the workforce at that time and since. Yet the rules of the program—and the "claims" of the trust fund—can be changed by Congress at any time.

Voters who believe that their benefits are secure are counting on one or both of two things: first, that legislators will not vote to raise the age of eligibility, lower benefits, or means-test eligibility; and second, that economic and productivity growth will fund future benefits even with a workforce that will be significantly smaller than the number of retirees. However, neither of those are sure things.

The Real Problem: Piling Up Debt

The United States has just seen a long period of tremendous economic and productivity growth. Yet in that period, from 1980 to 2008, the nation increased the national debt (including the bonds issued to the Social Security Trust Fund) from $900 billion to $10 trillion. In the same period, GDP grew from $2,790 billion ($2.8 trillion) to $14,265 billion ($14.3 trillion). Thus, in that period of tremendous growth, the national debt grew from about 32 percent of GDP to about 70 percent of GDP.

This amounts to economic idiocy. In a time of strong growth, *the nation chose policies that put it significantly deeper into debt.* Despite all the productivity gains attributable to an educated workforce, increased investment, technological innovation, and improved business processes, the U.S. national debt as a percentage of GDP *more than doubled.* This implies that future Social Security beneficiaries, at least those intending to retire in the next 20 years, should not count on increased economic growth and productivity to produce the funds that will redeem the bonds in the trust fund and pay for their benefits.

Why? Because, even with strong increases in economic growth and productivity *over a period of more than 25 years*, the government still ran up huge deficits and increases in the public debt. Americans have proven that they will not save enough to fund their retirement, and are not willing to pay taxes at rates that will fund both Social Security and other government programs.

That leaves "reforming" Social Security as the realistic option. Indeed, President Obama has put "tackling entitlement programs" on his To Do list. He may be just the man for the job. Just as the Republican anticommunist Richard Nixon could establish U.S. relations with the People's Republic of China, perhaps the Democrat Barack Obama can reform Social Security. He would need Congress to go along, but if Obama can lead the effort and sell it to the baby boomers, then increased eligibility ages and means-testing are the likely solutions to what will indeed be a crisis, albeit a slow-motion one.

Healing Medicare

Many observers and analysts see a *Medicare* crisis as even more likely in the near term. Medicare, the second largest U.S. social insurance program, covers 44 million beneficiaries and comprises a four-part plan: Part A, Hospital Insurance, covers bills for hospital stays and surgeries; Part B, Supplemental Medical Insurance, covers procedures not covered by Part A, including diagnostics and outpatient treatment; Part C, Medicare Advantage Plan, allows beneficiaries to obtain benefits through subsidized private insurance; Part D, Prescription Drug Benefit, provides subsidized medications, and was passed under George W. Bush.

WHAT'S THAT?

Medicare is a federal, single-payer health insurance program for U.S. citizens 65 years of age and over. The services are delivered mainly through private-sector caregivers, hospitals, and clinics, which are reimbursed for their services by the program. This is not to be confused with Medicaid, which is a state-level program for people under 65 who cannot afford care.

As noted earlier in this chapter, Medicare is funded out of federal payroll taxes, but also—in the cases of Parts B and D—by premiums paid by plan members (currently $96.40 per month). Like Social Security, this is a pay-as-you-go system in which current benefits are funded largely by taxes collected on current members of the workforce. Like Social Security, the system faces looming stress due to the aging of the baby boomers plus the additional pressures of rapidly rising health-care costs. Indeed, in its analysis of Medicare, the Congressional Budget Office (CBO) notes that rising health-care costs will contribute more to rising Medicare costs than the aging of the population. It also points out, logically enough, that policy changes can do more to affect the former than the latter.

Policy changes are certainly in order. CBO projections state that Medicare and Medicaid equaled 4 percent of GDP in 2007, but that figure will rise to 9 percent in 2032 and to 19 percent in 2082. Although 2082 is a long way off, the clear trend is for health-care costs to chew up an ever larger portion of the federal budget.

Obama proposed more effective plan administration and oversight, and pushed for voluntary health-care cost controls—the latter representing more a hope than a plan. The forces fueling Medicare growth lay in demographic trends and in the U.S. approach to paying for and delivering health care. About one third of total health-care costs are incurred in the last year of people's lives, which points to heavy medical intervention when it does little good. People who have Medicare or private insurance also have little incentive to curb their spending, which creates "overutilization." That problem is exacerbated by some physicians, who order unnecessary tests or "over-treat" patients due either to their medical philosophy or to the practice of defensive medicine, which provides some protection against malpractice suits.

The entire matter of financing health care—and, in particular, extending coverage to the 45 million Americans who have neither private nor public insurance—will be debated for some time. (It will also be covered in greater depth in Chapter 17.) The Obama administration has been committed to expanding coverage, as did the Bush administration with the prescription drug plan. The question is, how will the U.S. taxpayer be able to fund these plans? It's a particularly compelling question if longer-term economic growth slows and investors (that is, purchasers of securities) become more concerned about the level of U.S. debt.

In sum, deficit spending has costs associated with it, and Obama's projected shortfalls—as high as they are—depend on economic forecasts that may turn out to be optimistic. On the plus side, the economy has returned to growth, and the world still has faith in U.S. Treasury securities. On the downside, neither projected growth nor endless deficit spending represent surefire ways to finance spending. As Obama has said in other contexts, we need a "game changer," and it does not appear that one is on the immediate horizon.

The Least You Need to Know

- In the United States, the government plays a smaller role in the economy than governments in most other developed nations. Another difference is that U.S. tax policy emphasizes income taxes over taxes on goods and services.

- The federal budget is largely set by long-standing national priorities, as reflected in permanent departments created by the federal government (most recently, Homeland Security), and by legal obligations to fund entitlement programs.

- Deficit spending can stimulate growth, but if continued at high rates without commensurate investments in infrastructure and without the ensuing productivity growth, it increases the tax burden on future generations. Heavy deficit spending can also generate burdensome interest payments and even undermine a nation's currency.

- The Social Security Trust Fund is viewed by some as an actual trust fund that obligates the government to pay future beneficiaries the legally specified amounts, and by others as an accounting device that enables the federal government to spend the Social Security surplus on general outlays. In fact, the law can be changed to affect future benefits and the past surpluses have been spent on general outlays.

- Medicare faces serious funding difficulties as baby boomers age and health-care costs skyrocket. The only meaningful ways to address funding shortfalls in Medicare or Social Security are to increase taxes or to reduce outlays (by raising the age of eligibility, reducing payouts, or means-testing eligibility).

- Reducing entitlement spending requires elected officials to either raise taxes or reduce or limit extremely popular programs. Either way they risk their reelection chances, but they will have to risk implementing one or the other solution at some point in the near future.

Curing the Sickness of U.S. Health Care

In This Chapter

- What we mean by health care and health insurance
- Why the U.S. health-care system is hard to change
- Key challenges facing the U.S. health-care system
- Policy options for delivering health care

Few topics in U.S. economic policy are as complex, emotionally charged, and as vital to the nation's global competitiveness as health care. Yet many Americans are misinformed about national health-care policy and fail to comprehend the debate that surrounds it. That's understandable, given the many perspectives, technicalities, and distortions involved in the issue. Politicians haven't helped matters, with Democrats developing overly complex initiatives and Republicans arguing for the status quo.

This chapter sheds some light on the topic, while recognizing that there are no easy or inexpensive solutions to the U.S. health-care problem. I begin this chapter by distinguishing between health care and health insurance, a distinction that's rarely made clear. Then I present the challenges and the policy options the United States faces in these areas. My aim in this chapter is to provide guidance on the health-care debate so you can make up your own mind about the policies that might work best.

What does this have to do with the financial crisis and the Great Recession? In the recession, more than 8 million workers lost their jobs. Many of those workers had employer-paid (actually, partly employer-paid) health insurance as a benefit, for themselves and often for their families. When those workers lost those jobs, they and their families lost their health insurance, or had to start buying it on their own on the more expensive individual market. Indeed, in the recession, more than 4 million people lost their health insurance for various reasons.

Formidable fiscal challenges surround health care. Government costs incurred to fight the recession added to budget deficits that were piled up before the recession. As the portion of the 65 and over population grows, the costs of Medicare will also grow. In 2009, health care accounted for 17 percent of U.S. GDP—about twice what the average industrial nation spends—and U.S. outcomes are often no better, and in several areas worse, than in those nations.

Thus, the current U.S. system of health insurance—based mainly on private insurance partly paid by employers and on Medicare—is unsustainable. This is in contrast to all other industrial nations, each of which has either a national health-care system owned and operated by the government, like Britain, or a largely tax-funded health-insurance system, like Canada. This chapter will explain some options for, and obstacles to, addressing the situation.

The Current U.S. System

You may feel that basic health care is a right and should be available to people regardless of their ability to pay. If so, then you believe health care is what economists call a *public good* that, like national defense and primary and high school education, should be provided by the government. Or you may feel it is a *private good*, one that each of us is responsible for providing for ourselves. If so, you'll probably favor health care delivered through private entities, paid for by people directly from their incomes or with insurance purchased by them.

WHAT'S THAT?

A **public good** benefits everyone, but no one has an individual economic incentive to pay for or provide it; highways and national defense are two examples. A **private good** primarily benefits the individual, and individuals are willing to pay for it. Food and automobiles are two examples of private goods.

U.S. policy treats health care as a part-public, part-private good. It is a public good in that the government pays for health care for veterans of military service and for people 65 years of age and over. It is a private good in that everyone else, except people in poverty, who are often covered by state-run Medicaid programs, must pay for their own health insurance or health care. Most of those people do so with help from their employers, who deduct the cost of their insurance premiums from their taxable income. That, in a sense, amounts to a government subsidy.

Except for Veterans Administration hospitals, virtually all health care in the United States is delivered by private institutions and private practitioners. So as is often the case, the United States uses a mix of government and market mechanisms to deliver something that everyone needs. This is also the case with education and transportation, and it can be an effective system.

Health Care vs. Health Insurance

Many people—including many politicians—fail to distinguish between health care and health insurance, although they are two different businesses. I find it useful to think of *health care* as focused on delivering care to patients in hospitals, emergency rooms, and other clinical settings. Health care in this sense includes caregivers, their employers, and the enterprises that supply them with equipment, products, and services. That part of the U.S. health-care system is almost completely in the private sector, and no one is suggesting that should change.

What we call *health insurance* is a payment mechanism. Health insurance functions differently than most other lines of insurance. Insurance usually serves to spread risk (such as risk of death, auto accident, or fire) across a pool of insured people or entities. In exchange for premiums, the insurer agrees to compensate the insured for losses arising from the risk. The premium is calculated to reflect the risk and the potential compensation by actuarial methods, which calculate the premiums required to compensate those who will suffer the loss (deceased spouses, totaled cars, burned-down buildings) and to cover the insurer's expenses and profits.

However, health-insurance premiums typically don't compensate the insured for a specific amount—the $500,000 face amount of the life insurance policy; the loss of a $30,000 car; or the $2 million to replace a building. Rather, it pays for a level of care that can be quite open-ended, because nobody can foresee which disease, disorder, or physical illness a person may suffer, what treatment will cost, or for how long. The patient could become incapacitated and require care and payouts for the rest of his life. Indeed, doctors are generally committed to keeping patients alive and in the best possible health regardless of costs. Actuarial methods do enable health insurers to calculate premiums. But almost everyone becomes injured or ill at some time in their lives—and everyone dies and usually receives some level and length of care during the dying process.

Therefore, insurance is a payment mechanism in a way that life, auto, or fire insurance is not. After all, most buildings do not catch fire and not every motorist has an accident. Everyone does die, but that's why life insurance is written for a specific amount. The open-ended nature of health insurance—and of the insurer's commitment—has fueled high usage and high costs in the U.S. health-care system.

> **WHAT TO DO?**
>
> Never, ever, go without health-care insurance if at all possible. If you're young and healthy, strapped for cash, or both, you may be tempted to forego the expense. However, a serious illness or accident can happen to anyone, and without health insurance you can wind up with substandard care or in a financial mess.

Health-Care Reform or Insurance Reform?

No one has seriously proposed overhauling the U.S. *health-care* system but rather the *health-insurance* system. In the United States, health-care reform is actually health-insurance reform, although reducing the costs of health care is part of that reform. Many people seeking health-insurance reform want to reduce the role of the private insurers in the U.S. system, mainly for the following reasons:

- They want to de-link health insurance (and thus health care) from income.
- They want to de-link health insurance from employment.
- They feel the health-insurance industry doesn't add enough value.
- They want to improve cost controls and care.
- They want to improve U.S. companies' global competitiveness.

Private health insurance means that people pay for their insurance or health care out of their own pockets rather than through taxes. Thus, people with more money receive better health care. Supporters of health-insurance reform argue that health care is a public right, so it isn't fair that more money equals better health care.

In the U.S. system, employers pay part of their employees' premiums. If the employee loses her job or moves to an employer who doesn't offer health insurance, she must buy it on her own. Supporters of *portable health insurance* want to de-link insurance and employment.

Many people feel the health-insurance industry does only administrative work that the government could do more efficiently. This is arguably true and, in fact, insurers have an incentive *not* to pay for care. Private insurers account for about 15 percent of total health-care costs in the United States, but they deliver no actual care and provide mainly billing and administrative functions. You might think that would control costs, but it hasn't. In fact, Medicare has lower administrative costs than private health insurers (who have selling expenses), *and* Medicare does not have to turn a profit.

> **WHAT'S THAT?**
>
> **Portable health insurance** is health insurance that follows a person from employer to employer, and remains in effect even when the person has no employer. It is health insurance that does not depend on having a job. Although most people in the United States can purchase private insurance, relatively few can afford it without an employer's group plan (and rates) and the employer paying part of the premiums.
>
> **Evidence-based care** uses objective data and studies of illness, treatments, and outcomes to determine what treatments should be pursued and paid for. To some extent, evidence-based care can substitute for caregivers' judgments, but it can also simply inform and support those judgments.

Although insurers have done little to rein in costs, they have developed *evidence-based care* and consistent protocols. However, some of those efforts piggyback off work done by Medicare. The key issue in the costs-versus-care argument is that the insurer is a major third party between doctor and patient. Supporters of national health insurance believe that "government bureaucrats" will interfere less in that relationship than "profit-oriented corporate executives," and better control costs.

Every other major industrial economy has a national health or health-insurance program, funded by taxes. That means that companies in those nations do not have that expense. That expense helped to erode the competitiveness of the U.S. auto industry, and made health insurance a major bargaining point in the federal rescue of GM and Chrysler in early 2009. Of course, nations with national health insurance may devote more tax money to health insurance, but their overall cost of health care is lower. Having to pay for health insurance has made U.S. industry less competitive and has cost the economy manufacturing jobs.

Yet *nobody* in Congress or the Obama administration has proposed closing down the health-insurance industry or doing away with the right to pay for health care or health-care insurance privately. Even in Britain, which has true nationalized health care, an individual or family can purchase private insurance or pay their hospitals or caregivers directly. That said, an affordable national health-insurance program would certainly reduce the market share of health-insurance companies and drive some out of business. People who want national health insurance are okay with that, although even many of them would favor gradual introduction of national health insurance.

People who oppose universal government coverage often do so on the grounds that the government is inefficient compared with private industry. Yet they also claim that even offering everyone the option of a national health-insurance program would drive private insurers out of business. This argument lacks logic; a less-efficient operation cannot drive out a more-efficient operation in a market economy. If government subsidies make it more efficient—well, isn't efficiency what we're shooting for? Private colleges and universities thrive along with state colleges and universities. Private transportation operates alongside public transportation. Private investment and savings programs exist despite the presence of the Social Security program. Even private security firms thrive despite public police forces. A public health-insurance program in and of itself won't drive private insurers out of a market.

Also, no one has proposed a national system of health care—only health insurance. Private health insurance would remain available under all proposed reforms. In other words, anyone who says that health-insurance reform as proposed by the Obama administration is "socialized" medicine or health care is either mistaken or dishonest.

Why the U.S. System Is So Hard to Change

Despite skyrocketing costs, 47 million uninsured, and Medicare's financial problems, the U.S. system is quite hard to change. Many politicians have tried to change it over the past century, but without much success. The two main exceptions were President Johnson's passage of Medicare in the 1960s and George W. Bush's passage of the Medicare prescription drug benefit in the 2000s. (As I write this, the Obama health-care plan just passed, but most key provisions are not scheduled to take effect until 2014.)

There are four reasons that changing the U.S. health-insurance and health-care system is so difficult.

Health Care Is Complicated

When someone is seriously injured or ill, health care becomes a matter of life and death. It is also expensive, particularly in life and death situations. Caregivers, hospitals, nursing homes, clinics, insurers, government agencies, and patients all have their own, often competing interests. The procedures, cost structure, uncertainties about outcomes, political agendas, and insurance policies themselves add still more complexity.

Most People Are Happy

Forty-seven million people are without health insurance and the U.S. population is about 300 million. Thus, about 85 percent of the population has private health-care insurance or Medicare, and they are happy with that insurance and with their health care. They may not be happy with the cost of the insurance, and there are horror stories (many true) about people having their coverage pulled when they became ill or were denied coverage due to a real or trumped-up preexisting condition.

But most people, for now, are happy. They also fear that their private or Medicare coverage will change if the tens of millions of uninsured became insured. In other words, most of the roughly 250 million insured Americans see little reason to change the system.

People Feel Insulated from the Costs

The current insurance system encourages caregivers, institutions, and patients to use more rather than fewer services. In many diagnosis and treatment situations, there is very little incentive to limit the use of services. That's because the caregivers, institutions, and patients all see themselves as not paying for the services. All of the costs *appear to be* borne by the insurer.

Yet for-profit insurers must pass the costs onto their customers—the insured and their employers. Another factor boosting costs is *defensive medicine*, the procedures that caregivers recommend because they want to cover all their bases in the event of a malpractice suit.

WHAT'S THAT?

Defensive medicine is the practice of doctors and other caregivers ordering every test that might be applicable and "overtreating" patients in order to avoid potential malpractice lawsuits based on lack of thoroughness.

The Insurance Industry "Influences" Congress

The insurance industry, like scores of others, buys "influence" over lawmakers in the form of campaign contributions. They also often make implicit or explicit promises of employment in the industry or a lobbying firm when the legislator leaves office. U.S. campaign finance law and the revolving door between elected office and private industry enables industry to influence the laws legislators propose and pass. Indeed, parts of some bills are written by industry representatives.

Thus many politicians of both parties represent industries' financial interests rather than those of the average voter. All of this is generally legal and most of the relationships are disclosed for voters to research, and it amounts to a system of legal graft. Media reports of the "powerful health-insurance industry" refer to this system. With billions of dollars at stake, the industry spends huge amounts to influence legislators to do their bidding.

Thus most Republican and Democratic elected officials oppose essential reform of the U.S. health-care system. The following table lists amounts donated to federal elected officials and candidates by individuals and political action committees on behalf of Blue Cross/Blue Shield, which insures about 80 million people in the United States. (Essential reform would include universal access to a government-funded health-insurance program such as Medicare, the "public option.")

Contributions to Political Parties on Behalf of Blue Cross/Blue Shield (1998–2010, Dollars Rounded to Thousands)

Election	Total $	Percent to Dems.	Percent to Repubs.
2010*	550,000	58	42
2008	2,641,000	51	49
2006	2,060,000	36	64
2004	1,295,000	47	53
2002	2,432,000	27	73
2000	2,199,000	27	73
1998	1,381,000	34	66

As of September 2009

Source: www.opensecrets.org analysis of data reported to the Federal Election Commission

Note that the balance between donations to Democrats and Republicans shifted from favoring Republicans to a more equal distribution in the 2008 election cycle, and then to favor Democrats. A company does not, of course, spend and raise more than $1 million or $2 million in contributions for the joy of supporting the democratic process. They do it to influence people making laws that will affect their business.

Why the Current System Is Unsustainable

While a number of factors make the current U.S. system of health care and health insurance difficult to change, it is economically unsustainable. An unsustainable situation, behavior, or system will break down, fall apart, or come to an end unless it changes, adapts, or evolves in a way that addresses the forces working against it. The following forces are working against the U.S. system of health care and health insurance.

Growth of Costs

The cost of health care and health insurance has substantially outpaced inflation in most of the past 20 years. Health-insurance premiums more than doubled for the average U.S. worker from 2001 to 2007. This makes it harder for people to afford health care and health insurance and causes some to forego those expenses. If people forego health care, they can become sick and suffer, and can infect others. If people forego insurance and obtain care through emergency rooms, that simply passes their costs on to the rest of us.

Health Care's Disproportionate Claim on U.S. Productive Capacity

According to the U.S. Department of Health and Human Services, national health expenditures were expected to total 17.6 percent of GDP in 2009 and to reach 18.5 percent in 2014 and 20.3 percent in 2018. The United States devotes a larger share of its productive resources to health care than any other United Nations member except East Timor.

Thus the United States spends disproportionately on one area of the economy—an area in which one third of spending on patients occurs in the last year of life. Also, all this expenditure produces demonstrably inferior outcomes by many measures, including life expectancy and infant mortality, compared with nations that spend far less on health care.

WHAT TO DO?

Visit the site of the U.S. Department of Health and Human Services at www.hhs.
gov for information from the administration on health care and health-care
insurance.

Medicare Is in Trouble

As noted in Chapter 16, Medicare is potentially in even worse financial straits
than Social Security. Congressional Budget Office projections state that Medicare
(and Medicaid) equaled 4 percent of GDP in 2007, but that that figure will rise to
9 percent in 2032 and to 19 percent in 2082.

Although 2082 is a long way off, the trend is for health-care costs to chew up an ever
larger portion of the federal budget. There is a Medicare Trust Fund, but it is much
like the Social Security Trust Fund. As explained in Chapter 16, these funds hold
U.S. Treasury bonds but, as with the Social Security Trust Fund, these are merely
claims on future tax revenues. Those claims are rising fast as the U.S. population
ages. Worse, while Social Security can be limited to a defined payout, that's not the
case with medical expenses, which are more open-ended.

The U.S. Population Is Aging

The 76 million baby boomers (born from 1946 through 1965) start turning 65
in 2011. By 2030 they will all have turned 65 and all will, under current law, be
eligible for Medicare. Aging baby boomers will fuel rapid growth in the 65-and-over
cohort, boosting it from 12 percent of the population in 2010 to 19.3 percent in 2030
according to U.S. Census Bureau projections. Of course, older people require more
health care. This aging population is a chief reason for the Congressional Budget
Office projections that say that health care will consume more than 20 percent of
GDP by 2018, and 29 percent by 2030.

Current Cost Controls Aren't Working

Insurance companies assemble networks of providers and negotiate schedules for fees.
After that arrangement is in place, insurers tend to do one or more of the following:

1. Write a more or less blank check for a patient's care.

2. Set limits on the procedures that a caregiver can provide to a patient.

3. Deny or attempt to deny coverage of a patient's illness.

None of these patient-level measures have proven to be effective cost controls. In the first case, the patient has little incentive to refuse a recommended procedure, and doctors have little incentive not to recommend a potentially helpful one. In the second case, the insurer may override the doctor's judgment, which can be dangerous to the patient's health and to the insurer's relationship with the doctor, and generate patient lawsuits. In the third case, the insurer may be weaseling out of the contract or taking advantage of a patient's confusion.

The Current System Just Shifts Costs Around

While Medicare or private insurers may limit the reimbursement for a certain procedure, the doctor and hospital must still be paid for their true costs. They thus try to charge insurance companies more. Insurers resist that and try to get the institutions and caregivers to absorb the costs. Or they pass them on to employers, who may switch to cheaper insurance, charge employees for more of the premium, or hire fewer employees. Some employees lose their jobs. Others forego coverage and go to hospital emergency rooms for treatment, and if they cannot pay their bill (which is often the case) the hospital must shift that cost to another party.

You might argue that costs are always being shifted in various markets. That's true, but most markets do not deal in a necessity like health care, most do not involve an insurance system, and most do not have laws requiring an institution to deliver its product even if it might not be paid, which hospital emergency rooms are legally bound to do.

U.S. Global Competitiveness Is Being Undermined

It's difficult to obtain solid data on this, but even in the early 1990s, U.S. automakers were complaining that about $1,500 of the cost of every vehicle was health-insurance costs. When U.S. companies and workers must compete with those in nations with national health-insurance systems—and with nations that devote few resources to health care—they are at a disadvantage. There's a reason that every other industrial nation has a national program: it is sound, sustainable economic and industrial policy.

So for all these reasons, the current U.S. system will change, although most Americans do not want any changes to their health insurance. Yet as we saw in the housing and mortgage market meltdowns, change comes whether we want it or not.

So what are the policy options?

The Policy Options

There are several broad policy options for funding, paying for, and delivering health care. On one end of the continuum would be completely private health care and health insurance with no government assistance. At the other end of the continuum would be completely socialized medicine, with the government owning, operating, and paying for all health care. Most societies fall somewhere on that continuum.

National Health Care

National health care, socialized health care, or "socialized medicine" refers to a system in which the government owns the hospitals and equipment and pays the administrative staff and providers, who are actually government employees. This describes Britain's National Health Service. This is also the approach that the United States uses for veterans of military service. Veterans Administration (VA) hospitals are owned by the government and their staffs of doctors, nurses, and administrators are paid by the U.S. government. Despite some "horror stories," most patients are happy with the care they receive at VA facilities and all of them are happy with the fees, which are zero.

WHAT TO DO?

Avoid being confused or frightened by people who throw around the term "socialized" medicine or health care. The United States has not been seriously considering anything of the sort. However, by their definition, the United States does have "socialized" highways and police and fire departments and "nationalized" health care for military veterans.

National Health Insurance and Single-Payer Systems

National health insurance refers to a system in which the federal government provides health insurance to individuals and families, either out of general tax revenues or using tax receipts designated for the purpose. Single-payer programs amount to the same thing, in that a government agency, such as Health Canada, the single payer in Canada, pays for health care and is funded by taxes.

The United States currently has "national health insurance" for everyone 65 and over: Medicare, which is a single-payer program. Single payer refers to a system in which health insurance is provided to individuals and families through a government agency. In 2009, many health-insurance reform proponents (myself included, albeit with gradual adoption) wanted an optional, single-payer system of "Medicare for all," which would open the program to anyone who wanted to join. That would have been a workable, affordable "public option," but most politicians (including many doing the health-insurance industry's bidding) opposed it.

Mandates and Subsidies

Mandates are requirements that an individual purchase coverage or that an employer provide coverage. Usually, there is a certain mandated amount of coverage and certain qualifiers regarding who is subject to a mandate, such as individuals earning a certain level of income or employers with a certain number of employees.

Subsidies are financial assistance provided by the government. The approach currently used in Massachusetts to extend health-care coverage to all residents has used a combination of mandates and subsidies to achieve about 95 percent coverage. Most states mandate that all drivers have auto insurance.

Proposed 2009 Reforms

The issue of health care and health insurance gained momentum in the 2000s. President George W. Bush signed what at the time was the most significant and expensive legislation regarding Medicare since the program was created—the Medicare Prescription Drug Improvement and Modernization Act of 2003. That law created controversy, particularly around its prohibiting the government from negotiating prices of medications with pharmaceutical companies, but it did provide prescription drug coverage to all Medicare recipients. The cost of drugs had been cause for concern, with tales of senior citizens forced to choose between buying food or medications. Interestingly, the Bush bill—with an estimated price tag approaching $1 trillion and no attempt to pay for it with spending cuts or new taxes—was passed with minimal discussion by Republicans about its costs or increases to the deficit. There was nothing like the controversy surrounding the cost of reforms proposed in 2009 and 2010.

However, rising costs and access to care for the uninsured continued as major issues. The reforms proposed and passed by the Obama administration and the Democratic Congress aimed to address these issues. Republican opposition to the Democratic proposals essentially argued for keeping the current system. Republicans vehemently opposed Medicare in the 1960s. For example, in 1961, then private citizen Ronald Reagan was a spokesperson for the American Medical Association, which opposed a congressional bill called King-Anderson, which would have provided health care to senior citizens. In opposing that bill, Reagan said, "you and I are going to spend our sunset years telling our children and our children's children what it was like in America when men were free."

That proved to be nonsense. Medicare, created by the Social Security Act of 1965, as part of President Johnson's Great Society program, is among the most popular government programs. Moreover, rather than lamenting lost freedoms, beneficiaries in their sunset years reported higher levels of satisfaction with their insurance than privately insured patients, in both an April 2009 poll by the Kaiser Family Foundation and a 2007 survey by the Centers for Medicare and Medicaid Services.

Opponents of health-insurance reform use emotional speeches about lost freedom and creeping socialism because, from the economic and personal financial standpoints, a single-payer system similar to that in all other industrial nations is, actually, rationally superior. In politics, when people cannot win rational arguments, they often resort to emotional (and disingenuous) arguments. Moreover, private health insurance would still be available to anyone who wants to (and who is able to) purchase it, just like private schools, transportation, investment programs, and security services.

Democratic Proposals

The Democratic proposals of 2009 and 2010 aimed to extend coverage to most U.S. citizens and legal immigrants, mainly by requiring employers to offer health-care insurance (or suffer substantial penalties) and by requiring employees to enroll in health-care insurance plans. Employers would be required to pay for about 70 percent of the cost of the plan. The Democratic proposal would preserve the current system of private insurance and Medicare, while extending coverage to about 96 percent of the population.

The Democratic plan aimed to encourage greater competition in the health-insurance industry by opening up markets, which are generally defined by state boundaries, to more insurers. It attempted to reduce the cost of health insurance by enabling small businesses and individuals to join "co-ops" that would constitute the larger pools of insured individuals that enable insurers to provide lower rates. It also provided subsidies for people unable to afford private health-insurance premiums.

Under Democratic proposals, insurers could not drop policyholders who became ill or deny or delay coverage on the basis of sometimes flimsy preexisting conditions. This key provision does away with a major source of unfairness and distress for people with private insurance. Democratic proposals also did not limit a patient's ability to sue caregivers and hospitals.

Democratic proposals included cost-reduction measures ranging from having physicians' assistants rather than physicians deliver hospice care to possibly adopting HMO-style groups of caregivers within the Medicare program. According to the Congressional Budget Office (CBO), this proposal would cost about $1.1 trillion over the first 10 years, or an average of $110 billion a year.

Republican Proposals

Until November 2009, the Republican party did not offer any alternative to the Democratic proposals other than the status quo. They argued that the Democratic plan would represent government intrusion and socialized medicine and a new, major outlay for the taxpayer at a time of already high deficits.

The Republican proposal would limit patients' ability to sue caregivers and employers, but would not require employers to offer or require individuals to buy health insurance, nor would it provide subsidies for those who cannot afford to pay for coverage. It would expand the use of tax-sheltered medical savings accounts, allow people to purchase insurance outside their states, and make it easier for currently hard-to-insure people to obtain coverage. While out-of-state shopping brings a bit more competitiveness to the market, it could also send some employers and insurers searching for states with lighter insurance regulation, in what opponents call a "race to the bottom."

Over the first 10 years, the Republican proposal, which was judged even by Republicans to stand no chance of passage, would cost only $61 billion. It would leave the number of uninsured unchanged, and do even less than Democratic proposals to reduce rising health-care costs.

Problems in the Proposals

The fundamental problem in both the Democratic and Republican proposals is that they both take preserving the current system of private health insurance as their chief priority. Yet, insurers add tremendous bureaucracy and profit costs (again, accounting for about 15 percent of total health-care costs) while adding relatively little value—not *zero* value, but not value equal to the costs they place on the system, if one compares the results of the U.S. system with those of other nations.

Health-care insurance companies consist of administrators, not caregivers. They provide a payment mechanism, not "insurance" in the sense that life, fire, and property and casualty insurance companies do, as I explained earlier. That administrative function and payment mechanism could be provided by Medicare, as it now is for everyone 65 years of age or over.

However, political realities and the system of campaign financing currently obstruct the goal of "Medicare for all" and, thus, a single-payer system in the United States. This does not control costs or increase U.S. competitiveness in world markets, and the nation will continue to experience increasing costs and diminishing competitiveness until this system changes.

Given the political and financial realities in the United States, it is quite likely that health care will remain a problem for some years to come as the population ages, costs mount, and economic issues continue to accumulate.

The Least You Need to Know

- It's important to distinguish between the U.S. system of health care and its health-insurance system. The two are related, but the mix of private health insurance and Medicare leaves about 17 percent of the population without insurance and does not control costs effectively.

- Every other major industrial economy has a national health or national health-insurance program that is much more robust than the U.S. program. Most of those nations have health care as good as or better than the United States' by many measures, including life expectancy and infant mortality.

- People aiming to reform the U.S. health-insurance system want to de-link basic health care from income and employment, minimize the role of private insurers, control costs, and improve U.S. companies' global competitiveness.

- The current U.S. health-care system is hard to change because most people are insured and happy with their care, the issues are complex, they don't feel responsible for or affected by the cost consequence, and the health-insurance industry has many political allies.

- Democratic plans for health-insurance reform aimed to extend coverage to 96 percent of the population and reduce costs. The plan would add about $1.1 trillion to the U.S. federal budget over 10 years and leave the system of private health insurance largely in place.

- Republicans oppose health-insurance reform and offered no plan to extend coverage to the uninsured or to substantially reduce costs. There's a good chance that health care will remain an economic problem in the United States in the years ahead.

The Economics of Sustainable Growth

Chapter 18

In This Chapter

- The long-term determinants of economic growth
- Oil and sustainable energy sources
- Education and innovation as drivers of growth
- Problems of sustainability in the U.S. economy

As often occurs with a major event or new development, the Great Recession divided the world into two camps, in this case:

1. People who believe that the recession was only a cyclical downturn.

2. People who believe the recession was a cyclical downturn *and* a potential downward turning point for the U.S. economy.

Those in the second category believe that the recession exposed and underscored certain structural weaknesses in the U.S. economy. They believe the weaknesses had been concealed by consumer-led economic growth financed with massive private and public borrowing at artificially low interest rates. (I should say *we believe*, since I am in this camp.) People in this camp believe that a return to the rate and type of U.S. economic growth achieved in the past two expansions is not possible in the next few years, and that if it is achieved it will not be sustainable.

Sustainability, Politics, and Policies

I believe that those of us who are concerned about economic *sustainability* must do a better job of explaining our concerns. Let's start with the term sustainability itself. Sustainability, in an economic context, refers to the fact that certain practices of consumers, businesses, and governments can generate or at least contribute to long-term economic growth and others cannot. Practices that can generate long-term growth are sustainable and those that cannot are unsustainable. (Long-term generally means 10 or more years into the future, but usually less than 100.)

WHAT'S THAT?

In an economic context, **sustainability** refers to a set of practices by consumers, businesses, and governments that are consistent with long-term economic growth and prosperity. They generally have to do with conservation of natural resources, stewardship of the environment, support of public goods, development of nonfossil fuels, and, often, international economic cooperation.

In some cases, the practices themselves are not sustainable. For example, when a species of sea life is "fished out" to extinction, it is no longer available. The practice itself caused the extinction. Similarly, when the earth's oil reserves are completely depleted, then oil will no longer be available.

In other cases, the practices either are creating or may create more costs than benefits over the long term. The current, mainly market-driven system of U.S. health insurance is a good example. By some measures, such as infant mortality and life expectancy, this system is already generating results that are inferior to those of the public systems in other developed nations. This system has also put U.S. businesses (and workers) at a disadvantage in global markets, and has not curbed growth in health-care costs. Thus a practice that could theoretically go on indefinitely can become unsustainable on the basis of its costs.

This chapter examines various dimensions of sustainability. Although people often focus only on the important topics of sustainable energy or environmental sustainability, those are just aspects of the issue. Other aspects include practices of consumers, businesses, and governments unrelated to the environment and energy, such as investing, borrowing, education, and innovation.

That's a lot, and I cannot in this chapter cover every aspect of sustainability in depth. I can, however, give you a good overview of the topic and show how the U.S. economy might move to more sustainable practices. I won't, however, go deeply into the politics of sustainability here because the arguments around energy, education, and environmental issues are well-known and typically follow party lines. In general, people on the political right take a "pro-growth" approach and tend to oppose environmental and other government regulations. People on the left take a "pro-environment" or "green" approach to the environment and other aspects of sustainability and tend to favor regulation to achieve those ends.

Despite this divide, "pro-growth" and "green" are not mutually exclusive. *New York Times* op-ed columnist Tom Friedman, author of the best-seller *The World Is Flat*, has argued persuasively that green technologies and industries will probably become growth industries in the next couple of decades. In columns in September and October 2009, Friedman marveled at the fact that the world's largest solar panel factory is located in China, and wondered why it is not located in the United States. There are various reasons, but one is that there is little U.S. government support for alternative energy sources and other policies that favor sustainable growth.

WHAT TO DO?

If you don't already read Tom Friedman, check out his column in *The New York Times* at www.nytimes.com and his best-selling book *The World Is Flat*. He has become extremely concerned about U.S. global industrial competitiveness and is a major booster of U.S. policies that would promote that competitiveness.

Why would anyone oppose sustainable growth? In general, the economic argument against sustainable practices is that they increase current costs and thus reduce current profits and future growth (because future growth is financed through profits). The general economic argument for sustainable practices is that the long-term benefits will outweigh the costs. One of those benefits is that we pass on to future generations the advantages that we enjoyed, such as national parks, clean oceans, educated voters, and freedom from debt.

Either of these basic arguments can be correct when it is applied to a specific practice. In general, sustainable practices do increase near-term costs, but in anticipation of longer-term benefits. The choice for any society is whether the costs are outweighed by the benefits. Arguments that belittle environmentalists as "tree huggers" or portray pro-growth people as "whale killers" obscure this choice. There *are* costs associated with investing in environmental protection, alternative energy sources, education, innovation, and infrastructure. The question is whether those investments are worth making. That question should be answered analytically and rationally. Therefore, when you hear people making emotional appeals in this area, look at what's in it for them from the logical (and financial) standpoints.

Long-term investments tend to pay off in very tangible ways. Consider the U.S. system of interstate highways and then imagine life without it. Then try that exercise with the sewer system, power grid, Internet, telephone system, and public school system. They all came about as a result of public and private investment geared to the long term. That kind of investment, which supports sustainable growth, is desperately needed in the United States today. Without it, the U.S. economy will not be able to achieve sustainable long-term growth.

Aspects of Sustainability

By narrow definitions, sustainability measures the ability of the earth to support the human population. That measure is the *carrying capacity* of the planet. That concept poses the question, can the earth—which now supports some 6.8 billion people—support 15 billion, 20 billion, or 30 billion people? If it had to support that many, what steps must be taken to provide those people with a reasonable standard of living? What changes in diet, work, transportation, and other practices might be necessary?

WHAT'S THAT?

The **carrying capacity** of the planet is the number of people that the planet could support at a given lifestyle and level of consumption. That is the carrying capacity of an ecosystem. In other contexts, carrying capacity can refer to that of a transportation or communication system.

One of the most interesting things I've read in the past few years on this subject was a *New York Times* op-ed piece a few years ago in which the authors stated that if every person currently living on Earth were to achieve the lifestyle of the average North American or Western European, their usage of food, water, fuel, and other resources would equate to that of more than *70 billion* people. The authors pointed out that some experts believe the earth could support 15 or 20 billion people, but no one believes it could support 70 billion people with the lifestyle of the average North American or Western European.

However, I use sustainability here to indicate more than only carrying capacity. I define sustainability to mean sustainable economic growth and the factors related to it. This definition includes sustainable dietary, energy usage, and housing practices, and sustainable education, investment, and public financial policies.

For our purposes, sustainability relates to five broad areas of the economy:

- Environmental impact and natural resources

- Population and nutrition

- Energy availability and usage

- Infrastructure
- Innovation and education

Much of this has to do with the use of Earth's resources, particularly by the U.S. economy. As you may know, U.S. residents consume far more resources (and produce far more goods and services) than people elsewhere. Americans constitute 5 percent of the world's population. That 5 percent consume 25 percent of the world's energy, and produce and consume 22 percent of world GDP. The U.S. economic model is based on high consumption and high production. How sustainable is this economic model?

Examining these five areas will help us answer that question.

Environmental Impact and Natural Resources

The environmental impact of U.S. consumption and production practices far outweighs that of other nations, particularly developing nations, particularly when viewed in per capita terms. According to Vic Cox in his article, "U.S. Consumption Deserves Reappraisal," U.S. "CO_2 emissions rate 18 times greater than [those of] the low-income countries with 41 percent of the world's population."

According to www.mindfully.org, the average American generates 52 tons of garbage by age 75, and the U.S. throws out about 200,000 tons of edible food every day. Also, "50 percent of the wetlands, 90 percent of the northwestern old-growth forests, and 99 percent of the tall-grass prairie have been destroyed in the last 200 years." Oil production in the lower 48 states peaked back in the 1970s. In other words, although non–Native Americans arrived in the United States only about 200 years ago, they have used up most of a number of natural resources.

The Department of Energy's Energy Information Administration (EIA) reports that in 2005, U.S. energy-related carbon dioxide emissions amounted to about 21 percent of the world total. (Again, the United States has about 5 percent of the world's population.) U.S. carbon dioxide emissions are expected to decrease as a percentage of the world total in the next two decades, from 19.3 percent in 2010 to 16.2 percent in 2030. However, those emissions will still be increasing in volume. They will decrease as a percentage of world volume partly because China's share of world volume is projected to increase from 22.2 percent in 2010 (up from 19 in 2020) to 28.4 percent in 2030. China does, of course, have a population of about 1.3 billion people, or roughly four times the U.S. population, but emissions growth in China is among the world's major environmental concerns.

The problem of emissions and air quality has been the subject of clean air legislation in the United States and in other nations. The American Clean Energy and Security Act of 2009 passed the House in the summer but faced an uphill battle in the Senate in the autumn. This bill included *cap-and-trade provisions*, which are among the more practical and politically acceptable methods of controlling general air pollution.

WHAT'S THAT?

Cap-and-trade provisions set an overall target for air quality in a geographic area and then issue "permits" that allow each industrial entity in the area to emit a certain level of pollutants (that's the "cap" part). The entities are then allowed to buy and sell part of their emissions permits (that's the "trade" part). This rewards companies that get below their caps and enables those that cannot to make the transition at a pace they can afford.

In a cap-and-trade arrangement, an overall air-quality or emissions target is set and various sources of emissions are identified. Then various entities, such as factories, businesses, and power plants are permitted to emit a certain amount of pollutants. If they emit a lower-than-allowed level of pollutants (for instance, because they adopted better emission controls) then they can sell their "right" to pollute, the allowances, to other entities. This has the virtue of targeting levels of air quality, and then having the private sector sort out how that target will be reached. However, cap-and-trade can leave specific regions overly polluted even though overall targets are being met.

International efforts to control air and water pollutants, overfishing of the sea, logging in the rainforests, and killing of whales, seals, and dolphins meet with varying degrees of success. Individual nations generally resist international efforts to control their practices, and the United States has been no exception in recent years. One significant example of this was the United States' refusal to ratify and participate in the Kyoto Protocol, an international, United Nations–related agreement regarding emissions and global warming that has been ratified by more than 180 countries.

Population and Nutrition Issues

The American diet is high in protein, particularly animal protein as opposed to plant protein. This diet requires huge amounts of grain and water to produce the same amount of nutrition that could be had by eating smaller amounts of meat and larger amounts of beans, seeds, nuts, tofu, oatmeal, and spinach. The issue is not that eating meat is "bad" (although overconsumption of red meat is associated with higher cholesterol and heart disease—and, of course, the animals may be mistreated, and *are* being killed). The issue—or at least the economic issue—is that meat requires far more resources to produce a given amount of nutrition and provides more protein than people require.

According to www.mindfully.org, 80 percent of U.S. corn and 95 percent of U.S. oat production is fed to livestock, and 56 percent of available farmland is used for beef production. It takes 7 pounds of grain to produce 1 pound of beef. Grazing and cropland may appear to be a renewable resource, but that's not so. According to a 1997 Cornell University report, "about 90 percent of U.S. cropland is losing soil—to wind and water erosion—at 13 times above the sustainable rate."

In addition, factory farms and animal feedlots have become major sources of water pollution and serious threats to human (and animal) health. For example, runoff from chicken farms and accidents at hog waste "lagoons" have killed millions of fish and contaminated air and groundwater.

Although factory farming has made nutritious food readily available and affordable in the United States, the U.S. diet demands many land, water, fuel, transportation, and human resources to deliver levels of nutrition that could be had by consuming less animal protein and more plant protein. We may be approaching the upper limits of the farming system, when outbreaks of E. coli and salmonella have become more common and pollution of groundwater from hog waste has become problematic. However, sustainable farming would call for a U.S. diet far lower in animal protein.

Efforts to achieve sustainable farming have received little attention from legislators, but the market has spoken in many areas—or at least in affluent areas. The United States long ago ceased to support the family farm as an economic unit. However, the success of Whole Foods Markets and of organic and "natural" food products over the past 10 to 15 years shows there are alternatives to factory farming and heavily pro-cessed foods. Also, instances of food-borne infections have raised people's awareness of conditions that compromise food purity.

The farming, ranching, and processed foods industries, and the population's depen-dence on them, guarantee slow progress on this front. Yet people who can afford alternatives to highly processed foods (Whole Foods Markets are found only in afflu-ent neighborhoods), and who are educated enough to be aware of the dangers of high fat, sodium, and animal protein, often make changes along the lines of a "diet for a small planet." That phrase is from the title of a best-seller written by Frances Moore Lappé, the first popular book (1979) on the manmade causes of world hunger.

WHAT TO DO?

To get some perspective on food and nutrition issues, you might read *Hope's Edge: The Next Diet for a Small Planet,* by Frances Moore Lappé and Anne Lappé; *Fast Food Nation,* by Eric Schlosser; and *The Omnivore's Dilemma,* by Michael Pollan.

The issue of sustainability extends to the sea. Major fishing banks of the North Atlantic, such as Georges Bank, have become far less productive than in past decades. This has sparked battles between those favoring long-term planning and restricted fishing and those who resist regulation and restrictions. But nature will take its course. In his book, *The Big Oyster,* author Mark Kurlansky cites accounts from colonial times when the floor of New York Harbor was literally covered with oysters. Those days are long past, replaced now by efforts to bring native oysters back to those waters.

The current U.S. diet is unsustainable for a worldwide population and perhaps for the United States as well. Even if sustainable for Americans, it is clearly less economical and in certain ways less healthy than a diet based less on animal protein.

Energy Availability and Usage

I've discussed U.S. energy policy earlier in this book. That policy has been to allow markets and short-term considerations to determine energy usage. U.S. energy policy has not, however, been completely market driven. The nation has subsidized the petroleum industry (and the auto industry) by building highways, roads, bridges, and tunnels paid for at the local, state, and federal levels with tax dollars (including gasoline taxes and tolls). Moreover, oil has long been a major U.S. foreign policy consideration, as evidenced by support of Iranian dictator Shah Reza Palavi from the 1950s through the 1970s, U.S. protection of Kuwait from the 1990 invasion by Iraq, and U.S. invasion of Iraq after 9/11.

Combustion in engines for transportation and production and to produce electricity and heat generates huge amounts of greenhouse gases and other pollutants. The fossil fuels that drive combustion—oil, gasoline, coal, and natural gas—are nonrenewable resources. When they are gone, they are gone, and we are using them at increasing rates, globally. The extractive industries have contributed greatly to the growth of the U.S. and other economies, but a move toward *renewable* sources of energy appears to be called for at this time.

> **WHAT'S THAT?**
>
> **Renewable** sources of energy are those powered by natural resources that are not forever used up in the production of energy. These include solar, wind, hydro (waterfalls and rivers), wave and tidal, and geothermal (heat from the earth itself) sources. While some people consider biomass fuels (such as ethanol made from corn) "renewable," they aren't in the same sense as solar, wind, and tidal sources.

The growing economies of China and India are expected to ratchet up global demand for oil. Current world demand runs at about 85 million barrels per day, and known reserves of recoverable oil total about one trillion barrels. That's a bit over 30 years worth of oil, although new reserves are often discovered and new technology keeps redefining "recoverable oil." Optimistic estimates put global peak oil—the point at which oil production starts falling—at about 20 to 30 years from now. Pessimistic estimates say that the peak is here or just behind us. (Demand and production fell during the Great Recession.)

The Hirsch Report

A February 2005 report prepared for the U.S. Department of Energy (DOE) titled *Peaking of World Oil Production: Impacts, Mitigation, and Risk Management*, examined the issue of peak oil and its consequences in some depth. Known as the Hirsch Report after its author, energy expert and agency official Robert L. Hirsch, the document is summarized in "The Inevitable Peaking of World Oil Production" in the October 2005 bulletin of the Atlantic Council of the United States.

This summary makes five key points:

- World oil demand is forecast to grow by 50 percent by 2025 according to the DOE.

- Some experts are warning that world oil supply will not satisfy world demand in 10 to 15 years.

- Oil production is in decline in 33 of the world's 48 largest oil-producing countries.

- U.S. oil production peaked in 1970 despite sharp price hikes in the 1970s and technology advances in the 1980s and 1990s. (This peak was predicted.)

- Analysis of regions that have passed peak oil production, including Texas, North America, the United Kingdom, and Norway, shows that peaks can be sharp and unexpected.

With 90 percent of U.S. transportation depending on oil, Hirsch urges the nation (and world) to reduce dependence on oil, mainly for economic sustainability. Substitutes that he sites as promising in the near term include fuel-efficient transportation, heavy oil (which requires more resources to recover than conventional oil), coal liquefaction, enhanced oil recovery, and gas-to-liquids technologies. Although these all depend on fossil fuels, developing them would still require a "crash program."

Hirsch defines the overall problem as a "liquid fuels problem" rather than an energy crisis. His concern is that vehicles, planes, trains, and ships have no ready alternative to liquid fuels. He states that waiting until peaking occurs would leave the world with a significant liquid fuel deficit for two decades. Acting 10 years in advance of peak oil would create a 10-year deficit, and acting 20 years in advance—meaning now—would mitigate the deficit.

An even larger energy crisis also looms. While still relatively cheap, coal, which is used heavily in electricity generation, is the worst producer of greenhouse gases. Coal is neither a renewable nor a sustainable source of energy. Fortunately, early-stage projects in the United States and elsewhere are underway in technologies such as solar power and wind power. Also, while nuclear power generation has been controversial in the United States, it has an excellent overall safety record and is more commonly used in Europe, particularly France.

So there are steps the U.S. economy and other economies can take and alternatives to current sources of fuel. However, they must be invested in, researched, developed, and commercialized in the near future if those economies are to sustain their historic growth trajectories.

WHAT TO DO?

See *The Hirsch Report* for yourself at www.netl.doe.gov/publications/others/pdf/ Oil_Peaking_NETL.pdf.

Infrastructure

The term "infrastructure" means various things. Broadly, the term refers to the social infrastructure of government agencies, such as police, courts, corrections, tax collection, and education, and to the laws and legal system that enable people to make contracts, extend credit, and settle disputes. That "social infrastructure" extends to the banking system and financial markets. This infrastructure is still sound and reliable in advanced nations, but creating these institutions is a key challenge in war-torn third-world nations and dictatorships. Infrastructure also includes the military and defense capabilities.

Of more concern to people worried about U.S. economic sustainability is the infrastructure of power generation, air travel, telecommunications, ground transportation, and so on. Also known as "critical infrastructure," this includes the power grid, roads, bridges, tunnels, railways, subway and bus systems, hospitals and health care, wired and wireless telecommunication systems, the Internet, water supplies, sewage and sanitation, and fuel production and distribution.

These systems are potential targets of terrorist attack. Moreover, the United States has also invested less in some of these systems than it has in the past. Of course, it has also invested in important elements of the infrastructure, notably the Internet, wireless communications, and health-care technology. However, in recent decades the nation has underinvested in roadways, bridges, tunnels, railways, and power distribution. It has also arguably overinvested in defense and underinvested in education (a separate issue, covered shortly). A developed nation must maintain and continue to develop its infrastructure in order to sustain economic growth.

The United States has a costly health-care system, a highly politicized defense establishment (in which even outdated weapons programs are very difficult to end), substandard roadways, suboptimal power generation and distribution, and interstate railways that fall far short of European and Japanese rail systems. The United States must actively attend to this driver of economic well-being.

Innovation and Education

The United States has a long history of innovation that extends to this day, with the Internet among the most successful and revolutionary examples. In fact, the Internet represents an excellent, recent example of the three ways in which many major innovations have occurred in the United States:

- It was a public/private effort.

- It delivered true economic advantages.

- It has been a disruptive technology.

Many people don't realize that the Internet grew directly out of research and development (R&D) in a unit of the U.S. Department of Defense (the Defense Advance Research Projects Agency, or DARPA). Further R&D was funded by the U.S. government and conducted by academics in university labs. This work began in the 1960s, about two decades before commercialization even began and almost three decades before the launch of the World Wide Web.

The Internet made information access, communication, bill paying, shopping, advertising, workplace collaboration, and many other daily activities far more efficient and effective, unlike so many "innovations" that are mere product line extensions (Cool Ranch Doritos, Coke Zero) or that generate little actual value (cosmetic changes to cars). Hundreds of billions of dollars of value—in money saved and earned and in stock valuations of companies—have been generated by the Internet.

Disruptive technologies significantly change the playing field in one or more industries. Like the automobile, telephone, and television, they almost immediately outdate previous ways of doing things. This can change ways in which people do business and conduct their lives and can disrupt existing industries. Fear of disruption is why people in established industries often resist innovation, as is the case with energy and auto industries resisting development of alternative fuel technologies. But the fear often simply stifles innovation and retards progress.

Innovation occurs most often and most effectively when it is supported by investment and education. Investment is needed to fund innovation and to pay for R&D personnel, facilities, equipment, and activities. It can take decades to develop a new technology and years for a new technology to lead to profitable products. That's why public funding of basic R&D, for instance in university research laboratories, is so necessary. Education is equally important to sustained economic growth.

WHAT TO DO?

Broaden your thinking about what high technology means. Most of us think of it as information and communications technology, but high-tech industries actually include those in areas related to materials, superconductivity, radiation, nanotechnology, optics, imaging, chemistry, energy, and biotech, among many others.

Issues in U.S. Education and Investment

Scientific and technical knowledge is always advancing, and educated people—often highly educated people—advance it. Scientific and technical education, for instance in various branches of engineering, is important to innovation in medicine, electronics, materials, information technology, telecommunications, defense, production technology, and infrastructure improvement. Education in the humanities is important to innovation in music, art, literature, and cinema, as well as in management, health care, and education itself.

The United States has underinvested in education relative to certain other nations. This has become clear in international comparisons of student performance in areas such as days spent in school, test scores, and number of science and engineering graduates. The U.S. system of funding K–12 education mainly through local property taxes perpetuates separate pockets of affluence and poverty, a situation in which "the rich get richer and the poor have babies" (literally). This creates a huge waste of brainpower and an economic burden on society in terms of poverty, unemployment, and crime, with resulting impacts on health care, police, court, and corrections systems.

To sustain economic growth and quality of life, the United States must invest more in education and in R&D. The U.S. economy does not lack for investment funds, but rather for effective use of those funds. The short-term nature of corporate goals—and high rewards for short-term performance rather than long-term results—have undercut economic growth. So has the financial (and tax) system that rewards speculation (even with borrowed funds) and financial engineering, a term for "moving money around." In politics, 30 years of campaigns that belittle the government and most government spending have undercut public support for government investment in innovation as well as infrastructure.

Private and public innovation is essential to sustained economic growth, because markets constantly pressure companies to meet new needs and to meet old needs in better ways. Some people and companies are going to find ways to meet those demands. Economies with those people and companies will be the most prosperous over the long term, and continued long-term prosperity is an excellent definition of sustainability.

Factors Working For and Against U.S. Sustainability

The United States and other economies engage in a number of practices that undermine sustainable economic growth. If, with the support of the populace, the U.S. government were to take steps to curb, replace, or end these practices, the economy would be better able to generate sustainable growth. If the Great Recession were to play a role in triggering such change, then the crisis will not have gone to waste.

There has been evidence that the United States can change in ways that support sustainability, including these events and trends of the relatively recent past:

- U.S. legislative efforts on air quality include the Air Pollution Control Act of 1955, the Clean Air Act of 1963 and of 1970 and 1977, and 1990 amendments to the Clean Air Act of 1970.

- The Clean Water Act of 1972 did much to eliminate and control industrial pollution of U.S. lakes and rivers; the Comprehensive Environmental Response, Compensation, and Liability Act of 1980 ("Superfund legislation") led to the cleanup of 14,000 toxic waste sites.

- Efforts in the United States and elsewhere to develop alternative energy sources, such as wind and solar power, and to develop hybrid and electric cars appear quite promising.

- U.S. conservation, recycling, and pollution-control efforts have generally found support among consumers, particularly when upheld by the law.

- The United States continues to be a magnet for global investment due to its size, productivity, affluence, financial markets, and legal system.

In addition, reform of the U.S. health-insurance system has begun. Education became more of a focus at the federal level in the 2000s, with No Child Left Behind enacted (if feebly funded) and other legislation in the works. Infrastructure projects were part of the Obama stimulus program, but that area has received far less funding than it requires. For instance, a number of other nations far surpass the number of Internet connections in the United States—the nation that invented it.

Meanwhile, Around the World

The high-production, high-consumption U.S. economy may have become a victim of its own success. Americans developed and projected to the world an economic system in which individuals are free to follow their interests, impulses, and dreams. It's a system in which people can start businesses, create careers, and invest in themselves relatively free of government regulation, religious law, and family obligations. Largely as a result, Americans have—and expect to have—more, faster, and better products and services than most of the world. They have the largest homes and cars, the widest variety of products and services, the fastest pace of life, and the greatest consumption of resources.

Americans also have the largest waistlines, longest workweeks, fewest days off, flimsiest family ties, highest incarceration rates, highest medical bills, and highest debt. Vic Cox, in "U.S. Consumption Deserves Reappraisal," points out that, the richest 10 percent of Americans (about 25 million people) have an income greater than the poorest 43 percent of the world's people (2 billion). Though they sacrifice for their material success, Americans face serious questions about their way of life, particularly given threats of terrorism, levels of public and private debt, and questions of economic sustainability. For instance, in deciding to reduce taxes in the 2000s while increasing government expenditures—including two wars—the United States took on hundreds of billions of dollars in debt. Most of this debt was not used to build infrastructure or to launch R&D projects, but to fund wars and current expenses.

Such decisions, along with other factors, threaten U.S. economic sustainability. The world will not continue to purchase U.S. debt indefinitely, particularly if the value of the dollar falls. Oil-producing nations will not sell to their best customer but to the highest bidder. Emerging middle classes in China, India, and elsewhere will want the products that go with a middle-class lifestyle—few of which are produced in the United States. Water pollution, factory farming, and relentless overfishing cannot continue without increasing health hazards and economic costs.

As usual, the solution lies in policy decisions, but U.S. voters consistently reward politicians who misrepresent economic realities. Economic realities will eventually assert themselves, however, and they did in the financial crisis of 2008 and the ensuing recession. Yet even now, true re-regulation of financial institutions and health-care policies to make U.S. companies competitive with those of other industrial nations currently appear to be unachievable. Politicians of both parties, doing the bidding of their financially motivated contributors, ignore pressing economic needs and settle for compromise solutions that do not address financial mismanagement, misallocation of investment, and health-care cost increases and inequities.

A persistent focus on narrow, short-term interests—whether the next quarter's earnings for an executive or the next election for a politician—is not compatible with economic sustainability. Sustainability demands a focus on broad, long-term interests and that focus remains elusive.

The Least You Need to Know

- Broadly, sustainability refers to the "carrying capacity" of the planet, the number of people the earth could support. More specifically, economic sustainability refers to practices that contribute to continued economic growth.

- Five key aspects of sustainability are environmental issues and natural resources, population and nutrition, energy availability and usage, infrastructure, and innovation and education.

- The basic argument against sustainable practices is that they increase current costs and thus reduce current profits and future growth. The basic economic argument for sustainable practices is that the long-term benefits will outweigh the costs.

- Although arguments about sustainability are often couched in emotional or politically charged terms, the best policies come about through scientific and economic analysis and rational argument.

- The United States and other nations engage in various unsustainable practices, but there has also been encouraging progress in such areas as antipollution legislation, recycling, energy efficiency, alternative energy sources, and organic and natural farming.

The Economy Going Forward

At the end of the Great Recession, the U.S. economy stood at a crossroads, economically and politically. This created extraordinary uncertainty, which makes it harder for investors, businesses, and families to make decisions in the present and make plans for the future.

Few economists forecasted a robust economic recovery in the near term, and some feared that the economy could slip back into recession. Most economists, as well as most employers, investors, and workers (both employed and unemployed), expected a few years of sluggish growth. That means continued high unemployment, low growth in income, and a potentially slipping standard of living.

Politically, the nation appeared even more deeply divided and confused. Few voters seem to understand the relationship between economic policies and the severity and nature of the financial crisis and the ensuing recession. The politicians who made and supported the policies admitted no relation between their actions and the results. And those who came to office since the onset of the recession proved ineffectual when it came to either explaining what happened or addressing underlying problems.

This is not to say that they handled the crisis and the recession itself badly. The U.S. government's response to the crisis and to the immediate effects of the recession were sensible and effective under Presidents Bush and Obama. It is in changing the policies that contributed to the severity of the recession and in positioning the nation for genuine, long-term growth that they have failed so far.

The Financial System Recovers?

In This Chapter

- How the financial system weathered the crisis and recession
- U.S. Federal Reserve policies and positions
- Understanding interest rates and the economic cycle
- The state of financial system reform

Shortly after the financial crisis roiled the credit markets in the summer of 2008, governments around the world, particularly the U.S. government, acted to stabilize the system. As explained in Part 2, they shored up banks' capital by guaranteeing loans and providing funds, and facilitated purchases of weaker banks by stronger ones. The latter occurred in a number of nations including the United States, which for example "pushed" Merrill Lynch and Bank of America into a deal. Central banks also provided liquidity to the system in the form of new loan facilities and record low interest rates.

To this day, these measures remain controversial. This chapter does not revisit these controversies, but instead reports on the state of the financial system in late 2009 and early 2010, when the crisis had passed and the recession appeared to be over. This chapter looks at the Federal Reserve's (Fed) policies and their likely effects on the economy, and at the relationship between interest rates and the economy. It also examines specific criticisms that have been directed toward the Fed and the U.S. Treasury.

We begin with a quick look at the nature of the financial markets and why they are worth following.

The Nature of the Financial Markets

People who don't follow business or investments generally don't think much about the financial markets. In a sense, that's okay. If you buy a box of cereal, you don't need to think about farmers, grain buyers, cereal companies, and supermarket chains. You just want some cereal. Yet the *financial markets* trade money, the most useful and universal of all commodities, so events in the financial markets have far-reaching effects and warrant your interest.

WHAT'S THAT?

The term **financial markets,** broadly defined, refers to the buyers, sellers, brokers, institutions, funds, and other investors and speculators who buy, sell, trade, and invest in stocks, bonds, options, and contracts for commodities (such as precious metals and agricultural products). These markets now exist mainly in cyberspace, although there are still physical facilities, such as the New York Stock Exchange and the Chicago Board Options Exchange.

Money is pervasive and laden with meaning. When money changes hands—from depositors to lenders, from lenders to borrowers, from investors to business people, and from buyers of euros to sellers of dollars—people are expressing their thoughts, plans, feelings, and even dreams. Thus, the financial markets—where most of the world's saved, loaned, borrowed, and invested money is traded—are a repository for people's collective hopes and expectations for the future.

Consider your motivations when you purchase a stock or bond, buy a home or car, take out a loan to attend college or grad school, or use your savings to start a business. You are anticipating a future in which you will see a return on that stock or bond, hold onto the home or car, repay the student loan, or grow the business. Your expectations, and those of billions of other people, add up to the financial markets.

For these reasons, many people follow the financial markets not only because they're invested in them, but because they realize that movements in the markets reflect people's perceptions about the future of an economy. The markets also reflect people's perceptions of the risks in an economy.

Every investment presents a *risk-return tradeoff*. Investors put money at risk in the expectation of a return. The uncertainty of that return is related to the investment, the entity offering the investment, and economic conditions. Uncertainty surrounds all of these, so investors' perceptions of them affect the amount of risk they are willing to assume for a given return. In general, an investment with greater risk carries a higher return, and one with a higher return carries greater risk.

The stock, bond, commodity, and foreign-currency markets reflect investors' expectations of the future. As you know, expectations often become self-fulfilling. So examining the performance of a few key financial markets can provide real insight into an economy's prospects. The importance of the financial markets is underscored by the government's role in them as well.

WHAT'S THAT?

The **risk-return tradeoff** is the choice that investors face when they make an investment. In general, the higher the potential return on an investment—the higher the expected interest rate or dividend—the more risk there is associated with it. Similarly, the lower the risk, the lower the potential return. In other words, investors perceive a certain level of risk in an investment and must be compensated for that risk with a higher return.

The Government and the Markets

The government influences the markets mainly through monetary policy, implemented through the Fed. The Fed exerts less direct influence over the stock market than over the bond and credit markets. Stocks represent an investment in a company's future earnings, while a bond represents a loan to a company. Thus a stock's future returns are unknown, while a bond bears a known interest rate and stream of payments.

However, the Fed's interest rate policies do affect stock prices. In general, if the Fed lowers interest rates, investors tend to favor stocks over bonds, because low rates stimulate economic activity, which usually translates to rising stock prices. Investors also associate looser monetary policy with increased inflationary pressures, and most investors see stocks as offering more protection against inflation than bonds (although investors dislike inflation because it erodes the value of the currency and thus of most financial assets).

During the onset of the recession, the stock market fell as investors put money into the safest havens they could find. These included U.S. Treasury securities and the dollar, both of which have historically been very safe investments. As the recession wore on, investors realized that a depression would be avoided. So they moved money back into the stock market and out of the dollar. This generated rising stock prices and a falling dollar.

The U.S. Government and the Financial Crisis

I believe the U.S. government did a very good job of handling the financial crisis and, up to a point, the subsequent recession. This opinion does *not* apply to the government's handling of the economy in the years (and decades) before the crisis. Deficit spending undermined the federal budget. Tax cuts unmatched by spending cuts and misapplication of the Social Security and Medicare surpluses have weakened the long-term prospects for the U.S. economy. Easy money policies, light taxes on speculative investments, and the government's own example fueled low savings and high consumption. Policies allowed, and even encouraged, companies to move jobs to foreign locations, with no provision for new jobs or retraining.

When the crisis and the Great Recession arrived, the nation had few policy options. Yet the government generally responded well to the immediate crisis. U.S. and global depressions were averted. The financial system recovered fairly quickly considering the level of panic in 2008, and markets were healing by mid-2009. The Fed and the Treasury saw the financial system through difficult, uncertain times and helped the United States (and other nations) avoid an even deeper and more prolonged recession.

WHAT TO DO?

Please understand that I realize that it is easy to criticize policymakers and that it is far harder to balance economic demands and political realities. This realization is reflected in my "grades" for the government's programs in Chapter 21. Failure to be honest about economic realities is the major problem of policymakers, in my opinion. They would rather have their jobs than level with people.

The Critics Weigh In

Some disagree with my assessment of the Fed's performance, with the following as the major criticisms, together with my opinion of those views:

The Fed and Treasury bailed out their friends the bankers.

Critics on the left (and some on the right) believe that the Fed and Treasury enabled banks to survive largely out of political motivations. Meanwhile, they did far less for the auto industry and very little for workers in general. There's truth to this, in that the heads of the Fed and Treasury did favor some banks over others (particularly Goldman Sachs, which benefited greatly from federal support of insurer AIG). However, Bush, Obama, and Congress during both administrations extended unemployment benefits, and Obama and Congress did pass the stimulus package in February 2009.

The banks got government money but didn't lend it.

The Troubled Asset Relief Program (TARP) did not put cash into the economy, nor was it really meant to do so. I and other observers believed then and now that the chief purpose was not just to provide funds to the banks but, more importantly, to show that the U.S. government would not allow more major banks to fail. That calmed the markets and shored up faith in the system. The TARP funds were never really intended to be loaned out. If banks chose to lend them, fine. But they were never obligated to do so by the legislation.

The problem of toxic assets wasn't addressed.

A few months after TARP passed, it became apparent that the problem of the mortgage-related assets was not going to be solved by the program. Funds disbursed to the banks under TARP provided capital, but the banks did not have to write off or sell troubled loans or securities to obtain TARP funds. The mechanism for selling toxic assets ("legacy" loans and securities) was the Public-Private Investment Program (PPIP). That program was not actually announced until June 2009, and even in early 2010 it had not been a significant factor in shoring up the banks. Foreclosures remained high during the recession, and very little was done to help distressed homeowners. In other words, the banks continued to carry many troubled assets on their books through the recession, and it remains to be seen whether these assets cause them trouble.

Financial market reforms have been slow and weak.

This is the major problem I see in Obama's approach to the crisis. There has been far more talk than action in improving financial-market regulation and increasing the transparency of financial instruments (particularly derivatives). The problem in the bailouts and other assistance to financial institutions is that little genuine reform has been enacted. Even reforms that were enacted could have been stronger and put into effect far sooner. For example, the months-long lag from the passage of credit card reform to its taking effect was a joke on the public and a gift to the industry, which promptly jacked up rates in the interim.

Without a doubt, the financial services industry has politicians in its pocket. This is legal, thanks to our system of campaign financing, the power conferred on lobbyists, and the revolving door between the public and private sectors, as the credit card legislation demonstrated.

What the Financial Markets Said

The stock markets recovered much of their lost value in 2008. While they remained a long way off from the peak in the Dow of 14,000, they did recover to the 10,000 range and, equally important, held to that range. The stock markets tend to react quickly and often more emotionally than the bond markets. A bond pays a fixed rate of interest rather than a dividend that may or may not be declared (if indeed the company pays dividends at all, which many "growth companies" do not). For that reason, a bond's price fluctuates with investors' perceptions and expectations of future interest rates. Bond prices rise when interest rates are falling and fall when interest rates are rising. Those price fluctuations "adjust" the interest rate of a bond paying a fixed rate and thus reflect current and expected interest rates.

Let me explain. If a bond with a face value of $10,000 pays 4 percent interest a year, the investor receives $400 a year. But if interest rates are rising, the bond's price must fall to reflect that fact if the investor wants to sell the bond. So the price of the bond may fall to, say, $9,000, which means that it would then yield 4.4 percent (which is equal to $400/$9,000). Similarly, if rates are falling, the price of the bond would rise (for example, to $11,000), which means it would yield about 3.6 percent (which is equal to $400/$11,000). In this way, the bond market is an accurate gauge of investors' expectations.

Therefore, one way to gauge the economic situation is to monitor short-term, intermediate, and long-term interest rates. Accurate reads on rates are found in the markets themselves, where expectations of interest rates are readily visible. At the end of 2009, investors appeared to believe that the Fed did a good job managing the crisis and dealing with the recession. I say this because short-term and long-term interest rates were returning to their normal relationship and foretelling an economic expansion. Investors did not appear to be demanding extraordinarily high rates on U.S. securities. And the stock market appeared healthy, with prices neither too low nor too frothy.

The one indicator of skittish investors may have been the price of gold, which at the end of December 2009 stood near its record high reached earlier that month. Also, the dollar, which is covered in Chapter 20, took quite a hit in 2009. But here we focus on interest rates.

Why Interest Rates Are of Interest

Interest rates are the price of money. The price of money depends on the money supply, and on the demand for money (in the form of credit) by businesses, consumers, and the government. Apart from supply and demand, the lengths of time over which borrowers want to borrow and lenders want to lend will affect rates. Usually, the longer the borrowing period, the higher the rate. Another factor is lenders' views of the likelihood of repayment, but each lender makes that decision case by case.

These forces work together in the credit markets to generate short-term, intermediate, and long-term rates. The credit markets are the parts of the financial markets where companies, banks, and governments lend and borrow funds. Short-term borrowings occur through commercial paper (for companies and banks), reserves held with the Fed (for banks), and Treasury bills (for the U.S. government). Long-term borrowing occurs through bonds issued by all types of entities.

Debt securities are traded in the public credit markets, and you can learn about investors' expectations of future economic conditions by examining the *yield curve*. The yield curve is a graph that shows the interest rates of debt instruments of the same quality but different maturities, arranged from shortest to longest maturity.

 WHAT'S THAT?

The **yield curve** is a graphic representation of interest rates for government bonds at different maturities. As such, it is a measure of the risks that investors perceive in the economy as they look to the future.

The yield curve most commonly referred to is that defined by U.S. Treasury securities. Because U.S. Treasuries are considered risk-free, they provide a "pure" reading of interest rates as "the time value of money," because there is no credit risk (the risk of not being repaid). Generally, maturities are shown for 1-, 3-, and 6-month Treasury bills; for 1-, 2-, 3-, 5-, 7-, 10-, and 20-year Treasury notes; and for the 30-year Treasury bond.

What the Yield Curve Means

The yield curve can be positive (pointing upward from left to right), flat, or negative. The slope of the yield curve results from investors' behavior in the bond markets, and the three different curves—positive, flat, or negative—hold different implications.

The yield curve is positive when long-term rates are higher than short-term rates. That is the normal state of affairs given that the longer the maturity of a bond, the more risk is involved because repayment is further in the future.

The yield curve is flat when there is minimal difference between short-term and long-term rates. The curve flattens (from a positive position) when investors shift from short-term to long-term securities. Their increased demand for long-term securities bids up the price of long-term securities, drives down the yield, and brings long-term rates down closer to short-term rates.

The yield curve is negative when long-term rates are lower than short-term rates. This "inverted yield curve" usually means that a recession is ahead. This reflects investors' pessimism about the future. They want to be in a secure investment for the long term. When money moves from short-term paper to long-term paper, short-term yields rise to attract more investors to those instruments. That actually results in short-term rates being higher than long-term rates.

The following table shows the yields for selected Treasuries at the end of each year from 1999 through 2009. (We won't plot the curve here, but it results when you graph the interest rates for the various maturities on a given date. Thus the curve for the rates dated 12/31/99 in the table would be plotted from 5.33 percent to 6.83 percent and be upward sloping.)

U.S. Treasury Yield Curve Rates (Percent)

Date	3-mo.	1-year	5-year	10-year	20-year
12/31/99	5.33	5.98	6.36	6.45	6.83
12/29/00	5.89	5.32	4.99	5.12	5.59
12/31/01	1.74	2.17	4.38	5.07	5.74
12/31/02	1.22	1.32	2.78	3.83	4.83
12/31/03	0.95	1.26	3.25	4.27	5.10
12/31/04	2.22	2.75	3.63	4.24	4.85
12/30/05	4.08	4.38	4.35	4.39	4.61
12/29/06	5.02	5.00	4.74	4.71	4.91
12/31/07	3.36	3.34	3.45	4.04	4.50
12/31/08	0.11	0.37	1.55	2.25	3.05
12/31/09	0.06	0.47	2.47	3.85	4.58

Source: U.S. Treasury

The table shows a positive yield curve at the end of 1999. Then during 2000, the yield curve turned slightly negative—the 3-month T-bill yield (5.89 percent) was higher than that on the 20-year note (5.59 percent). This accurately foretold the brief, mild recession of 2001. One reason it was brief is that the Fed ratcheted down rates in 2001. By the end of that year, as the table shows, the yield curve had returned to normal, with the 3-month T-bill rate at 1.74 and the 20-year note at 5.74.

A positive yield curve prevailed until 2005. By the end of that year, the curve had flattened to the point at which the 3-month rate of 4.08 percent was only about one half of 1 percent lower than the 20-year rate of 4.61.

By the end of 2006, the 3-month rate of 5.02 slightly exceeded the 20-year rate of 4.91. Like the inverted curve of 2000, this interest rate picture foretold a recession— the Great Recession of 2008–2009. Seeing economic conditions deteriorate in 2007, the Fed reduced rates throughout that year and throughout the recession.

The good news is that at the end of 2009, the yield curve was sharply positive. The 3-month T-bill stood at 0.06 and the 20-year rate at 4.58. That curve points to an expansion, which indeed was already underway in the third quarter of 2009.

You can gauge credit market conditions by monitoring the spread between the 3-month rate and the 20-year note rate. A narrowing spread means the yield curve is flattening and investors expect slower growth. If the short-term rate exceeds the long-term rate, they probably expect a recession. If the spread is widening, then the yield curve is becoming more positive. That means investors expect growth to commence or to continue, which was the state of affairs at the end of 2009.

Back to a Bubble?

The most immediate risk to the economic expansion in early 2010 was the threat of a double-dip (W-shaped) recession. In this scenario, high unemployment, troubled housing markets, and the end of fiscal stimulus result in low demand and economic contraction. Yet another risk is that of another asset bubble in the future. If the Fed keeps rates too low for too long, another stock market or, perhaps less likely, housing bubble could result.

Some observers believe the gold market at the end of 2009 exhibited characteristics of a bubble. The price of gold reached a record high of $1,226 per ounce in December 2009, seemingly well above the intrinsic value of the metal. Indeed, a price correction occurred after that early December peak, settling in the $1,100 range. This is up from about $870 at the end of 2008 and $835 at the end of 2007.

Gold generally rises when the dollar is weak and investors worry about inflation and the safety of securities. But if gold prices enter a bubble, they can rise just because prices are rising. When the expansion truly takes hold and unemployment falls and incomes rise, the price of gold should stabilize. At the end of 2009, most of the money to be made in gold during this cycle had likely been made.

Trends to Expect in Financial Services Regulation

Financial services regulation will remain a work in progress. No single set of regulations can be applied across the board indefinitely. Even some sound principles, such as not allowing "too big to fail" banks, or clearly separating depository and investment institutions, may not always be applicable. For instance, if some nations permit "too big to fail" banks and support or subsidize them (as the United States, United Kingdom, and Switzerland did in 2007–2008), then other nations may feel the need to as well. That said, here are a few trends to expect.

Companies Will Grow Large, but Boutiques Will Survive

The U.S. government actually helped make banks larger by pushing mergers between certain banks, such as Bank of America and Merrill Lynch, and Wells Fargo and Wachovia; so banks that are "too big to fail" will remain with us. They are arguably needed to compete against other nations' massive banks. However, *boutiques*, small community banks and small investment funds of various types, will proliferate and add vigor and choice to the financial industry.

WHAT'S THAT?

In finance, a **boutique** is a relatively small, independently operated fund or investment advisory firm. Among the most popular in the 2000s were hedge funds (which trade currencies, stocks, derivatives, and other financial instruments) and private equity funds. The latter generally invest in publicly and privately held companies in order to help them either to restructure their finances or improve their operations (or both) and then sell them.

Increasing Regulation (at Times)

The real issue with "too big to fail" banks is that they require strict regulation, which the U.S. government does not seem prepared to provide. In 2009 there was much talk about more regulation, but far less action. There was talk of a "systemic regulator" for the U.S. financial system and yet another regulatory agency. I believe that systematic regulation by *existing bodies*—the Fed and Congress—could have averted the crisis. Even if regulation increases, it will almost certainly be uneven, politicized, and perhaps done badly.

Increasing Transparency (for a While)

Investors have supposedly demanded greater transparency, more disclosure, understandable products, and less risk. Many of us would like to believe that they will invest accordingly, but over the past 30 years they have consistently sought high, fast returns, even with high risk that they did not fully comprehend. While investors have been chastened, there's reason to believe these lessons will be forgotten when the next high-return (and supposedly low-risk) investment vehicle comes along.

Better Risk Management (We Hope)

Banks themselves may begin to do a better job of risk management. After all, through poor risk management, they lost billions in value and brought government intervention and public scrutiny upon themselves. As business people, they should have a lively interest in understanding risks, and managing them better. Finance essentially *is* risk management, so we can hope that banks have learned some lessons, even if investors have not.

WHAT TO DO?

If you invest in a company, particularly a bank or other financial institution, or rely on one as an employer or major customer, try to familiarize yourself with its risk-management policies. From its public statements and annual report, try to get a sense of how much risk it takes on and how it goes about managing risk. Some companies are just very careful about the risks they assume. They may be less profitable, but their earnings may be less volatile and they may be around longer.

Greater Internationalism and Convergence of Standards

The complexity and risks of the global financial system became clear in the financial crisis. In response, accounting bodies, international banking groups, industry associations, and regulatory agencies have pushed for greater coordination of regulatory policies and accounting standards. For example, the SEC has mandated adoption of International Financial Reporting Standards by the United States, which will move American and European accounting standards closer together, in 2014.

Let's all hope that these trends will skew toward the positive, because a healthy global economy depends to a large extent on a healthy global financial system. I am not as pessimistic as some other observers who decry the role of the banks and Wall Street in the U.S. economy. I agree that their role may be too large and their earnings have been disproportionate to the actual value they have generated in recent years. But I am also hopeful that they will respond positively to the challenges of capital allocation and risk management in the years ahead.

This leads me to a (slightly) more optimistic, or at least less pessimistic, view of the U.S. economy than many other observers hold. I'll present that view in Chapter 21. In the next chapter, Chapter 20, we pull back to view the global economy and the major forces that will shape it in the next few years.

The Least You Need to Know

- The U.S. and global economies achieved growth in the last half of 2009, although it was difficult to judge how sustained the recovery would be.
- Central banks, and particularly the U.S. Federal Reserve, largely did a good job of managing the financial crisis and averting far worse developments in the financial markets.
- Interest rates and the bond market can actually be a better barometer of investor sentiment and the economy's growth prospects than the stock market.
- The interest rate yield curve—the rates for various maturities of U.S. securities—is usually positive, but flattens as investors become pessimistic and turns negative when they expect a recession. In late 2009, the yield curve was positive.
- Regulation of the U.S. financial services industry will not be revolutionary and may indeed be geared more toward protecting the interests of the banks than those of investors or customers.

Ongoing Global Economic Forces

Chapter 20

In This Chapter

- The changing U.S. role in the global economy
- Changes for the worse in the U.S. balance of trade
- Movements in the U.S. dollar and what they mean
- The effects of high global debt on growth

In Chapter 6, I commented on the global economic picture and presented forecasts for several major non-U.S. economies. This chapter examines key forces at work in the global economy, what they mean, and their likely effects as the future unfolds.

This chapter looks at the world economy in terms of its dynamics rather than the performance of specific economies. Those dynamics occur in markets and express themselves in investment flows, trade patterns, currency movements, and international economic relations.

We begin by considering the flow of money in the world economy, then turn to the changing role of the United States in the global economy. This chapter also examines the U.S. dollar in relation to other currencies. That will in turn lead us to a discussion of the global economy and where it is headed, with a particular focus on China, a large and populous nation that is determined to continue its rapid growth and expand its presence in the world economy.

Global Liquidity Dynamics

The global economy as a whole is a market economy, and, in a market economy, investors will put their money where it will earn the highest return for the risk involved. That is, the risk-return trade-off determines investors' behavior. Some investments are virtually risk-free, and because they are, they produce almost certain but relatively low returns. Riskier investments produce less certain but higher returns. U.S. Treasury securities are considered risk-free because they are backed by the taxing power of the U.S. government, which oversees the world's largest *national economy*. The U.S. private sector has also generally been a good place to invest. U.S. companies have a long record of innovation and growth, and U.S. financial markets have usually been transparent and well-regulated compared with those of many other nations.

 WHAT'S THAT?

The term **national economy** refers to the economy of a country, as opposed to a regional economy or that of an economic union, such as the European Union (EU). The United States has the largest economy of any nation, but the EU GDP is larger.

Of course, many other nations have vibrant economies and financial markets. For instance, when the European Union (EU) adopted the euro and lowered internal trade barriers, Europe as a whole became more competitive with the United States. Apart from Japan, Asia (particularly China) has made tremendous economic gains in the past two decades. In general, the world economy has been on an upswing over the past 10 to 15 years.

However, the financial crisis and recession of 2008–2009 had three major effects on the global economy. First, it knocked most national economies off their growth trajectories. Most developed nations went into recession, and fast-growing developing economies saw reduced growth. Second, there had been a global upsurge in liquidity—that is, in the amount of money in the world economy—due to low interest rates and government stimulus packages, which also fueled investment (and speculation). Third, government policies, such as deficit spending to stimulate economic growth, have increased the national debt of many nations.

The second and third points in the preceding paragraph raise a question in some people's minds. If there's so much money around, why is there so much debt? The answer is that much of the money has been created by debt: by central banks' efforts to shore up the credit markets and stressed banks. Central banks expand the money supply in their economies by lowering interest rates, lowering reserve requirements, paying interest on reserves, purchasing or guaranteeing troubled securities, and creating new loan facilities so banks can borrow from them.

The U.S. Federal Reserve (Fed) and other central banks took such measures in response to the crisis, and most of these measures—lowering interest rates, lowering reserve requirements, purchasing securities, and creating loan facilities—make it easier to obtain credit. They increase the money supply through *credit creation*, and thus increase debt. In addition to such expansionary monetary policy, most major economies have engaged in expansionary fiscal policy: deficit spending to stimulate their economies. In some economies—including the U.S. economy—the government already was in high debt relative to historic standards before the crisis.

WHAT'S THAT?

Credit creation occurs when a central bank lowers reserve requirements or takes other measures, such as instituting new loan facilities, that enable the banking system to make new loans. Those lower requirements or new loan facilities enable the bank to make loans beyond the amounts that it could based upon its existing deposits. This credit creation expands the money supply and promotes growth.

As a result, the global economy and a number of economies within it are more fragile than most economists and policymakers would prefer. They are fragile for the same reason that a household or business in high debt becomes fragile—a portion of current and future earnings must be directed to paying interest and principal on money spent in the past. If those payments become burdensome (for instance, when income falls), they can threaten the financial stability of the household, business, or nation.

Does the debt in the United States or other national economies, such as Greece and the United Kingdom, threaten their economic recoveries? Yes, to an extent. To examine the extent for the United States, let's look at the role of the United States in the world economy and at U.S. patterns of borrowing and trade.

The United States in a Global Context

The United States accounts for about 25 percent of the world's GDP. Thus, the pace of global economic recovery depends in part on the pace of the U.S. recovery. If U.S. consumers, businesses, and government temper their spending, growth could remain sluggish in nations that export heavily to the United States.

This reflects a lack of balance in the world economy, largely due to the massive role of the United States. The U.S. economy has been a major international force due to its innovativeness, business success, political system, cultural climate, and sheer size. (In a sense, the EU was formed as something of a "United States of Europe," so its nations could collectively compete more effectively against the United States.) Although its role may have diminished a bit since its peak in the past century, the United States has long been the dominant producer, market, and destination for investment.

Criticisms of the United States are numerous and well-documented. They include its companies' and banks' global expansion, its heavy use of resources, its tendency to abstain from some international agreements, its influence over international organizations, its tendency to lecture other nations on economic policy, and its tendency to export its cultural values. Since the war in Vietnam, its military policies have also been widely criticized.

On the other hand, many EU and Asian companies have also expanded internationally, Europe and Japan have benefited greatly from the *U.S. defense umbrella*, and Americans have been eager consumers (perhaps too eager) of other nations' exports. Yet the U.S. role in the global economy has been and is still undeniably large, and the United States does act, at times, with less than a full sense of the responsibilities that may entail. For instance, it is no coincidence that the U.S. subprime mortgage crisis set off a global financial crisis.

All of that said, the role of the United States in the world economy has changed over the past 30 to 40 years in one very significant way. The United States has moved from being a supplier of exports and a lender of funds to being an importer and a debtor.

WHAT'S THAT?

The **U.S. defense umbrella** is the European and global system of military bases and weaponry created during the Cold War to keep the Soviet Union and other potentially aggressive nations in check. This system enabled Europe and Japan to spend less on defense than it otherwise would have had to spend.

U.S. Outflows Versus Inflows

Since 1976, the United States has run a trade deficit with the rest of the world in goods and services. (A trade deficit occurs when a nation's imports exceed its exports, either overall or in a specific category, such as of goods or services. A trade surplus occurs when a nation's exports exceed its imports, overall or in a specific category.)

Actually, the deficit is in goods, because the United States runs a trade surplus in services. That is, the United States imports more goods than it exports, and it exports more services than it imports. (These services include investment and commercial banking services, and engineering, legal, medical, and other professional services.) But for the United States the total amount of imported goods and services far exceeds the total amount of exported goods and services.

Trade in goods and services between the United States and other nations is tracked in the balance of international payments, or balance of payments, for short. (I am going to omit most technicalities of international trade, but they are explained in more detail in *The Complete Idiot's Guide to Economics*, which I also wrote.) The balance of payments includes three accounts, of which the current account and the financial account are the most important:

- The *current account* includes mainly imports and exports of goods and services.

- The *financial account* includes trade in fixed assets, such as real estate, and in financial assets, such as stocks, bonds, and government securities.

- The *capital account* includes forgiveness of loans and a few other small items, and it is by far the smallest of the three accounts that make up the balance of payments.

Current-account deficits and financial-account deficits can be calculated collectively (that is, for the United States in relation to the rest of the world), or individually for the United States in relation to any other nation. The values cited here are based on collective calculations between the United States and the rest of the world.

WHAT TO DO?

Check out the balance of payments yourself from time to time by visiting the website of the Bureau of Economic Analysis at www.bea.gov/international/ and clicking on the desired links.

In 2007 and 2008, the total current-account deficit was about $700 billion in each year. In any given year, the current-account deficit—the amount by which U.S. imports exceeds U.S. exports—must be financed somehow. U.S. households, businesses, and government must pay foreign suppliers for their exports (which are U.S. imports). That occurs through payments by the United States to those suppliers in other nations or loans to or investments in the United States by other nations. Thus, in 2007 and 2008, the United States had to pay, borrow, or obtain investments of about $700 billion from other nations to finance its purchases of imports. Much of that money was borrowed.

Over the years, current-account deficits have generated the $3 trillion in U.S. Treasury securities that was held by foreign entities at the end of 2009. Increasing oil imports and large U.S. federal budget deficits since the late 1970s are two key reasons for the balance-of-payments deficit. Also, given the offshoring of millions of manufacturing jobs, the United States must import a huge amount of goods. This was the result of U.S. companies choosing to move manufacturing jobs to foreign locations with low production costs, and U.S. consumers choosing to pay lower prices than they would have for U.S.-made goods.

That's all well and good, and I am not—repeat, *not*—arguing for protectionist trade policies. However, that policy decision should have taken into account the relatively high-paying manufacturing jobs that would be lost in the process and included measures that would shore up the U.S. economy. Instead, the United States offshored much of its manufacturing base and left the replacing of those jobs to market forces.

Unfortunately, the market did not create enough high-paying jobs to replace those that were lost. That is the main reason that the middle class has seen little growth in real income over the past two decades and the nation has become mired in debt. In a very real sense, the United States actually did borrow from China to buy Chinese goods. That dynamic makes the United States and China highly dependent on one another.

Historical Highs

The current-account deficits of the 1980s and 1990s were considered high even back then. From 1980 through 1989, the cumulative current-account deficit totaled $846 billion, an average of $85 billion a year. From 1990 through 1999, the cumulative trade deficit totaled $1.1 trillion, an average of $105 billion a year. Until 1971, the United States had always run a current-account surplus—it had always exported more than it imported. So the reversal of that trend to deficits in 1971 was a surprise. (Since then, only 1973 and 1975 have been years of U.S. current-account surpluses.)

However, as high as the current-account deficits of the 1980s and 1990s seemed, they pale in comparison with those of the 2000s. For the nine years from 2000 through

2008, the cumulative current-account deficit totaled $5.1 trillion, an average of about $572 billion (or more than *half a trillion*) a year. That is five times the annual average of the 1990s.

The current-account deficit is financed through the financial account within the balance of payments. When other nations loan or invest more in the United States than the United States invests in those nations, the financial account runs a surplus. That surplus finances the current-account deficit (the payments for the excess of imports over exports). Despite the name, this surplus is not necessarily good. It means that the United States is in debt to or owned by foreign entities more than it has loaned to or invested in foreign entities. It means that foreigners own more U.S. financial securities or real assets (such as factories or real estate) than the United States does in foreign nations.

The United States, the world's largest economy, has become a debtor nation. The United States is a net user of funds rather than the net supplier of funds—as it was before the 1970s. Normally, one would expect a wealthy, developed nation to be a net supplier of funds to less developed nations: a lender to and investor in other nations, and a collector of interest and dividend payments. Of course, the United States does lend to and invest in other nations, but not to the extent that they do in the United States—and not, in my opinion, to the extent that it should.

Ask yourself: Why would the most developed national economy in the world, with a $14 trillion economy, owe a trillion dollars to China, a developing economy with a $4 trillion economy?

The answer is that the United States wants China's inexpensive goods (and it wants expensive oil from elsewhere), and that U.S. taxation, spending, and industrial policy decisions have left the nation very short of money. The United States runs a current-account deficit and a financial-account surplus with China and with the world as a whole. That is one, but only one, of the causes of the fall in the U.S. dollar in late 2009.

The Fall of the Dollar

Examining the forces that affect the value of nations' currencies is beyond the scope of this book. So is an explanation of the ways in which foreign exchange rates are set. (Again, these are explained in *The Complete Idiot's Guide to Economics*.) However, the fall of the dollar as an effect of the recession and of U.S. economic policies is definitely worth discussing here.

A foreign exchange rate is the price of a currency in terms of another currency. For instance, when the euro was introduced as the currency for the EU in 1999, its value was set at the equivalent of $1. You could buy €100 for $100. Since then, the dollar has risen and fallen in terms of the euro (or "against the euro"). These movements occur in the *foreign exchange market*, where banks and companies buy and sell foreign currencies to purchase goods and services, and where speculators "bet" on the future movements of currencies.

WHAT'S THAT?

The **foreign exchange market** is not a physical market located in a building, but rather a virtual market made up of buyers and sellers of currencies. These traders, investors, and speculators include professionals working for major financial institutions as well as others working for independent funds, such as hedge funds.

In some periods, particularly shortly after the euro was introduced, the dollar *rose* against the euro and the euro *fell* against the dollar. That means that a given number of dollars would purchase *more* euros and a given number of euros would purchase *fewer* dollars than before the change in the exchange rate. Accordingly, you could purchase, say, €100 for $90, and vice versa. In other periods, the dollar fell against the euro and the euro rose against the dollar.

When the dollar (or any currency) gains against another currency, it is said to be "strong" in relation to that currency. When it falls against another currency, it is said to be "weak." But a strong dollar is not necessarily good for everyone, nor is a weak dollar bad for everyone.

Effects of U.S. Dollar Movements

In general, there are two key things to know about foreign currency movements (using the U.S. dollar as an example of movements applicable to any currency).

- A *strong dollar* means that U.S. consumers *pay less for imports*. It also means that foreign consumers must pay more for U.S. exports, which tends to *reduce* U.S. exports. That tends to decrease U.S. production and employment.

- A *weak dollar* means that U.S. consumers *must pay more for imports*. It also means that foreign consumers will pay less for U.S. exports, which tends to *increase* U.S. exports. That in turn tends to increase U.S. production and employment.

So a strong dollar and a weak dollar each have positive and negative effects. A strong dollar helps U.S. consumers because it makes foreign goods cheaper. But it hurts U.S. exports and thus U.S. production and employment. A weak dollar makes U.S. exports less expensive for foreigners and thus boosts U.S. exports. That tends to help U.S. producers who sell goods to foreign markets. Also, a weak dollar makes the United States a more attractive travel destination for foreign visitors, while a strong dollar makes it less attractive.

The value of the dollar also affects foreign lenders and investors. Foreign lenders and investors like a strong dollar because it enables them to buy more of their own currency when they convert the dollar loan or investment back into their own currency. Foreign lenders and investors generally dislike a falling dollar because when they are paid interest or convert the loan or investment back into their own currency, they get less of it.

Given the amount of dollars held in the form of loans, government bonds, and other investments outside the United States, other nations generally want a strong U.S. dollar. The strong dollar also keeps demand for their exports to the United States high. (Think about the billions of dollars paid by the United States to oil exporting nations annually, for over 15 million barrels of imported oil *each day*. At $75 dollars a barrel, that's roughly $800 billion a year leaving the United States. Clearly, oil exporting nations benefit from a strong dollar.)

Also, the U.S. dollar is the world's major reserve currency—the currency in which most nations prefer to hold their foreign exchange reserves. They are holding dollars, and they don't want to see the value of those holdings diminish. That's another reason that the falling dollar in 2009 became a cause for concern around the world. (Subsequently, in 2010 the dollar regained some of its lost value against the euro as Greece's debt came to light and the EU struggled with the decision to bail out the nation.)

Currency Events

During the Great Recession and after the U.S. government's response to it, the dollar fell against other major currencies. The key factors decreasing the value of the dollar have been:

- High U.S. trade deficits
- High U.S. budget deficits
- Loose monetary policy

Although the dollar's fall accelerated in 2008 and 2009, the United States had been running high trade deficits for most of the 1990s and 2000s. Oil imports are a major reason. As noted previously, when a nation imports more than it exports, it must finance that current-account deficit. To do so, the nation must borrow internationally or sell more assets to foreigners. Constant borrowing can weaken a nation's currency because foreign lenders will worry about being repaid by a country going ever more deeply into debt.

As documented in this book and many other sources, the U.S. government has run high budget deficits for decades. During the 2008–2009 recession, tax receipts decreased and spending increased. Budget deficits have to be financed, and foreign borrowers do a good portion of the financing. In the long term, budget deficits can erode a currency because domestic and foreign investors in government securities become concerned about inflation. They come to worry that the government may print money to pay the bills. When inflation occurs, the currency's value against other currencies generally falls.

Many economists believe a monetary policy of low U.S. interest rates and an expanded money supply contributed to a weaker dollar. That's because an expanding money supply (or "printing money") can boost demand and create "too many dollars chasing too few goods." During the U.S. expansions of the 1990s and 2000s, the United States ran current-account deficits. Doing so can enable a nation to "export its inflation" in higher prices for its exports.

Many economists believe that the weakening of the dollar in 2009 represented a correction in its value. They believe that high trade and budget deficits and loose monetary policy created a situation in which the dollar *should* be falling. The falling dollar can help the United States increase its exports; however, no one expects an "export-led recovery" in America. Rather, the world looks to the United States to purchase imports.

Net-net, the risks of a weakening dollar probably outweigh the benefits. The one bright side is that a weakening dollar may—repeat, *may*—force additional discipline on the Fed, which runs U.S. monetary policy, and on Congress and U.S. presidents, who run fiscal policy. In the near term, the United States can do little about its trade deficit. Yet when recovery begins in earnest, it can exercise restraint in fiscal and monetary policy. That would help to stabilize the dollar and restore the world's faith in the government that stands behind it.

WHAT TO DO?

Buy American—or don't. The prevalence of U.S. campaigns to buy American-made goods appears to have diminished over the past couple of decades. Realistically, when making purchase decisions, and particularly major purchase decisions such as cars, people are going to purchase the goods that represent the best value for their money. They are not about to support manufacturers of inferior goods. However, if those goods are consistently imports, they are in fact providing jobs for foreign workers. The only answer is for the United States to remain competitive and to produce the best possible goods.

China's Position on the Dollar

As the single largest holder of U.S. government debt and a major exporter to the United States, China has a vested interest in a strong dollar. The Chinese government has in recent years occasionally cautioned the United States to get its financial house in order. Moreover, China has adopted a policy of keeping its currency, the renminbi, at a fixed rate vis-à-vis the dollar. That means that, as the dollar fluctuates against other currencies, the renminbi also does, but its value against the dollar remains fixed.

The optimal U.S. "dollar policy" would balance the pros and cons of a strong and weak dollar, and take the economies of our trading partners into account. Through trade policies that encourage exports and less expansionary monetary policies, the United States could have exerted better control over the dollar over the past 30 years. Also, an energy policy based on something other than increasing oil imports might help, as would getting the federal budget deficits under control. Of course, a recession is not the time to focus on deficit reduction.

Given that these measures were not enacted during the past three expansions (in the 1980s, 1990s, and 2000s) it may be naïvely optimistic to expect them to be enacted now. In fact, enacting measures to strengthen the dollar could hamper U.S. economic recovery in some ways, and a weak dollar may therefore be preferable. For example, a weaker dollar lowers the price of U.S. exports and may encourage U.S. job growth. While it may be unrealistic to expect an export-led U.S. economic recovery, increased exports certainly won't hurt the U.S. economy.

A World of Debt

The United States and a number of EU governments took on huge amounts of debt while trying to stimulate their economies. At the end of 2009, those efforts were apparently qualified successes, but the debt overhang remained significant. These levels of debt have prompted concern among some parties, including the rating agencies that judge the creditworthiness of governments, companies, and banks. For example, *The Wall Street Journal* noted on December 9, 2009, that "Fitch Ratings cut Greece's credit rating a notch to the lowest level in the 16-nation euro zone."

As the article, titled "Countries' Debt Woes Pose Risk to Upturn," noted, "Even as a fledgling recovery takes hold, the deterioration of some governments' balance sheets represents a continuing risk." The article cited Greece as the most urgent EU case, potentially putting the EU in the position of either bailing out the country or allowing a debt crisis. In the latter case, the debt would have to be restructured and Greece's future borrowing potential would be undermined. The article also reported that, "Moody's also said that the UK's rating would be at risk if it didn't lower its budget deficit." In the early months of 2010, both Greece and to a lesser extent the United Kingdom saw their debt problems approach crisis proportions. (Meanwhile, the United States has some individual states in similarly dire straits, as noted in Chapter 14.)

In late November 2009, the United Arab Emirate (UAE) of Dubai rocked the financial world with the news that it would delay payments on the debt of a government-owned company. Over the previous 10 years, Dubai had launched ambitious efforts to become a luxury destination, conference center, and second-home site for the world's wealthy. This Xanadu, which included an indoor ski slope and manmade islands, was to anchor Dubai's economy in the absence of significant oil deposits. That plan has been derailed, or at least stalled, by the global recession. At the end of 2009, most observers believed that Abu Dhabi, another UAE nation, would cover the debt.

Yet into 2010, the prospect of a default on some nation's sovereign debt remained a real possibility. Even with a restructuring of debt, the nation issuing the debt in question will see its future ability to borrow impaired. That could undermine that nation's development and almost certainly its fiscal policy flexibility.

A sovereign default could also ripple around the world. In the past, the failure of a single financial institution, such as Barings Bank, Bear Stearns, or Lehman Brothers, has had widespread effects. That's because of the interconnectedness of financial institutions and of the risks they take. It's also because the failure of a major bank, let alone default by a nation, can spread panic throughout the financial markets over the possibility of another, more devastating failure. That panic can become a self-fulfilling expectation as massive sell-offs of securities and indiscriminate runs on banks occur.

Of course, other sovereign governments can step in to assist a troubled nation. However, that can strain the finances of the governments that do so, causing more deficits and increasing the competition for funds and the risk of those governments running aground, and perhaps the risks to the financial system.

For all these reasons, many governments (and many households and banks) should undergo deleveraging to bring down their levels of debt and risks of default.

About Deleveraging

In general, *deleveraging* involves paying off debt or selling it and using the proceeds to build up cash reserves or to purchase productive assets. That last point is important. If a government or a company uses debt to invest in productive assets, such as when the U.S. government invests in the nation's infrastructure (or a project that gives rise to something like the Internet), that is a good use of debt. Bailing out reckless bankers is less so. However, even bailing out bankers can (and should) perpetuate institutions that will continue to provide stability, jobs, and tax revenues.

WHAT'S THAT?

Deleveraging is the process by which a business, bank, or government decreases its levels of debt. It is commonly used even when the entity has not actually been using leverage as formally defined in Chapter 3 (to increase the return on an investment), and is sometimes applied to households as well. Deleveraging involves paying down debt or, in the case of a business or bank, raising investment funds to replace the debt.

However, it's also necessary to have an exit strategy—a way of deleveraging, of liquidating the debt and lowering the risk to the nation, the recovery, and the taxpayers (or, in a bank or company, the shareholders). The Fed has an exit strategy, as discussed in Chapter 5, but the Fed is part of the banking system, controls reserve requirements, and can set interest rates. It has far more flexibility than the administration or Congress in changing policy.

For the U.S. government to actually "deleverage," it must either increase taxes or reduce spending. But the public dislikes both of those options. Even a politician courageous enough to propose either one would face the fact that increasing taxes or reducing spending could dampen economic growth. Few governments want to jeopardize fragile economic recoveries. Even banks have been reluctant to reduce their debt. (The one exception is the eagerness of U.S. banks to pay back funds from the Troubled Asset Relief Program [TARP]. However, that appears to be related to their desire to avoid government oversight of their policies, particularly compensation policies.)

Households, however, have been reducing their debt. They want to back off their record high levels of credit card and other borrowings, and are expected to shop more carefully and less often in the months and years ahead. That may lead to a more sluggish recovery, but also to higher savings rates and a more firmly grounded U.S. economy, in which consumers do not live paycheck to paycheck or carry high levels of debt to finance lifestyles they cannot afford.

Spinning into the Future

Economic facts of life will continue to assert themselves. No nation, no matter how productive, can continue to borrow without those supplying the funds eventually putting on the brakes in one way or another. The most likely way for them to do so would be to demand higher interest rates. However, higher rates could jeopardize the ability of the United States to service its debt, which could hurt holders of U.S. debt.

The markets will set the rates and, if competition for investment funds from other economies increases, the United States will either have to curtail borrowing or pay the higher rates. Indeed, the higher rates themselves will force fiscal discipline on the United States. Also, the lenders themselves, such as China, could force fiscal discipline on the United States by reducing its purchases of new U.S. debt.

Meanwhile, consumers and producers in emerging economies will demand their share of the global economic pie. They will want motor vehicles, comfortable homes, and the full range of products and services of middle-class life. As the populations of the United States, Canada, and Europe continue to age, they will face fiscal budgetary pressures of their own. Retirement and health-care expenses will have to be addressed in a serious manner. The U.S. dollar will probably not enjoy quite the status that it has for much of the past 60 years, but that will be part of the rebalancing that will occur as global economic growth and expansion proceeds.

In fact, rebalancing may be the watchword for observers of the global economy over the next several years and beyond. Watch for changes in trade flows, currency values, fiscal policies, and private sector demand, with an eye toward what the changes mean—on balance—for national economies and for global economic growth.

The Least You Need to Know

- At the end of the recession, the global economy was heavily in debt. This came about as central banks lowered interest rates and governments engaged in deficit spending in order to battle the recession.

- The possibility of a sovereign debt default by a relatively small nation, such as Greece or Dubai, remained a real possibility at the end of 2009.

- Once a provider of exports and investment funds to the world, the United States has become a debtor nation. With an economy more than three times the size of China's, the United States owes that nation about $1 trillion.

- When a nation's currency weakens, that nation's exports become cheaper, which boosts exports and can boost employment. However, it can also disappoint foreign lenders and investors, who will receive less when they convert the loan or investment back into their own currency.

- When a nation's currency strengthens, that nation's exports become more expensive and imports become cheaper. That can create trade deficits of the kind that the United States experienced from the mid-1970s onward.

The Shape of
Things to Come

Chapter 21

In This Chapter

- Forces working for and against U.S. economic growth
- The U.S. economy as the Great Recession ended
- Is there a "new normal" ahead?
- Why the U.S. economic strength will continue

In the introduction to this book, I noted that U.S. citizens may face a lower standard of living for years to come.

This chapter discusses that prospect. Certain public policies, coupled with global economic forces, have created serious challenges for the U.S. economy. The near-term challenge is to establish growth that is less dependent on consumer spending and credit. The longer-term challenge is to put the middle class on a solid financial footing and to gain global competitiveness in areas that will lead to sustainable growth.

This chapter examines factors that will determine the course of the U.S. expansion over the next several years and beyond. It looks at U.S. economic performance as recovery appeared to be underway in early 2010, and at the factors that will affect any expansion. It also provides a "report card" on the policies launched in response to the crisis and the recession. We begin, however, with a look at economic performance at the end of 2009 and in early 2010.

Although the U.S. economic recovery remained fragile in early 2010, the third quarter of 2009 was in all likelihood the turning point in the business cycle that ended the first decade of the new century. The U.S. economy grew by 2.2 percent in that quarter, and then by an encouraging 5.9 percent for the fourth quarter of 2009. However, in late 2009 and early 2010 bad news continued on the employment front.

The unemployment rate fell marginally from October's 10.2 percent to 10 percent in November, where it remained in December, and then dropped to 9.7 percent in January.

As noted, few economists forecasted a return to robust growth, despite some good news in other data. Retail sales for the 2009 holiday season were encouraging. The January 8, 2010, *New York Times* reported that, for November and December combined, "the industry posted a 1.8 percent sales increase for stores open at least a year … a marked contrast from the 5.6 decline in 2008," according to the International Council of Shopping Centers. Most reports noted that consumers were continuing their frugal ways. Retailers had expected this, however, and managed their inventories conservatively to avoid deep discounts as Christmas approached.

Sales of autos and light trucks remained sluggish at the end of 2009. For that year, "U.S. sales of cars and light trucks plunged 21 percent to 10.4 million" according to a January 8, 2010, Reuters report. That same report noted that for the first time ever residents of another country purchased more cars and light trucks than Americans: China, with sales of about 12.7 million cars and light trucks during 2009.

The key to increased consumer spending in retail, autos, and other sectors is increased employment. High unemployment saps the spending of the unemployed (and those unemployed but no longer counted as such) *and* curbs the spending of the employed. Many people with jobs fear they may lose them, particularly if the economy recovers slowly or, worse, dips back into recession.

Housing at the End of the Recession

At the end of 2009, housing remained a real question mark and a potential trouble spot. The number of distressed homeowners remained extremely high, with 14.4 percent of residential borrowers in foreclosure or delinquency in September 2009, according to the Mortgage Bankers Association. This reflects the high unemployment rate, as well as the underemployment and long-term unemployment not reflected in the widely reported rate.

On a brighter note, in October 2009, sales of *existing* homes reached their highest levels since February 2007, the end of the housing bubble. Sales of existing homes usually increase before residential homebuilding and construction increase. In January 2010, residential *building permits* and *housing starts* increased from year-earlier levels. Permits rose by about 17 percent over the January 2009 level, and housing starts for the month increased by about 21 percent over the year-earlier level.

WHAT'S THAT?

Building permits are required by most locations in the United States and are a good indicator of future housing starts. **Housing starts** are instances in which ground has been broken for the footings or foundation of a residential structure. The U.S. Census Bureau tracks on both of these measures of housing activity.

In general, however, even with the first-time homebuyer tax credit, housing remained slack in 2009. For banks with troubled mortgage-related assets, the "plan" seems to have been to carry the assets until the economy improved. The longer banks could avoid massive charge-offs and prop up their balance sheets, the better—in their eyes and, presumably, the government's.

Housing will certainly recover. The demographics of the baby boom "echo" will see to that. But it will take years to counter the effects of the excessive building, valuation, and lending of the housing bubble, particularly in markets like Miami, San Diego, Las Vegas, and others that boomed during the bubble. Because housing drives a lot of economic activity, the lingering effects will include slow employment and income growth. Thus, housing may remain a drag on the economy.

WHAT TO DO?

Track housing and employment activity at your state and, if possible, local level. Check out the official website of your state and of state agencies related to labor and employment. Also, the U.S. Census Bureau (www.census.gov) and the Bureau of Economic Analysis (www.bea.gov) report many economic indicators at state levels. For local information, follow your local business press.

The Postrecession U.S. Economy

Economists disagree about the prospects for the U.S. economy in the next several years, but very few forecast a rapid return to robust growth. There are three main reasons for that: weak consumer spending, structural industry problems, and government fiscal problems.

Consumer Spending Will Remain Relatively Weak

Burdened by high debt, high unemployment, and job insecurity, consumers alone cannot be expected to pull the U.S. economy into a strong expansion. Growth in consumer spending will return only when the employment picture improves substantially, which is not likely in the near term.

One alternative would be yet another asset bubble along the lines of tech stocks in the 1990s and housing in the 2000s. That would put money into people's pockets and boost consumer spending. But it would depend on the Fed keeping rates low and pumping liquidity into the financial system even after a reasonable recovery begins. Also, as we have seen, bubbles can be dangerous, and many analysts and advisors (and the Chinese) will warn the Fed if it tends to keep rates too low for too long.

So employment growth remains critical to the future of the economy. However, employment is closely linked to the strength and structure of U.S. industries.

Structural Problems in U.S. Industries

Although the U.S. economy contains copious productive capacity, little of it is devoted to manufacturing anymore, compared to the decades in which the U.S. middle class expanded rapidly. Those high-paying manufacturing jobs helped to fuel the mid-century growth of the American middle class. No more.

U.S. auto manufacturing, once a major engine of middle-class expansion, will take several years to restructure into a smaller, less unionized domestic industry. The housing industry will also change as the population ages and homebuilders seek alternatives to business models based on high square-footage. Real estate sales and mortgage origination and lending will also take years to regain their peaks. All of this will weigh on the economy. In circular fashion, weak employment growth means weak income growth, which means weak consumer spending growth, which means weak economic growth, which means weak employment growth.

Fiscal Problems at All Levels of Government

Rising federal deficits are a problem because the levels of debt are becoming extremely high and the world will not continue to purchase U.S. Treasury securities indefinitely. People who tell you this is not a problem are like the people who said housing prices wouldn't decline in the 2000s. The U.S. government cannot continue to spend money it does not have and to issue debt in the expectation that the market for it is insatiable.

Moreover, fiscal problems are not limited to the federal government. Individual states are required by their constitutions to balance their annual budgets, and they have only three ways of doing so when they are over budget: increase taxes, reduce spending (that is, services), or issue debt. Increasing taxes is unpopular and can drive households and businesses out of the state. Reducing services is also unpopular and can also drive away households and businesses. People want good schools, sanitation, and low crime, and they flock to states that provide them. (Some of the highest tax areas of the nation—New York City, Long Island, New Jersey, and California—are also the most densely populated.)

Issuing debt is another option for states (and large cities), but markets are sensitive to their creditworthiness. If a state issues high debt relative to its tax base, it will have to pay higher interest rates, which further expands expenditures and calls for higher taxes.

The recession worsened budget deficits at the federal and state levels because tax collections decreased due to lower economic activity. Also, government had to increase services for the poor and unemployed. There is no easy path out of the fiscal dilemma. Services will probably have to be reduced or taxes increased at federal, state, and municipal levels. Those are difficult political choices, but they cannot be postponed forever.

Looking Ahead

In a sluggish or uneven recovery, economic indicators "bounce around" for awhile. Housing starts might be strong for a quarter or two, then weaken. Consumer spending and auto sales might do the same. That's because pent-up demand for housing, durable goods, and cars will be released, and then subside, while sustainable build-ups in sales, inventories, and production remain in the future. In other words, pent-up demand cannot create a sustainable recovery or overcome the structural weaknesses in the U.S. economy.

WHAT TO DO?

View economic indicators over time and in groups. These data track various types of economic activity and performance, but you shouldn't view them in isolation and you should track them over time. In other words, don't rely on one piece of data, such as the unemployment rate or housing starts or GDP growth. Instead, look at the data together and examine it over time. Two observations may be the start of a trend, but it's not really a trend. Also, listen to the explanations of changes in the data, but listen critically and make your own logical connections.

So the essential difficulty in the U.S. economy over the next few years will probably be sluggish or uneven growth (or both). It will likely be a few years before a strong, sustainable growth trajectory is reestablished.

I strongly doubt that the U.S. economy will enter a downward spiral. While the cyclical downturn that began in early 2008 morphed into the worst recession since World War II, it was still a cyclical downturn. High household debt, the housing price bubble and subprime mortgage crisis, previous low interest rates, and deficit spending left the nation with few options for fueling recovery. Thus the Fed could not engineer a "soft landing" by gradually lowering interest rates, nor could the government stimulate strong growth by lowering taxes or increasing spending.

However, the Bush and Obama administrations did a good (not great) job of dealing with the crisis and the downturn. Still, many Americans believe that the nation will not recover with genuine strength in the years immediately following the recession, although a fairly strong recovery would be the normal course of events, as it was after the early 1980s, 1990s, and 2000s recessions.

Is There a "New Normal"?

Can the U.S. economic booms of the past be replicated? Will the economy "go back the way it was"? Or is there going to be a "new normal," in which Americans have lower incomes, spend less, use less debt, and experience a lower standard of living?

The answer to the latter is quite possibly, "yes." In fact, that forecast, which I am not alone in making, is based on five observable trends:

- **Incomes have stagnated.** As I've documented in this book, real incomes have stagnated for much of the middle class. In the past two decades, only the top 20 percent gained in its share of income, with the top 1 percent gaining a hugely disproportionate share.

- **Unemployment will persist.** Some jobs simply will not come back. Automotive, retail, and real estate jobs are three areas that are not expected to recover their early 2000s peak anytime soon. New industries will arise, but will they create highly paid jobs here or lower paid jobs in other, lower-cost nations?

- **Asset values have declined.** Home prices will take years to return to former peaks. Stocks recovered a good portion of lost value, but many people not only saw "paper losses" on their 401(k) accounts but also had to tap them—and other savings—to survive the recession. Many baby boomers will have to save a lot over the next 10 to 20 years to finance what retirement they will have.

- **Foreign competition will increase.** When the middle class expands in nations that previously had small ones, those people will need oil, other resources, and capital. The United States will not remain dominant without developing a new political consensus based on building up the middle and working classes. Such a consensus seems unlikely.

- **Political paralysis.** While many expected a new—or at least more productive—approach to politics in Washington with the election of Barack Obama, it did not emerge as he faced two major tests of political will: health-care reform and financial-services reform. Although the election of an African American to the nation's highest office is indeed a milestone, once he took office, politics as usual prevailed. Health-care reform was a windfall for the health-insurance industry, and financial-services reform has not been vigorous and will not stop banks from taking risks if taxpayers stand ready to bail them out.

Many Americans have become frustrated with policies that have undercut the middle class, yet they often fail to realize that the majority of voters supported (and continue to support) these policies. They voted for politicians of both parties who favored lower taxes without reductions in services or benefits, and thus favored large deficits. They voted for politicians who favor a "more competitive" America in which people "don't have the government on their backs" (or a livable minimum wage) and where the "free market" determines winners and losers. It's sad when the free market produces more losers than winners, but it often does. But when it does, the losers don't seem very interested in "taking responsibility for their lives."

The policies I'm talking about benefited investors—the top 20 percent of households—often at the expense of wage earners. When Democrats realized they couldn't get elected on "liberal" policies, they moved to the right. Regardless of what politicians and pundits say, there are very few "liberals" in U.S. politics. That, of course, is why health-care reform will deliver huge benefits to the insurance companies, and why financial-services regulation will probably remain toothless.

The consensus that prevailed in the 30 years after World War II is gone, partly due to divisive politics and partly due to the new and outsized influence of money and lobbyists in politics. However, the government showed that it could respond to an economic crisis when it was absolutely necessary.

Report Card on Initiatives

Given that the recession officially began in December 2007, and recessionary conditions (especially high unemployment) continued through 2009, we have had a two-year period in which we can examine the performance of the federal government in response to an economic crisis. Here are my grades for the government's specific efforts.

Troubled Asset Relief Program (TARP) (Grade: B)

The passage of TARP in 2008 and distribution of bailout funds showed that the government would not let major financial institutions (other than Bear Stearns and Lehman Brothers) fail. That calmed the markets and forestalled runs on banks.

But TARP did not address troubled assets in a timely or substantial manner, and the bailouts had a mysteriously preferential quality. To address troubled assets, TARP should have ensured that "toxic" mortgage loans and related securities were restructured, charged off, or sold off for whatever they were worth, rather than being carried on balance sheets indefinitely. Unfortunately, many of those assets have been carried because the banks have been afraid of finding out what they were worth and absorbing the loss.

As to the preferential quality of the bailouts, the reasons that Bear and Lehman were allowed to fail while others were not has never really been explained. Worse, the bailouts asked very little of the banks. By showing banks that they don't have to bear all of their losses, the government may have set the stage for the next meltdown. That said, the goal at the time—to calm the markets—*was* achieved.

Bailouts of GM and Chrysler (B+)

Controversial for the strings (and bankruptcies) attached and for the differences in the treatment of the Midwest versus Wall Street, these bailouts came under TARP. TARP was not created to bail out auto companies or unions; however, as a political move, it was sensible. The United States could use two domestic car companies, but it did not have to save Chrysler because Ford required no bailout. Time will show how economically sound (and how fair or unfair to Ford) these bailouts were. But they did save a major domestic industry, and many of its jobs, for the time being.

Public-Private Investment Program (PPIP) (C)

PPIP has been a minor factor in the banking system's recovery. Designed to help banks sell troubled, mortgage-related loans and securities, the program was slow to be formulated, late to be announced, and minimal in the use that banks made of it relative to the amount of troubled securities they presumably carried.

> **WHAT TO DO?**
>
> Visit the U.S. Treasury site at www.ustreas.gov and search on PPIP for information on the Public-Private Investment Program, which went into effect under TARP.

Mortgage-Relief/Restructuring Program (C)

In autumn 2008, Federal Deposit Insurance Corp. Chairman Sheila Bair and other experts called for a mortgage-relief package for distressed homeowners. Although the TARP legislation called on the Treasury to enact mortgage relief, controversy arose regarding the "morality" of bailing out people who bought more house than they could afford.

Given the risks taken by savvy investment bankers, beating up on unsophisticated homebuyers in the same kind of trouble seems excessive. Also, although tens of thousands of mortgages were restructured, it paled next to the banks' bailouts, loans, and guarantees. Hundreds of thousands of people have lost their homes due to government and industry inaction.

American Recovery and Reinvestment Act of 2009 (ARRA) (A)

The ARRA (the "stimulus package") featured payroll tax cuts, direct aid to states, and creation of infrastructure jobs. Those on the left called for a far larger package, and those on the right called for a far smaller one (or none)—and for more tax cuts. Despite Republican opposition, ARRA worked as intended, helping states stay afloat and putting money into people's pockets. It also provided for jobs via infrastructure spending in 2010 and 2011. With ARRA, the government acted to bolster the economy and at least kept it from sinking lower, which also helped tax receipts.

Other Legislative Efforts (A-)

Over some Republican opposition, Congress extended unemployment benefits and the periods during which unemployed workers could apply to purchase health insurance on their own from the plans they belonged to while employed (under COBRA). The up to $8,000 credit for first-time homebuyers and the "Cash for Clunkers" program showed that the government was acting, and did benefit the people who bought and sold those homes and cars.

Also, although it was not a new initiative, the federal food-stamp program (the Supplemental Nutrition Assistance Program) was assisting some 36.5 million (or 1 in 8) Americans as of August 2009—an increase of more than 30 percent over 2008 levels.

Banking Reform (D)

As of early 2010, two years after the onset of the recession and almost two years after the failure of Bear Stearns, no financial-services reform worthy of the name had taken place. Even the most ardent supporter of the free market cannot (logically and morally) support bailouts and debt guarantees for banks when their risk taking causes them trouble without supporting tighter regulation. But that is exactly what many people, including many politicians, do support. Heads, bank executives and investors win; tails, taxpayers lose. It's quite sad, or laughable, depending on your point of view.

Taxing away part of executive bonuses or passing a "consumers' bill of rights" would be good, but the real issue is this: Does the United States permit the existence of banks that are too big to fail, and guarantee their continued existence at taxpayer expense? Or does the United States limit the size of banks, regulate them so that they cannot take excessive risks, or refuse to bail them out? As was proven from the Great Depression until the 1980s, sound regulation is possible. But U.S. politicians and the industry are resisting it.

Federal Reserve Programs (A-)

The U.S. central bank instituted facilities and measures to provide liquidity to the commercial paper and other credit markets and to the banking system as a whole. That the funds (and the TARP funds) were not loaned to households and businesses is a minor issue given that demand for credit and for goods and services was low and debt was already high. The key was to bolster the confidence of investors, the business community, and foreign governments in the U.S. banking system and in the Fed's willingness and ability to play its role of lender of last resort during those uncertain days. The Fed accomplished this.

Overall Grade: B

You may think that I am being too generous in grading the overall efforts by the government a "B," and in my grades for some of the specific programs. But please keep the context in mind. Recall that a number of the measures, such as TARP, the auto industry bailouts, and the stimulus package, were enacted to address pressing situations when we knew far less (and feared far more) than we do now. Much could have been done differently, but those early steps (unlike banking reform, a later opportunity) were handled well.

As of 2010, however, the U.S. economy faced several major risks.

The Risks Are Significant

Even with a "new normal" of lower consumer spending and a lackluster recovery expected, things could be worse—and may still be. Indeed, the U.S. economy faces several significant longer-term risks:

- Structural federal budget deficits could hobble growth and undercut the public sector.

- Loose monetary policy could generate another credit-fueled asset bubble.

- Investors could continue to allocate too much capital to speculation rather than to investment.

- Restructuring of the U.S. economy could take 5 to 10 years, leaving the United States behind other nations for the next decade or two.

- U.S. companies could find it hard to compete on world markets unless U.S. education improves and genuine health-care reform occurs.

- Political divisiveness and lack of direction could continue to generate bad policies.

The biggest "risk" may not be a risk, but rather a proven historical phenomenon: nations and economies have lifecycles. They go through a period of inception and initial organization, growth and prosperity, maturity and expansionism, and diminishment and decay. Many observers have noted similarities between the United States and faded empires such as Rome, Spain, and Britain. Some similarities are superficial, but their sheer number is disturbing. Signs of U.S. decline include bloated budgets, lack of leadership, corruption in the public sector, obsession with past glories, inability to address long-standing problems (education, infrastructure, health care), an overextended military, and a frivolous populace focused on sensation rather than serious issues.

The United States has been blessed with a durable form of government, tremendous natural resources and geographical advantages, and waves of immigrants who built the national character and culture. The United States has made many real and important contributions to the world, from fighting two world wars not of its own making to defining a culture in which individuals can pursue their own goals by their own means.

That culture continues to yield significant benefits. Yet some U.S. advantages of the twentieth century—an isolated domestic market, seemingly unlimited natural resources, and greater political consensus—have faded. Freedom to innovate and to act independently has also spawned the most violent culture in the industrial world, the highest incarceration rates, and persistent, significant poverty, even in families long established in the nation.

Several important commentators have bemoaned diminished American optimism. On November 17, 2009, *New York Times* columnist David Brooks noted the sense of optimism in China and a lack of one in the United States. Many people wonder how the nation that helped Europeans free themselves of Hitler's tyranny could become bogged down for years in Iraq and Afghanistan. Why has the United States been unable to build something, *anything* on the site of the World Trade Center in New York City?

I have suggested that some ideas adopted about 30 years ago have undermined U.S. consensus and unity of action. The approach of the political right has gone well beyond the goal of "getting government off our backs." It has overreached into "pelvic politics," becoming obsessed with gay people, and using emotional wedge issues such as abortion and immigration to distract people from economic policies. Yet the failure of the right resembles that of the left. Neither party levels with voters about the choices they face. Neither party tells voters what things will really cost and what trade-offs are involved.

Why? Because it works. They know voters don't like bad news. They also know most voters lack the interest, knowledge, and time to sift through policies. When politicians don't reveal their true agendas and the true costs and trade-offs of policies, and people cannot or will not analyze their policies, voters cannot vote in their own best interests. Wage earners will vote for policies that hurt wage earners and benefit investors. Workers will vote for policies that enable companies to move their jobs to foreign locations.

Self-styled *populist* media figures and splinter political groups tap the anger of U.S. voters. But the proper target of voter anger may be voters themselves, who supported a system that does not benefit them. Maybe they are justified in feeling betrayed. Or maybe they have no more justification than greedy marks who believe con men. Voters wanted something for nothing—lower taxes without reduced services, wars without national sacrifice (even higher taxes, let alone a draft), and debt without repayment. Does anyone really believe that is the way the world works?

WHAT'S THAT?

The term **populist** and the related ideology populism can be quite ambiguous. Traditionally, it has referred to political figures who champion the interests of "the little guy"—that is, the average voter rather than the wealthy "elites." However, like many words, this one has become somewhat corrupted. Some figures who claim to oppose the elites actually attained and remained in office by representing them. Somewhat ingeniously, the Republican party has managed to portray itself as "populist" while pushing policies that have benefited the top 20 percent of households and employers over employees. Somewhat stupidly, the Democratic party has abandoned the working class, which it had represented from the Great Depression until the 1980s, in favor of representing—well, I'm actually not sure.

We Will Survive

All of this said, the U.S. and European Union (EU) economies are not going to fall apart anytime soon. Both remain extremely large sources of demand and production. Both have the advantage of stable, open systems of governance and vigorous financial markets.

Most EU nations have many public programs, ranging from universal health care to child daycare, as well as safeguards for workers facing potential layoffs. These cost money and can create certain costs, such as less flexible labor markets. However, there is greater consensus in those nations regarding government's role in the economy. The major question is whether those nations will be able to continue to afford those programs and policies if their populations age and their economies grow more slowly.

A similar question faces the United States. On the downside, the government seems unable to reduce expenditures. Also, the aging U.S. population has indeed been betrayed by the use of their Social Security and Medicare tax proceeds by both parties over the past three decades for other purposes. On the upside, however, the U.S. economy remains tremendously productive and flexible. That flexibility has been amply demonstrated in the ability of U.S. companies to adopt numerous innovations. These include Total Quality Management and other programs that improved productive quality, just-in-time inventory management and other cost-cutting methods, flatter organizations that are more responsive to change, and management methods that boost productivity.

With more than $14 trillion in GDP, the United States remains by far the largest national economy and market. An entity that large can absorb a lot of shock and remain standing. In addition, although they can be faulted for their myopia, American voters can change their leadership. To serve their broader economic interests, they may even change the system that puts politicians in the pockets of commercial interests. That is a necessary step to putting the U.S. economy back on a strong, long-term growth trajectory.

Another necessary step, however, would be to develop a viable vision of a national economic future. That vision must include ways of creating competition without making 50 to 80 percent of households economic "losers," ways of funding education as an investment in innovation, ways of choosing government programs that benefit those that actually need such programs, and ways of funding them without running up trillions in debt. It is possible to do such things, and there are good examples in U.S. history and around the world (and directly to the north). The final question is, must the United States weather more financial crises and harsh recessions before Americans can face their actual problems and start functioning as a team?

We will see.

The Least You Need to Know

- The turning point for an upswing in the late 2000s business cycle was, in all likelihood, the third quarter of 2009, when growth of 2.2 percent was achieved. That was followed by a healthy rate of 5.9 percent growth in the fourth quarter of 2009.

- However, in early 2010, economists disagreed about the prospects for the postrecession U.S. economy, and few forecast a return to robust growth. The main reasons were slow consumer spending, structural economic problems, and government fiscal problems.

- Rather than a strong recovery or a return to prerecession growth rates, some analysts forecast a "new normal" of slower growth and, perhaps, a lower standard of living.

- Key reasons for forecasts of a "new normal" include stagnant incomes, persistent unemployment, low asset values, increased savings, rising foreign competition, and political paralysis.

- Many U.S. citizens have voted against their economic interests over the years, and the "free market" has created many losers who weren't warned of that possibility by politicians who enacted "pro-business" policies for decades. The future of the U.S. economy now largely depends on a new political consensus, which does not appear to be on the horizon.

- Given its size, innovativeness, productivity, and history of achievement, the U.S. economy (and that of the European Union) will remain viable and vigorous for the foreseeable future. But they may not grow as fast as more recently developing economies determined to expand their middle classes.